# Behavioral Finance and Investor Types

# Behavioral Finance and Investor Types

*Managing Behavior to Make Better Investment Decisions*

## MICHAEL M. POMPIAN

WILEY

John Wiley & Sons, Inc.

Published by John Wiley & Sons, Inc., Hoboken, New Jersey.
Published simultaneously in Canada.

For general information on our other products and services or for technical support, please
contact our Customer Care Department within the United States at (800) 762-2974, outside
the United States at (317) 572-3993 or fax (317) 572-4002.

Wiley also publishes its books in a variety of electronic formats. Some content that appears in
print may not be available in electronic books. For more information about Wiley products,
visit our web site at www.wiley.com.

*Library of Congress Cataloging-in-Publication Data:*

Pompian, Michael M., 1963–
  Behavioral finance and investor types : managing behavior to make better investment
decisions / Michael M. Pompian.
      p. cm.—(Wiley finance series)
  Includes index.
  ISBN 978-1-118-01150-8 (cloth); ISBN 978-1-118-22181-5 (ebk);
  ISBN 978-1-118-23560-7 (ebk); ISBN 978-1-118-26048-7 (ebk)
  1. Investments—Psychological aspects.   2. Investments—Decision making.   I. Title.
  HG4515.15.P657 2012
  332.601'9—dc23

                                                                          2011052854

10  9  8  7  6  5  4  3  2  1

*This book is dedicated to my brother Dave and his family, Hali, Tyler, and Sascha.*

# Contents

# Foreword

**F**ishermen often use the expression "to set the hook" and that is what I hope to do for *Behavioral Finance and Investor Types*. Michael Pompian graciously asked me if I would write this Foreword and, in a blink, I agreed. Why? Because the investing pond is full of investors who need to take the hook Michael is presenting here.

You are about to read and solve a mystery of sorts. It lifts the curtain on what lurks behind investment choices—improperly formulated choices that so often derail expectations. This book takes the often tedious and prover-bial "scraping and sanding before painting" and makes it the intriguing cornerstone of investing. Ben Franklin, always insightful about visionaries, wrote in the 1769 *Farmers' Almanac*, "There are three things extremely hard: steel, a diamond, and to know one's self." To make sound choices, you must know yourself in order to know what decisions your personality can withstand when building and implementing an investment policy and process. You must know yourself, or the organization for which you serve, well enough to convey the beliefs, preferences, and biases about those whom you have chosen to advise you on investment decisions. This includes bro-kers, consultants, investment advisors, and so on. To be unable to do so is a prescription for inappropriate asset selection and portfolio composition—a far too common outcome. This is true from both an expected return and an expected risk perspective.

It is hard to imagine how much effort and knowledge was required to create this book. To focus effectively on what drives different types of personalities and match those personalities with an appropriate, fitted in-vesting solution requires a long and patient observer and practitioner, like Michael Pompian. After many years in the consulting business, Michael has honed a deep psychological understanding of investor personalities, and ac-curately characterizes and classifies them into types. He is a rare breed with his deep knowledge of what drives investors and what drives portfolios—an elementary alignment that is the missing ingredient for the vast majority of investors—both individuals and institutions.

*Behavioral Finance* is about the psychology that drives financial or in-vestment choices in an uncertain future environment. Behavioral finance has been mostly under the wing of the academic community whose research has become prolific enough to offer a source of meaning and direction for investors. Twenty years ago behavioral finance was mostly a nebulous, certainly unrequited, and scattered collection of research by those who dared to tamper with classical views of finance. Recognizing the overwhelming role of psychology in decision making has forever changed the role of individuals and groups in making investment choices! Way back in the 1930s, John Maynard Keynes wrote of "animal spirits," a now bantered catch-all for our behavior as investors. Then, in 2002, Daniel Kahneman put behavioral finance front and center by winning the Nobel Prize in Economics. Kahneman is a psychologist and points out that he has never taken a course in economics. Since that event, interest in behavioral finance has catapulted to become a source of rationale for investors' decisions.

Michael has done yeoman's service in taking years of academic research and his own practitioner insights to illuminate the mandatory need to understand the virtues of the physiological implications of choice. He is bringing these essential findings to the forefront of untangling everyday investment thinking with the clear mandate of implementing sound investment decisions. His combined knowledge of the inherent drivers of investor behavior, and years of careful observation, clearly illuminates that shoe sizes, so to speak, vary a great deal. He has effectively "typed" investors—be they individuals or institutions—as a way to narrow and clarify what choices would be best for them. This "sanding and scraping" provides compatibility between investor expectations and ultimate results.

So, who should read this book? If we start with every investor and every consultant or broker, the answer is all of them. The psychological insights into personality types developed from the building blocks of beliefs, preferences, and behavioral biases are now essential for developing appropriate recommendations. All the agents involved in this process now realize what Ben Franklin described as one of the hardest things in life—to know one's self. Portfolios must reflect both the personality of their clients and their needs in order to create a thoughtful, sound investment program. Otherwise, investors and their advisors will join the majority of those who do not have the benefit of the practical blueprint that *Behavioral Finance and Investment Types* so effectively provides.

ARNOLD WOOD
*President and Chief Executive Officer*
*Martingale Asset Management*

# Preface

**O**ver the past 20-plus years of working in the investment advisory business, I have been lucky enough to establish and build satisfying relationships with many different kinds of people. When I say "different," I mean in terms of temperament, occupation, economic circumstances, social strata, gender, and other factors. I've learned that human psychology is complex (big surprise!) and that people form their attitudes and habits in multi-faceted ways; attitudes and habits about everything from eating, to approaches to working, to interpersonal relationships and—you guessed it—money and investing are all part of the intricate web of the human mind. When working with something as important as a person's money, it is extremely helpful to understand what behaviors might be affecting their decision making processes.

These decisions are based on two basic psychological ideas: emotions and cognitions. Emotions generally have to do with how people feel while cognitions have to do with how people think. At first blush, this distinction may not appear overly helpful, but it is. It provides a framework for understanding how people think and act in relation to their money. The book will cover this emotional-cognitive idea in due course. But first, an introduction to the overall thinking behind the book is in order.

## AN IMPERFECT SCIENCE

Although it might seem to be an impossible task to try to categorize people by their behaviors, many thoughtful people have tried to do so. Many of the people who have tried to do this are quite well known—Freud, for example—while others are quite unknown. Several chapters of this book are devoted to an historical view of personality theory and the research that has gone into this subject. After reading this work, what one quickly realizes is that the study of personality is an imperfect science. Unlike hard sciences like physics and chemistry, which have elegant mathematical formulas for explaining naturally occurring phenomena, social science is less precise.

This book is certainly closer to being imprecise than it is to being precise based on this fundamental idea. The ideas in the book are an attempt to categorize investors by their behavior—something that by definition cannot be precise. Therefore, the book should be used to gain insights into one's basic behaviors and learn how to counteract the potentially negative outcomes associated with biased investment decision making. Don't get too caught up in the categories or classifications. Moreover, identifying your own type is only valuable if you can do something with the information!

In order to do something with the categorization of investors by their behavior, I created a term called "Behavioral Investor Types" (also known as BITs), which is used throughout the book. There are four BITs used to describe the most commonly found investor personalities. Undoubtedly you will find some discrepancies—but fret not. BITs were created to make behavioral finance easier to apply in practice. Before jumping into the nuts and bolts of how to diagnose clients into BITs, as is done in the book, it is important for readers to understand the depth of thought that went into creating them; I will do so because I want you to feel confident about using this material in practice.

BITs build on key concepts I outlined in some of my early papers, including one published in the *Journal of Financial Planning* in March 2005 entitled "The Future of Wealth Management: Incorporating Behavioral Finance into Your Practice," as well as my book, published in 2006, entitled *Behavioral Finance and Wealth Management,* and a subsequent second edition of the same book published in 2012. In those two works, I outline a method of applying behavioral finance to private clients in a way that I now refer to as "bottom-up." "Bottom-up" means that in order for an advisor to diagnose and treat behavioral biases, he or she must test for all behavioral biases in the client first, and then determine which ones a client has before being able to use bias information to create a customized investment plan. For example, in *Behavioral Finance and Wealth Management,* I describe 20 of the most common behavioral biases that an advisor is likely to encounter, explain how to diagnose a client's biases, show how to identify types of biases, and finally show how to plot this information on a chart to create the best practical allocation for the client. Some investors and advisors may find this bottom-up approach too time-consuming or complex. With the introduction of BITs in this book, however, I take a simpler, more efficient approach to bias identification.

The BIT identification process is a multi-step diagnostic process that results in clients being classified into one of four behavioral investor types. Bias identification, which is done near the end of the process, is narrowed down for the advisor by giving the advisor clues as to which biases a client is likely to have based on the client's BIT. BITs were designed to help advisors make rapid yet insightful assessments of what type of investor they are dealing with before recommending an investment plan. The benefit of defining what type of investor an advisor is dealing with up-front is that client behavioral surprises that result in a client wishing to change his or her portfolio that arise as a result of market turmoil can be mitigated. If an advisor can limit the number of traumatic episodes that inevitably occur throughout the advisory process by delivering smoother (read: expected) investment results because the advisor had created an investment plan that is customized to the client's behavioral make-up, a stronger client relationship is the result. BITs are not intended to be absolutes but rather guideposts to use when making the journey with a client; dealing with irrational investor behavior is not an exact science. For example, an advisor may find that he or she has correctly classified a client as a certain BIT, but finds that the client has traits (biases) of another.

In the book, I provide descriptions of the four behavioral investor types: Preservers, Followers, Individualists, and Accumulators. The book will include a diagnostic for isolating behavioral biases, and advice for dealing with each BIT. Each BIT is characterized by a certain risk tolerance level and a primary type of bias—either cognitive (driven by faulty reasoning) or emotional (driven by impulses or feelings). One of the most important concepts advisors should keep in mind as they go through the book is that the least risk-tolerant BIT and the most risk-tolerant BIT are driven by emotional biases, while the two BITs in between these two extremes are mainly affected by cognitive biases. Emotional clients tend to be more difficult clients to work with, and advisors who can recognize the type of client they are dealing with prior to making investment recommendations will be much better prepared to deal with irrational behavior when it arises.

At the end of the day, the purpose of classifying your clients into BITs is to build better relationships with them. The essence of being a great advisor is to be a great people person. Naturally, one absolutely needs to be technically competent in their chosen specialty in the business—but to get really great one needs to be able to sense how a relationship is going and make strides to build the relationship, and at the same time be versatile enough to work with people from all walks of life and backgrounds. This is the fun part of working in the investment advisory business for some people; it is for me. For those of you who are familiar with my work, you will know that I am a big believer in the power of behavioral finance to help explain investor behavior to improve investment outcomes. The key benefit of learning the details of behavioral finance is that one can know when one is making biased investment decisions or help clients to see that they are making biased decisions. Understanding how people behave can be a critical component to not only improving investment outcomes for oneself but also in building lasting relationships with others.

## WHY THIS BOOK?

This book was conceived only after many hours, weeks, and years of researching, studying, and applying behavioral finance concepts to real-world investment situations. As a wealth manager, I have found the value of understanding the behavioral investor types of clients and have discovered some ways to adjust investment programs for the biases I witness. You will learn about these methods. By writing this book, I hope to spread the knowledge that I have so that other advisors and clients can benefit from these insights. Up until now, there has not been a book available that has served as a guide to investor personalities for the advisor or sophisticated investor.

Although I have been saying this for a decade, investment advisors have never had a more challenging environment in which to work. Many advisors thought they had found nirvana in the late 1990s, only to find themselves in quicksand in 2001 and 2002. And the bull market of the 2000s and subsequent meltdown in 2008 puts one now in a low-return environment. As has been the case for years now, advisors are continuously peppered with vexing questions from their clients:

"Why is this fund not up as much as that fund?"

"The market has not done well the past quarter—What should we do?"

"Why is asset allocation so important?"

"Why are we investing in alternative investments?"

"Why aren't we investing in alternative investments?"

"Why don't we take the same approach to investing in college money and retirement money?"

"Why don't we buy fewer stocks so we can get better returns?"

Advisors and investors alike can benefit from a book that helps to identify BITs and deal with the behavioral and emotional sides of investing so that they can help their clients understand why they have trouble sticking to a long-term program of investing.

## PLAN OF THE BOOK

Part One of the book is an introduction to behavioral finance. These chapters include an overview of why reaching financial goals is difficult, an overview of behavioral finance concepts, and an introduction to behavioral biases. Part Two of the book is a comprehensive review of personality theory, complete with an introduction to the subject and a review of the history of personality testing. Also in Part Two is background information on the Behavioral Investor Type theoretical framework and Behavioral Investor Type Diagnostic Testing. Part Three of the book is an explanation of each of the Behavioral Investor Types. Part Four is called "Plan and Act" and the chapters offer practical advice on capital markets and asset casses, asset allocation, financial planning, and investment advice for each Behavioral Investor Type.

## WHO SHOULD USE THIS BOOK?

The book was originally intended as a handbook for wealth management practitioners who help clients create and manage investment portfolios. As the book evolved, it became clear that individual investors could also greatly benefit from it. The following are additional target audiences for the book:

- *Traditional wire-house financial advisors.* A substantial portion of the wealth in the United States and abroad is in the very capable hands of traditional wire-house financial advisors. From a historical perspective, these advisors have not traditionally been held to a fiduciary standard, as the client relationship was based primarily on financial planning's being "incidental" to the brokerage of investments. In today's modern era, many believe that this will have to change, as "wealth management," "investment advice," and brokerage will merge to become one. And the change is indeed taking place within these hallowed organizations. Thus, it is crucial that financial advisors develop stronger relationships with their clients because advisors will be held to a higher standard of responsibility. Applying behavioral finance will be a critical step in this process as the financial services industry continues to evolve.
- *Private bank advisors and portfolio managers.* Private banks, such at U.S. Trust, Bessemer Trust, and the like, have always taken a very solemn, straight-laced approach to client portfolios. Stocks, bonds, and cash were really it for hundreds of years. Lately, many of these banks have added such nontraditional offerings as venture capital, hedge funds, and others to their lineup of investment product offerings. However, many clients, including many extremely wealthy clients, still have the big three—stocks, bonds, and cash—for better or worse. Private banks would be well served to begin to adopt a more progressive approach to serving clients. Bank clients tend to be conservative, but they also tend to be trusting and hands-off clients. This client base represents a vast frontier to which behavioral finance could be applied because

these clients either do not recognize that they do not have an appropriate portfolio or tend to recognize only too late that they should have been more or less aggressive with their portfolios. Private banks have developed a great trust with their clients and should leverage this trust to include behavioral finance in these relationships.

■ *Independent financial advisors.* Independent registered representatives (wealth managers who are Series 7 registered but who are not affiliated with major stock brokerage firms) have a unique opportunity to apply behavioral finance to their clients. They are typically not part of a vast firm and may have fewer restrictions than their wire-house brethren. These advisors, although subject to regulatory scrutiny, can for the most part create their own ways of serving clients; and with many seeing that great success is growing their business, they can deepen and broaden these relationships by including behavioral finance.

■ *Registered investment advisors.* Of all potential advisors that could include behavioral finance as a part of the process of delivering wealth management services, it is my belief that registered investment advisors (RIAs) are well positioned to do so. Why? Because RIAs are typically smaller firms, which have fewer regulations than other advisors. I envision RIAs asking clients, "How do you feel about this portfolio?" "If we changed your allocation to more aggressive, how might your behavior change?" Many other types of advisors cannot and will not ask these types of questions for fear of regulatory or other matters, such as pricing, investment choices, or others.

■ *Consultants and other financial advisors.* Consultants to individual investors, family offices, or other entities that invest for individuals can also greatly benefit from this book. Understanding how and why their clients make investment decisions can greatly impact the investment choices consultants can recommend. When the investor is happy with his or her allocation and feels good about the selection of managers from a psychological perspective, the consultant has done his or her job and will likely keep that client for the long term.

■ *Individual investors.* For those individual investors who have the ability to look introspectively and assess their behavioral biases, this book is ideal. Many individual investors who choose either to do it themselves or to rely on a financial advisor only for peripheral advice often find themselves unable to separate their emotions from the investment decision making process. This does not have to be a permanent condition. By reading this book and delving deep into their behaviors, individual investors can indeed learn to modify behaviors and to create portfolios that help them stick to their long-term investment programs and, thus, reach their long-term financial goals.

## WHEN TO USE THIS BOOK

First and foremost, this book is generally intended for those who want to apply behavioral finance to the asset allocation process to create better portfolios for their clients or themselves. This book can be used:

- *At the outset of a financial advisory relationship.* Understanding the type of investor one is *before* creating an investment program is highly recommended. If you are an advisor and you deal with many different types of people, this book can be very helpful in terms of dealing appropriately with the unique personalities that make up your client base.
- *When there is an opportunity to create or re-create an asset allocation from scratch.* Advisors know well the pleasure of having only cash to invest for a client. The lack of such baggage as emotional ties to certain investments, tax implications, and a host of other issues that accompany an existing allocation is ideal. The time to apply the knowledge learned in this book is at the moment that one has the opportunity to invest only cash or to clean house on an existing portfolio.
- *When a life trauma has taken place.* Advisors often encounter a very emotional client who is faced with a critical investment decision during a traumatic time, such as a divorce, a death in the family, or job loss. These are the times that the advisor can add a significant amount of value to the client situation by using the concepts learned in this book.
- *When wealth transfer and legacy are being considered.* Many wealthy clients want to leave a legacy. Is there any more emotional an issue than this one? Having a frank discussion about what it possible and what is not possible is difficult and is often fraught with emotional crosscurrents that the advisor would be well advised to stand clear of. However, by including behavioral finance into the discussion and taking an objective, outside counselor's viewpoint, the client may well be able to draw his or her own conclusion about what direction to take when leaving a legacy.

Naturally, there are many more situations not listed here that can arise and where this book will be helpful.

Now that you have a good sense for the thinking behind the book and the reasons for creating Behavioral Investor Types, my hope is that you can take what you learn in this book and put it to use in practice. The volatility in markets is very high and the expectation is that it will stay that way for a long time. Understanding how investors behave can go along way toward improving investment outcomes. Whether you are an investor or an advisor, your aim should be to actually apply the ideas and concepts in the book to real world situations. So please—get started! If you have any questions or comments related to this book please feel free to e-mail me at my personal e-mail, which is mpompian@hotmail.com. If you have any questions related to investment consulting or working with ultra-affluent clients, my office e-mail is michael.pompian@mercer.com. Thanks for reading!

# Acknowledgments

I would like to acknowledge all my colleagues, both present and past, who have contributed to broadening my knowledge, not only in the topic of this book but also in wealth management in general. You know who you are. In particular, I would like thank my proofreader, Cristina Hensel, and her brother, Will Hensel, for their contributions to the book. Cristina was invaluable to the organization and structure of the book and contributed in so many ways to the book's overall quality. Will Hensel was instrumental in researching and helping to create the sections on Personality Theory and the History of Personality Types. I would also like to acknowledge my colleague, Jack Dwyer, who helped immensely on (read here: did a majority of the research for) Chapter 12, Capital Markets and Asset Classes. I would also like to acknowledge all of the behavioral finance academics and professionals who have inspired me with their brilliant work. Finally, I would like to thank my parents and extended family for giving me the support to write this book.

M.P.

# Introduction to Behavioral Finance

The purpose of this book is to identify various types of investors and how best to deal with managing their behavioral attributes for the purpose of reaching financial goals. The foundational elements of each type are the behavioral biases that each investor exhibits. In order to understand the origins of the biases and how to use them, it is critical to learn about the subject of behavioral finance. Part One of the book provides both an introduction to the subject of behavioral finance and also an introduction to 20 of the most common investor biases. Part One starts with a discussion of why attaining financial goals is so difficult for so many people around the world.

# Chapter 1

# Why Reaching Financial Goals Is Difficult

*I'd like to live as a poor man, with lots of money.*
—Pablo Picasso

W hy are so many people across the United States and other developed (and currently developing countries) in a position to accumulate wealth but have such a difficult time doing so? More often than not, the reason for this failure is that one's own financial choices and behaviors sabotage otherwise well-intentioned efforts to achieve stated financial goals—assuming one's goals are stated. For the purposes of this book, we will leave aside any discussion of the current outlook for the global economy, take no notice of the wealth distribution or wage levels, and stick primarily to the subject of personal financial management.

Intuitively, most people know that saving money is a good thing, but our desire for material goods and spending on services often overrides otherwise good instincts. Understanding why behavior is so difficult to control is actually quite simple—it is a lack of self-discipline driven by psychological and/or environmental factors—but the solutions are often complex and illusory. Later in the book, we will examine some of these complexities in detail and attempt to find solutions. In this chapter, however, we start by examining some simple examples of self-defeating behavior, two of which are nonfinancial and three of which are financial examples. By doing so, we gain a common understanding of the challenges involved in controlling behavior and emphasize the importance of why behavior must be carefully managed. At the end of the chapter, I provide information about how this chapter relates to the other two chapters in this section, as well as some comments.

## NONFINANCIAL EXAMPLES OF
## SELF-DEFEATING BEHAVIOR

In order to get a clearer understanding of self-defeating behavior in the financial realm, it can be helpful to see examples of nonfinancial self-defeating behavior. The following examples are intended to be generic and purposefully not meant to shed a negative light on anyone matching this description.

### Example 1: The Yo-Yo Dieter

Everyone knows someone who is overweight and has tried on numerous occasions to lose weight but has not been successful. I'm not talking about the rare individual with such a severe problem that gastric bypass surgery or other drastic measure is needed, but rather the person who is 30 to 50 to 100 pounds overweight and systematically fails at weight loss. And I'm also not talking about the uneducated person who does not know the amount of calories contained in food or the unhealthy effects of carrying around extra pounds. The people I am considering know that what they are putting into their bodies is what is making them overweight.

These unfortunate folks have often been traveling on a yo-yo or riding on a rollercoaster of diets: losing pounds then gaining pounds, gaining then losing, and back again. Through the dieting process, these people get educated on the calorie count of food and, by doing so, consciously know how much extra food is going into their bodies in terms of calories they eat per day. They also know that they don't eat enough fruits and vegetables (or none at all) or exercise enough (or not at all). Attempts at a quick fix are therefore attractive, however unsustainable these types of diets may be. We've all heard about diets such as all meat or no meat or a host of others that work for a while but eventually fail as the old behaviors and the accompanying pounds come back. At some point these folks just give up and say to themselves that they can't do it, and they just go on with life with the extra pounds. There are a number of psychological and physiological reasons for overeating. Although the following list[1] is targeted at women, and may not be completely exhaustive, it contains some key reasons why people overeat (and much of the information is applicable to men as well).

- Boredom: You eat when you're bored or do not have anything interesting to do or to look forward to. TV is a favorite pastime, especially when you are alone at home and bored. When food commercials are running 200 images per hour into our cerebral cortex, it is difficult not to be drawn toward the refrigerator. If food commercials are a trigger, you should watch nature shows or commercial-free TV.

■ Feeling deprived: You feel deprived of the foods you enjoy, which leaves you craving for them even more. The media's attitude toward emphasizing thinness as the ideal has led to restrictive dieting and avoidance of entire groups of foods. Unfortunately, because the foods we are urged to avoid are abundantly available, and food visibility and availability are powerful eating stimuli, restrictors often break the plan and eat forbidden foods. Once this happens, overwhelming guilt followed by feelings of low self-esteem motivate the individual to go on overconsuming the avoided food in an attempt to numb these negative feelings.

■ Glucose intolerance: This is a physiological trigger. In a healthy body, carbohydrates are converted to glucose and a blood glucose level of ~60–120mg/dl is maintained without thought to the dietary consumption of carbohydrate. In the glucose intolerant population, carbohydrates are readily converted to glucose, and the pancreas responds to this shift in blood sugar by secreting an excessive amount of the hormone, insulin. Insulin's job is to remove the glucose from the blood stream and help it to enter the body cells. If done properly, the blood glucose level returns to the normal range regardless of the amount of carbohydrate consumed. If this system is not working correctly, a quick rise in blood glucose followed by an over-production of insulin occurs. The excessive insulin is not recognized by the body cells so it is unable to remove the glucose from the blood stream. The result is an increase in blood insulin levels, which has an appetite stimulating effect. The person is driven to eat, and if simple carbohydrates are chosen, the cycle continues.

Other factors include a lifestyle that is constantly draining your energy; desire for comfort; feelings of being overwhelmed, upset, or hurt; and the big kicker: a lack of will power. Whatever the case, the basic facts are that there are too many people who know what they need to do to cut weight but cannot find the behavioral tools to succeed. This, naturally, is in contrast to the dieter-exerciser who eats right and exercises regularly and manages to get weight under control. It should be simple, right? For the record, I am a few pounds overweight and am guilty of several of the behaviors mentioned here, but the difference is that I am doing something about it, because I realize that *I* am in control of my diet and exercise and not the other way around. Figure 1.1 illustrates that as we age our weight is destined to go up (there are those who manage to keep it off their whole lives but not that many!). However, if we stick to a healthy diet and exercise frequently we will likely keep to a more even weight loss and, if we do, we will likely weigh less than those who are on the roller coaster. Easier said than done! (See Figure 1.1.)

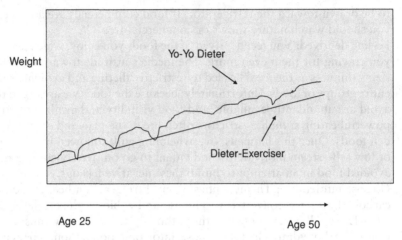

**FIGURE 1.1**    The Dieter-Exerciser versus the Yo-Yo Dieter

## Example 2: The Educated Smoker

Have you ever met a doctor or other health professional who is also a smoker? This one sort of astounds me. How can it be that a person who has devoted their lives to the health and well-being of others can treat their body so carelessly? I can remember that, as a teenager, I would play sports with my friends in my backyard and witness my next-door neighbor, a doctor, chain-smoking on her porch. I knew even at that age the health risks of smoking and I could not understand for the life of me why she smoked (I knew *she* had to know the risks involved). Later, when she was in her forties, I heard she had died of lung cancer. This shocked me, but when I thought about it I realized it shouldn't have come as a surprise. To this day, I still remember a poster in the hall of my middle school that showed an elderly, wrinkled, lifeless person holding a cigarette with the caption "Smoking is very debonair" across the bottom, which was meant to deter youngsters from smoking. It was shock treatment at an early age, and it worked. So how is it that a well-trained doctor, with full knowledge of the health risks of smoking, chain-smokes him- or herself to an almost certain death? As with the yo-yo dieter, there are psychological as well as physiological reasons why people who know smoking is bad still engage in the act.[2]

For many people, smoking is a reliable lifestyle coping tool. Although every person's specific reasons to smoke are unique, they all share a common theme. Smoking is used as a way to suppress uncomfortable feelings, and smoking is used to alleviate stress, calm nerves, and relax. No wonder that when you are deprived of smoking, your mind and body are unsettled for a little while. Below is a list of some positive intentions often associated with smoking.

- Coping with anger, stress, anxiety, tiredness, or sadness.
- Smoking is pleasant and relaxing.
- Smoking is stimulating.
- Acceptance: being part of a group.
- As a way to socialize.
- Provides support when things go wrong.
- A way to look confident and in control.
- Keeps weight down.
- Rebellion: defining self as different or unique from a group.
- A reminder to breathe.
- Something to do with your mouth and hands.
- Shutting out stimuli from the outside world.
- Shutting out emotions from the inside world.
- Something to do just for you and nobody else.
- A way to shift gears or changes states.
- A way to feel confident.
- A way to shut off distressing feelings.
- A way to deal with stress or anxiety.
- A way to get attention.
- Marking the beginning or the end of something.

The National Institute on Drug Abuse (NIDA) reports that people suffering from nicotine withdrawal have increased aggression, anxiety, hostility, and anger. However, perhaps these emotional responses are due, not to withdrawal, but to an increased awareness of unresolved emotions. If smoking dulls emotions, it's logical that quitting smoking allows awareness of those emotions to bubble up to the surface. If emotional issues aren't resolved, a reformed smoker may feel overwhelmed and eventually turn back to cigarettes to deal with the uncomfortable feelings.

Instead, when you smoke, the carbon monoxide in the smoke bonds to your red blood cells, taking up the spaces where oxygen needs to bond. This makes you less able to take in the deep, oxygen-filled breath needed to bring life, to activate new energy, to allow health and healing, or bring creative insight into your problems and issues. The bottom line here is that once again, even though it is well known and documented that smoking is an entirely unhealthy activity, there are a myriad of reasons why people smoke. Self-defeating behavior is the culprit; intellectually, we know that smoking is bad. But somehow the will to stop just isn't there.

## FINANCIAL EXAMPLES OF
## SELF-DEFEATING BEHAVIOR

Now that we have reviewed some nonfinancial examples of self-defeating behavior, we can turn to financial examples of behaviors that should be equated with poor investment performance but are repeated by investors month after month, year after year, cycle after cycle.

### Number 1: The Return Chaser

One of the most basic of human investment instincts is to be in the know regarding the latest investment trend. How silly we feel when we are at a cocktail party or barbeque in our community and we join a conversation in progress about how your neighbor just made a killing on XYZ stock that participates in ABC hot industry. Why am I not participating in this money making opportunity, you ask yourself? This occurred with Internet stocks in the late 1990s and then with real estate during the subsequent decade, and now back to the Internet bubble of the late 1990s with social networking companies that are creating, in my view, another irrational valuation bubble that some investors wish they could be involved with and, undoubtedly, someday will be glad they never invested in.

At one time or another we have all seen someone who epitomizes this type of investor—or maybe this is our own behavior! These folks follow the latest trend, paying no attention to valuation. They have no rational basis for making an investment and jump in without an exit strategy, or they plan to get out when a profit has been made, if one is ever made. The investment may go up, but since no plan is in place, the investment ultimately turns sour and losses ensue.

As investors, we must resist the urge to participate in such schemes and steer clear of these money-losing opportunities. Our own behavior is often the culprit, and we need to overcome our natural instincts to participate in less-than-rational investment schemes, or at least we should have an exit strategy if the decision is made to participate. Later in the book we will look at individual behaviors that account for chasing returns, as has been described here, and devise strategies for overcoming these behaviors.

### Number 2: The Overconfident Gambler

It is not uncommon to come across the type of investor who thinks they are smarter than the average market participant, who enjoys the thrill of trading in and out of the market (like the thrill associated with gambling), and is more often than not on the losing end of the trade (with the occasional win to keep them in the game). And being on the losing end of the trade often

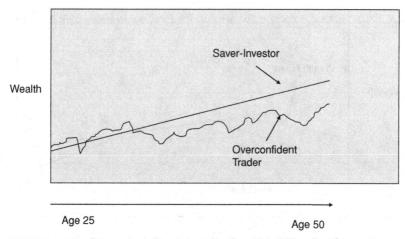

**FIGURE 1.2** Saver-Investor versus the Overconfident Trader

causes even more of the gambling behaviors to kick in, so that they engage in the same risky trading behavior in an attempt to get back to even. This example is in contrast to the person who avoids such behavior (or keeps it to such a modest amount that it does not affect long-term wealth creation) and manages to save and invest over long periods of time to build wealth gradually. Notice a pattern here? This example is, of course, nearly identical to the yo-yo dieter in the nonfinancial examples who attempts to lose weight quickly on a regular basis only to gain it back. In this case it's the opposite situation: The person attempts to gain wealth quickly, only to "lose it back." Figure 1.2 illustrates the overconfident gambler versus the opposite type of investor, whom I will call the saver-investor. Both start at 25 years old and are currently 50 years old. Figure 1.2 extends out in time to show that there are still opportunities to change behavior even at mid-life.

Naturally, this chart does not represent reality perfectly, but you get the point: It's not hard to tell which kind of person you want to be. So, why can't we do it? The answer is that we can, but we first need to identify the key factors that are rendering us incapable of engaging in good behavior.

## Number 3: The "Too Conservative" Investor

Although it is not as common, there exists a class of investors who are too conservative in their thinking. They are so afraid of losing money to a down stock market, whether through previous personal experience or not, that they simply won't accept any amount of risk. The failure with this approach is that people who cannot accept some amount of risk also risk outliving their money. The diagram in Figure 1.3 illustrates. Early into one's career,

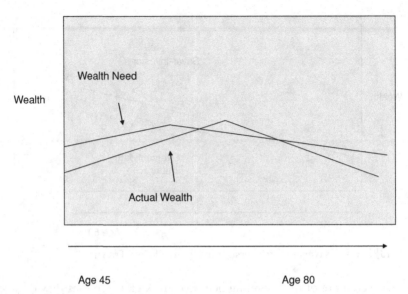

**FIGURE 1.3**    The Risk-Averse Investor

earning may not keep pace with the demand for funds due to expenses like college and housing. At some point during mid-career, these expenses may be surpassed by earnings and debt is reduced. Then later in life, one's working career can end either voluntarily or not, and cash needs should be surpassed by income. But if one does not accumulate enough of a nest egg and invest it wisely, there can be a situation where one may outlive one's assets. This is demonstrated in Figure 1.3. Certain people in this situation intuitively know that they need to increase risk, but they simply cannot take action to do it. They know about concepts such as inflation and low yields on bonds, but they will not take the risk this is necessary to build wealth.

Like the previous figure, this chart does not represent reality perfectly, but you get the point: You don't want to be in a situation where you don't have enough money as age increases. Taking risk in this case is advisable. In other cases advisors spend a good deal of time talking people out of taking risk.

We have reviewed three very basic situations in which we have identified a type of investor. The intent was not to go into great detail but to illustrate a situation in which it is difficult to control one's impulses toward a certain action or behavior. As we saw with the nonfinancial situations, people know they are taking actions that are not in their best interest. Similarly in the financial examples, we saw that people can make financial decisions that are not in their best interest even when they know they should take a different path. In many other cases, people may not be aware of their irrational behavior, and they need their advisors or other close relations to help them understand that they are making mistakes.

## SUMMARY

The remainder of Part One is devoted to helping readers to (1) understand the history and the basic concepts behind behavioral finance—that is, rational versus irrational investor behavior; and (2) reviewing 20 of the most common behavioral biases advisors and investors come across when making financial decisions. Why is this important? It's important because this information will help readers to gain a foundation for understanding concepts presented later in the book; specifically, to identify what key behaviors are impeding advancement towards attaining financial goals. The mechanisms for identifying and managing unwelcome behaviors are presented in the book in the form of investor personality types or, as I call them, Behavioral Investor Types (also known as BITs.) If you can identify what basic type of investor you are, and then diagnose your unique irrational behaviors, you will be in a much better position to overcome these behaviors and, ultimately, reach your financial goals. If you are a financial advisor, and you understand the behaviors that lead to poor financial performance—either yours or your clients'—you will be well positioned to advise your clients to behave better. Figure 1.4 describes this idea in basic, yet I hope beneficial, terms.

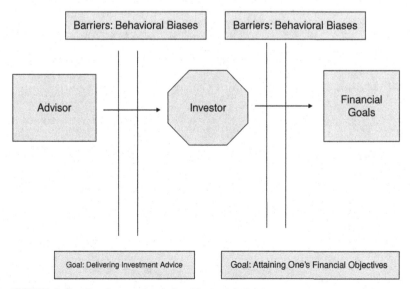

**FIGURE 1.4** Barriers to Attaining Financial Goals

Now that we have examined self-defeating behavior examples, both financial and nonfinancial, we will move on to the rest of Part One by first examining the background of the study of investor psychology, or *behavioral finance,* in Chapter 2.

## NOTES

1. "Top 10 Triggers for Over-Eating," Women Fitness—A Complete Online Guide to Achieve Healthy Weight Loss and Optimum Fitness (Fitness Women, Women's Fitness, Women Health, Woman Health, Health, Womensfitness), www.womenfitness.net/over-eating.htm (accessed July 5, 2011).
2. Annette Colby, "When Was the Last Time You Felt Fantastic?: Imagine Living Your Most Perfect Life and Feeling Better Than You Ever Thought Possible!" www.annettecolby.com (accessed July 5, 2011).

# Chapter 2

# Overview of Behavioral Finance

*People in standard finance are rational. People in behavioral*
*finance are normal.*

                —Meir Statman, PhD, Santa Clara University

**A**t its core, behavioral finance attempts to understand and explain actual investor and market behaviors versus theories of investor behavior. This idea differs from traditional (or standard) finance, which is based on assumptions of how investors and markets should behave. As Professor Statman's quote puts it, standard finance people are modeled as "rational," whereas behavioral finance people are modeled as "normal." This may be interpreted to mean that "normal" people may behave irrationally—but the reality is that almost no one (actually I will go so far as to say absolutely no one) behaves perfectly rationally. Fundamentally, behavioral finance is about understanding how people make decisions, both individually and collectively. By understanding how investors and markets behave, it may be possible to modify or adapt to these behaviors in order to improve economic outcomes. In many instances, knowledge of and integration of behavioral finance may lead to superior results for both advisors and their clients.

In the context of this book, we will be focusing on the development of individual investor biases or irrational behaviors. These biases will help to define the behavioral investor types reviewed later in the book. This chapter will focus on key developments that have occurred over the years that have led to discovery and use of behavioral biases. For a more complete review of the history of behavioral finance, readers can refer to my recently published second edition of *Behavioral Finance and Wealth Management*. We begin this chapter with an overview of the two main branches of the study of behavioral finance: Behavioral Finance Micro (BFMI), which examines behaviors or biases of individual investors, and Behavioral Finance Macro (BFMA), which has to do with the behavior of markets that are made up of individual investors. Next, there is a basic review of an ongoing debate between those people who believe that people do not act rationally (standard finance) and those people who believe that people act irrationally (behavioral finance). This chapter finishes with a summary of the role of behavioral finance in dealing with private clients and how the practical application of behavioral finance can enhance an advisory relationship.

## BEHAVIORAL FINANCE: MICRO VERSUS MACRO

Behavioral finance is commonly defined as the application of psychology to finance and it has become a very hot topic, generating credence with the rupture of the tech-stock bubble in March 2000 and pushed to the forefront of both investors' and advisors' minds with the financial market meltdown of 2008–2009. Although the term behavioral finance is bandied about in books, magazine articles, and investment papers, many people lack a firm understanding of the concepts behind behavioral finance. Additional confusion may arise from a proliferation of topics resembling behavioral finance, at least in name, including: behavioral science, investor psychology, cognitive psychology, behavioral economics, experimental economics, and cognitive science, to name a few. Furthermore, many investor psychology books that have entered the market recently refer to various aspects of behavioral finance but fail to fully define it. This section will try to communicate a more detailed understanding of the term "behavioral finance." First, we discuss some of the popular authors in the field and review the outstanding work they have done (not an exhaustive list), which will provide a broad overview of the subject. We then examine the two primary subtopics in behavioral finance: Behavioral Finance Micro and Behavioral Finance Macro. Finally, we will observe the ways in which behavioral finance applies specifically to wealth management, the focus of this book.

As we have observed, behavioral finance models and interprets phenomena ranging from individual investor conduct to market-level outcomes. Therefore, it is a difficult subject to define. For practitioners and investors reading this book, this is a major problem, because our goal is to develop a common vocabulary so that we can apply to our benefit the very valuable body of behavioral finance knowledge. For purposes of this book, we adopt an approach favored by traditional economics textbooks; we break our topic down into two subtopics: Behavioral Finance Micro and Behavioral Finance Macro.

1. Behavioral Finance Micro (BFMI) examines behaviors or biases of individual investors that distinguish them from the rational actors envisioned in classical economic theory.
2. Behavioral Finance Macro (BFMA) detects and describes anomalies in the efficient market hypothesis that behavioral models may explain.

As wealth management practitioners and investors, our primary focus will be BFMI, the study of individual investor behavior. Specifically, we want to identify relevant psychological biases and investigate their influence on asset allocation decisions so that we can manage the effects of those biases on the investment process.

Each of the two subtopics of behavioral finance corresponds to a distinct set of issues within the standard finance versus behavioral finance discussion. With regard to BFMA, the debate asks: Are markets "efficient," or are they subject to behavioral effects? With regard to BFMI, the debate asks: Are individual investors perfectly rational, or can cognitive and emotional errors impact their financial decisions? These questions are examined in the next section of this chapter; but to set the stage for the discussion, it is critical to understand that much of economic and financial theory is based on the notion that individuals act rationally and consider all available information in the decision making process. In academic studies, researchers have documented abundant evidence of irrational behavior and repeated errors in judgment by adult human subjects.

Finally, one last thought before moving on. It should be noted that there is an entire body of information available on what the popular press has termed "the psychology of money." This subject involves individuals' relationship with money—how they spend it, how they feel about it, and how they use it. There are many useful books in this area; however, this book will not focus on these topics.

## STANDARD FINANCE VERSUS BEHAVIORAL FINANCE

This section reviews the two basic concepts in standard finance that behavioral finance disputes: rational markets and rational economic man. It also covers the basis on which behavioral finance proponents challenge each tenet and discusses some evidence that has emerged in favor of the behavioral approach.

On Monday, October 18, 2004, a significant but mostly unnoticed article appeared in the *Wall Street Journal*. Eugene Fama, one of the pillars of the efficient market school of financial thought, was cited admitting that stock prices could become "somewhat irrational." Imagine a renowned and rabid Boston Red Sox fan proposing that Fenway Park be renamed Yogi Berra Stadium (after the colorful New York Yankees catcher), and you may begin to grasp the gravity of Fama's concession. The development raised eyebrows and pleased many behavioralists. (Fama's paper, "Market Efficiency, Long-Term Returns, and Behavioral Finance," noting this concession at the Social Science Research Network, is one of the most popular investment downloads on the website.) The *Journal* article also featured remarks by Roger Ibbotson, founder of Ibboston Associates: "There is a shift taking place," Ibbotson observed. "People are recognizing that markets are less efficient than we thought."[1]

As Meir Statman eloquently put it, "Standard finance is the body of knowledge built on the pillars of the arbitrage principles of Miller and Modigliani, the portfolio principles of Markowitz, the capital asset pricing theory of Sharpe, Lintner, and Black, and the option-pricing theory of Black, Scholes, and Merton."[2] Standard finance theory is designed to provide mathematically elegant explanations for financial questions that, when posed in real life, are often complicated by imprecise, inelegant conditions. The standard finance approach relies on a set of assumptions that oversimplify reality. For example, embedded within standard finance is the notion of "Homo Economicus," or rational economic man. It prescribes that humans make perfectly rational economic decisions at all times. Standard finance, basically, is built on rules about how investors *should* behave, rather than on principles describing how they actually behave. Behavioral finance attempts to identify and learn from the human psychological phenomena at work in financial markets and within individual investors. Behavioral finance, like standard finance, is ultimately governed by basic precepts and assumptions. However, standard finance grounds its assumptions in idealized financial behavior; behavioral finance grounds its assumptions in observed financial behavior.

## Efficient Markets versus Irrational Markets

During the 1970s, the standard finance theory of market efficiency became the model of market behavior accepted by the majority of academics and a good number of professionals. The Efficient Market Hypothesis had matured in the previous decade, stemming from the doctoral dissertation of Fama. Fama persuasively demonstrated that in a securities market populated by many well-informed investors, investments will be appropriately priced and will reflect all available information. There are three forms of the efficient market hypothesis:

1. The "Weak" form contends that all past market prices and data are fully reflected in securities prices; that is, technical analysis is of little or no value.
2. The "Semistrong" form contends that all publicly available information is fully reflected in securities prices; that is, fundamental analysis is of no value.
3. The "Strong" form contends that all information is fully reflected in securities prices; that is, insider information is of no value.

If a market is efficient, then no amount of information or rigorous analysis can be expected to result in outperformance of a selected benchmark. An efficient market can basically be defined as a market wherein large numbers of rational investors act to maximize profits in the direction of individual securities. A key assumption is that relevant information is freely available to all participants. This competition among market participants results in a market wherein, at any given time, prices of individual investments reflect the total effects of all information, including information about events that have already happened, and events that the market expects to take place in the future. In sum, at any given time in an efficient market, the price of a security will match that security's intrinsic value.

At the center of this market efficiency debate are the actual portfolio managers who manage investments. Some of these managers are fervently passive, believing that the market is too efficient to "beat"; some are active managers, believing that the right strategies can consistently generate alpha (alpha is performance above a selected benchmark). In reality, active managers beat their benchmarks only roughly 33 percent of the time on average. This may explain why the popularity of exchange traded funds (ETFs) has exploded in the past five years and why venture capitalists are now supporting new ETF companies, many of which are offering a variation on the basic ETF theme.

The implications of the efficient market hypothesis are far-reaching. Most individuals who trade stocks and bonds do so under the assumption that the securities they are buying (selling) are worth more (less) than the prices that they are paying. If markets are truly efficient and current prices fully reflect all pertinent information, then trading securities in an attempt to surpass a benchmark is a game of luck, not skill.

The market efficiency debate has inspired literally thousands of studies attempting to determine whether specific markets are in fact "efficient."

Many studies do indeed point to evidence that supports the efficient market hypothesis. Researchers have documented numerous, persistent anomalies, however, that contradict the efficient market hypothesis. There are three main types of market anomalies: Fundamental Anomalies, Technical Anomalies, and Calendar Anomalies.

**Fundamental Anomalies**  Irregularities that emerge when a stock's performance is considered in light of a fundamental assessment of the stock's value are known as fundamental anomalies. Many people, for example, are unaware that value investing—one of the most popular and effective investment methods—is based on fundamental anomalies in the efficient market hypothesis. There is a large body of evidence documenting that investors consistently overestimate the prospects of growth companies and underestimate the value of out-of-favor companies.

One example concerns stocks with low price-to-book-value (P/B) ratios. Eugene Fama and Kenneth French performed a study of low price-to-book-value ratios that covered the period between 1963 and 1990.[3] The study considered all equities listed on the New York Stock Exchange (NYSE), the American Stock Exchange (AMEX), and the Nasdaq. The stocks were divided into 10 groups by book/market and were reranked annually. The lowest book/market stocks outperformed the highest book/market stocks 21.4 to 8 percent, with each decile performing more poorly than the previously ranked, higher-ratio decile. Fama and French also ranked the deciles by beta and found that the value stocks posed lower risk and that the growth stocks had the highest risk. Another famous value investor, David Dreman, found that for the 25-year period ending in 1994, the lowest 20 percent P/B stocks (quarterly adjustments) significantly outperformed the market; the market, in turn, outperformed the 20 percent highest P/B of the largest 1,500 stocks on Compustat.[4]

Securities with low price-to-sales ratios also often exhibit performance that is fundamentally anomalous. Numerous studies have shown that low P/B is a consistent predictor of future value. In *What Works on Wall Street*, however, James P. O'Shaughnessy demonstrated that stocks with low price-to-sales ratios outperform markets in general and also outperform stocks with high price-to-sales ratios. He believes that the price/sales ratio is the strongest single determinant of excess return.[5]

Low price-to-earnings (P/E) ratio is another attribute that tends to anomalously correlate with outperformance. Numerous studies, including David Dreman's work, have shown that low P/E stocks tend to outperform both high P/E stocks and the market in general.[6]

Ample evidence also indicates that stocks with high dividend yields tend to outperform others. The Dow Dividend Strategy, which has received a great deal of attention recently, counsels on purchasing the 10 highest yielding Dow stocks.

**Technical Anomalies**  Another major debate in the investing world revolves around whether past securities prices can be used to predict future securities prices. "Technical analysis" encompasses a number of techniques that attempt to forecast securities prices by studying past prices. Sometimes, technical analysis reveals inconsistencies with respect to the efficient market hypothesis; these are technical anomalies. Common technical analysis strategies are based on relative strength and moving averages, as well as on support and resistance. While a full discussion of these strategies would prove too intricate for our purposes, there are many excellent books on the subject of technical analysis. In general, the majority of research-focused technical analysis trading methods (and, therefore, by extension, the weak-form efficient market hypothesis) find that prices adjust rapidly in response to new stock market information and that technical analysis techniques are not likely to provide any advantage to investors who use them. However, proponents continue to argue the validity of certain technical strategies.

**Calendar Anomalies**  One calendar anomaly is known as the January Effect. Historically, stocks in general and small stocks in particular have delivered abnormally high returns during the month of January. Robert Haugen and Philippe Jorion, two researchers on the subject, note that "the January Effect is, perhaps, the best-known example of anomalous behavior in security markets throughout the world."[7] The January Effect is particularly illuminating because it hasn't disappeared, despite being well known for 25 years (according to arbitrage theory, anomalies should disappear as traders attempt to exploit them in advance).

   The January Effect is attributed to stocks rebounding following year-end tax selling. Individual stocks depressed near year-end are more likely to be sold for tax-loss harvesting. Some researchers have also begun to identify a December Effect, which stems both from the requirement that many mutual funds report holdings as well as from investors buying in advance of potential January increases.

   Additionally, there is a Turn-of-the-Month Effect. Studies have shown that stocks show higher returns on the last and on the first four days of each month relative to the other days. Frank Russell Company examined returns of the Standard & Poor's (S&P) 500 over a 65-year period and found that U.S. large-cap stocks consistently generate higher returns at the turn of the month.[8] Some believe that this effect is due to end-of-month cash flows (salaries, mortgages, credit cards, etc.). Chris Hensel and William Ziemba found that returns for the turn of the month consistently and significantly exceeded averages during the interval from 1928 through 1993 and "that the total return from the S&P 500 over this 65-year period was received mostly during the turn of the month."[9] The study implies that investors making regular purchases may benefit by scheduling those purchases prior to the turn of the month.

Finally, as of this writing, during the course of its existence the Dow Jones Industrial Average (DJIA) has never posted a net decline over any year ending in a "five." Of course, this may be purely coincidental.

Validity exists in both the efficient market and the anomalous market theories. In reality, markets are neither perfectly efficient nor completely anomalous. Market efficiency is not black or white, but rather it varies by degrees of gray, depending on the market in question. In markets exhibiting substantial inefficiency, savvy investors can strive to outperform less savvy investors. Many believe that large-capitalization stocks, such as GE and Microsoft, tend to be very informative and efficient stocks but that small-capitalization stocks and international stocks are less efficient, creating opportunities for outperformance. Real estate, while traditionally an inefficient market, has become more transparent and, during the time of this writing, could be entering a bubble phase. Finally, the venture capital market, lacking fluid and continuous prices, is considered to be less efficient due to information asymmetries between players.

## Rational Economic Man versus Behaviorally Biased Man

Stemming from neoclassical economics, *Homo economicus* is a simple model of human economic behavior, which assumes that principles of perfect self-interest, perfect rationality, and perfect information govern economic decisions by individuals. Like the efficient market hypothesis, Homo economicus is a tenet that economists uphold with varying degrees of stringency. Some have adopted it in a semistrong form; this version does not see rational economic behavior as perfectly predominant but still assumes an abnormally high occurrence of rational economic traits. Other economists support a weak form of Homo economicus, in which the corresponding traits exist but are not strong. All of these versions share the core assumption that humans are "rational maximizers" who are purely self-interested and make perfectly rational economic decisions. Economists like to use the concept of rational economic man for two primary reasons: (1) Homo economicus makes economic analysis relatively simple; naturally, one might question how useful such a simple model can be; (2) Homo economicus allows economists to quantify their findings, making their work more elegant and easier to digest.

If humans are perfectly rational, possessing perfect information and perfect self-interest, then perhaps their behavior can be quantified.

Most criticisms of Homo economicus proceed by challenging the bases for these three underlying assumptions—perfect rationality, perfect self-interest, and perfect information.

1. *Perfect Rationality.* When humans are rational, they have the ability to reason and to make beneficial judgments. However, rationality is not the sole driver of human behavior. In fact, it may not even be the primary driver, as many psychologists believe that the human intellect is actually subservient to human emotion. They contend, therefore, that human behavior is less the product of logic than of subjective impulses, such as fear, love, hate, pleasure, and pain. Humans use their intellect only to achieve or to avoid these emotional outcomes.

2. *Perfect Self-Interest.* Many studies have shown that people are not perfectly self-interested. If they were, philanthropy would not exist. Religions prizing selflessness, sacrifice, and kindness to strangers would also be unlikely to prevail as they have over centuries. Perfect self-interest would preclude people from performing such unselfish deeds as volunteering, helping the needy, or serving in the military. It would also rule out self-destructive behavior, such as suicide, alcoholism, and substance abuse.

3. *Perfect Information.* Some people may possess perfect or near-perfect information on certain subjects; a doctor or a dentist, one would hope, is impeccably versed in his or her field. It is impossible, however, for every person to enjoy perfect knowledge of every subject. In the world of investing, there is nearly an infinite amount to know and learn; and even the most successful investors don't master all disciplines.

Many economic decisions are made in the absence of perfect information. For instance, some economic theories assume that people adjust their buying habits based on the Federal Reserve's monetary policy. Naturally, some people know exactly where to find the Fed data, how to interpret it, and how to apply it; but many people don't know or care who or what the Federal Reserve is. Considering that this inefficiency affects millions of people, the idea that all financial actors possess perfect information becomes implausible.

Again, as with market efficiency, human rationality rarely manifests in black or white absolutes. It is better modeled across a spectrum of gray. People are neither perfectly rational nor perfectly irrational; they possess diverse combinations of rational and irrational characteristics, and benefit from different degrees of enlightenment with respect to different issues.

## THE ROLE OF BEHAVIORAL FINANCE WITH PRIVATE CLIENTS

Private clients can greatly benefit from the application of behavioral finance to their unique situations. Because behavioral finance is a relatively new concept in application to individual investors, investment advisors may feel reluctant to accept its validity. Moreover, advisors may not feel comfortable asking their clients psychological or behavioral questions to ascertain biases, especially at the beginning of the advisory relationship.

One of the objectives of this book is to position behavioral finance as a more mainstream aspect of the wealth management relationship, for both advisors and clients.

As practitioners increasingly adopt behavioral finance, clients will begin to see the benefits. There is no doubt that an understanding of how investor psychology impacts investment outcomes will generate insights that benefit the advisory relationship. The key result of a behavioral finance–enhanced relationship will be a portfolio to which the advisor can comfortably adhere while fulfilling the client's long-term goals. This result has obvious advantages—advantages that suggest that behavioral finance will continue to play an increasing role in portfolio structure.

## PRACTICAL APPLICATIONS

Wealth management practitioners have different ways of measuring the success of an advisory relationship. Few could argue that every successful relationship shares some fundamental characteristics:

- The advisor understands the client's financial goals.
- The advisor maintains a systematic (consistent) approach to advising the client.
- The advisor delivers what the client expects.
- The relationship benefits both client and advisor.

So, how can behavioral finance help?

### Formulating Financial Goals

Experienced financial advisors know that defining financial goals is critical to creating an investment program appropriate for the client. To best define financial goals, it is helpful to understand the psychology and the emotions underlying the decisions behind creating the goals. Upcoming chapters in this book will suggest ways in which advisors can use behavioral finance to discern why investors are setting the goals that they are. Such insights equip the advisor in deepening the bond with the client, producing a better investment outcome, and achieving a better advisory relationship.

## Maintaining a Consistent Approach

Most successful advisors exercise a consistent approach to delivering wealth management services. Incorporating the benefits of behavioral finance can become part of that discipline and would not mandate large-scale changes in the advisor's methods. Behavioral finance can also add more professionalism and structure to the relationship because advisors can use it in the process for getting to know the client, which precedes the delivery of any actual investment advice. This step will be appreciated by clients, and it will make the relationship more successful.

## Delivering What the Client Expects

Perhaps there is no other aspect of the advisory relationship that could benefit more from behavioral finance. Addressing client expectations is essential to a successful relationship; in many unfortunate instances, the advisor doesn't deliver the client's expectations because the advisor doesn't understand the needs of the client. Behavioral finance provides a context in which the advisor can take a step back and attempt to really understand the motivations of the client. Having gotten to the root of the client's expectations, the advisor is then more equipped to help realize them.

## Ensuring Mutual Benefits

There is no question that measures taken that result in happier, more satisfied clients will also improve the advisor's practice and work life. Incorporating insights from behavioral finance into the advisory relationship will enhance that relationship, and it will lead to more fruitful results.

It is well known by those in the individual investor advisory business that investment results are not the primary reason that a client seeks a new advisor. The number one reason that practitioners lose clients is that clients do not feel as though their advisors understand, or attempt to understand, their financial objectives—resulting in poor relationships. The primary benefit that behavioral finance offers is the ability to develop a strong bond between client and advisor. By getting inside the head of the client and developing a comprehensive grasp of his or her motives and fears, the advisor can help the client to better understand why a portfolio is designed the way

it is and why it is the right portfolio for him or her—regardless of what
happens from day to day in the markets.

## NOTES

1. Eugene Fama, "Market Efficiency, Long-Term Returns, and Behavioral Finance,"
   *Wall Street Journal,* October 18, 2004.
2. Meir Statman, "Behaviorial Finance: Past Battles and Future Engagements," Association for Investment Management and Research, 1999.
3. Eugene Fama and Kenneth French, "The Cross-Section of Expected Stock Returns," *Journal of Finance* 47, no. 2 (1992): 427–465.
4. Dreman Value Management website: www.dreman.com.
5. James O'Shaughnessy, *What Works on Wall Street* (New York: McGraw-Hill
   Professional, 2005).
6. Dreman Value: www.dreman.com.
7. Robert Haugen and Philippe Jorion, "The January Effect: Still There After
   All These Years," *Financial Analysts Journal* 52 (1) (January–February 1996):
   27–31.
8. Russell Investment Group website: www.russell.com/us/education_center.
9. Chris R. Hensel and William T. Ziemba, "Investment Results from Exploiting
   Turn-of-the-Month Effects," *Journal of Portfolio Management* 22, no. 3 (Spring
   1996): 17–23.

# CHAPTER 3

# The Building Blocks:
# Behavioral Biases

T he dictionary defines the word "bias" in a number of ways, including: a statistical sampling or testing error caused by systematically favoring some outcomes over others; a preference or an inclination, especially one that inhibits impartial judgment; an inclination or prejudice in favor of a particular viewpoint; an inclination of temperament or outlook, especially a personal and sometimes unreasoned judgment. In the context of this chapter, we are considering biases that result in irrational financial decisions caused by faulty cognitive reasoning or reasoning influenced by emotions. This classification—distinguishing between biases based on faulty cognitive reasoning (cognitive errors) and those based on reasoning influenced by feelings or emotions (emotional biases) is an important one and one that we will return to repeatedly throughout the book. Although researchers in the field of psychology have developed many different classifications and identifying factors to categorize and better understand biases, it is reasonable to place biases within these two categories.

Although there is a complex methodology to identifying and classifying biases, in short, cognitive errors stem from basic statistical, information processing, or memory errors; cognitive errors may be considered the result of faulty reasoning. Emotional biases stem from impulse or intuition and may be considered to result from reasoning influenced by feelings. Behavioral biases, regardless of their source, may cause decisions to deviate from the assumed rational decisions of traditional finance. In this book, behavioral biases are classified as either cognitive errors or emotional biases. This distinction is not only simple and easily understood, but it also provides a useful framework for understanding how behavioral investor types, introduced later, are created.

Although it might not be obvious, in my experience cognitive errors are more easily corrected than emotional biases. Individuals are better able to adapt their behaviors or modify their processes if the source of the bias is logically identifiable, even if the investor does not fully understand the specific investment issues under consideration. For instance, an individual may not understand the complex mathematical process involved in updating probabilities when presented with an everyday financial decision, but may comprehend that the process he or she used was not complete or correct. Cognitive errors can also be thought of as blind spots or distortions in the human mind. Cognitive errors do not result from emotional or other predispositions toward certain judgments, but rather from either subconscious mental procedures for processing information or irrational perseverance in one's own beliefs. Because cognitive errors stem from faulty reasoning, better information, education, and advice can often correct for them.

On the other hand, because emotional biases stem from impulse or intuition—especially personal and possibly unreasoned judgments—they are less easily corrected. It is generally agreed that an emotion is a mental state that arises spontaneously rather than through conscious effort. Emotions are related to feelings, perceptions, or beliefs about elements, objects, or relations between these things, and they can be a function of reality or of the imagination. In the world of investing, emotions can cause investors to make suboptimal decisions. Emotions may be undesirable to those feeling them; they may wish to control the emotions but often cannot. Thus, it may only be possible to recognize an emotional bias and adapt to it. When investors adapt to biases, they accept them and make decisions to recognize and adjust for them (rather than making an attempt to reduce or eliminate them).

The cognitive–emotional distinction will help determine when and how to adjust for behavioral biases in financial decision making. However, it should be noted that specific biases may have some common aspects and that a specific bias may seem to have both cognitive and emotional aspects. Researchers in financial decision making have identified numerous and specific behavioral biases. This chapter will not attempt to discuss all identified biases. Rather, it will discuss some of the more publicized and recognized biases within the cognitive-emotional framework. This framework will be useful in developing an awareness of biases, their implications, and ways of using them later in the book.

In the next two sections, we discuss specific behavioral biases. The purpose of this chapter is only to describe biases; interpretation and use of the biases are done in later chapters. Cognitive errors are discussed in the next section and emotional biases in the following section. For each bias we (1) describe the bias, including evidence supporting the existence of the bias; and (2) describe the consequences of the bias. Advice for overcoming biases are presented in later chapters. We limit our focus to gauging the presence or absence—not the magnitude—of each bias that we review. That is, we do not try to measure how strongly the bias is exhibited, but rather we define each bias and its potential consequences. In detecting a bias, we identify statements or thought processes that may be indicative of the bias. Diagnostic tests with varying degrees of complexity are available to detect biases and can be found in *Behavioral Finance and Wealth Management*, published by John Wiley & Sons.

## COGNITIVE BIASES

We will now review 13 cognitive biases and their implications for financial decision making. Cognitive biases are classified into two categories. The first category contains "belief perseverance" biases. Belief perseverance in the context of behavioral biases is the tendency to cling to one's previously held or recently established beliefs irrationally or illogically. Investors continue to hold and justify the belief because of their bias toward belief in themselves or their own ideals or abilities. The second category of cognitive error has to do with how people process information either illogically or irrationally in financial decision making.

Note: In this book, the individuals discussed are called "financial market participants" (FMPs), and are engaged in financial decision making. These include both individual investors and financial services professionals engaging in financial markets.

### Belief Perseverance Biases

The belief perseverance biases we discuss are conservatism, confirmation, representativeness, illusion of control, hindsight, and cognitive dissonance.

**Conservatism Bias** Conservatism bias is a belief perseverance bias in which people maintain their prior views or forecasts by inadequately incorporating new information that arises. Academic studies have demonstrated that conservatism causes individuals to overweigh initial beliefs about outcomes and underreact to new information; in other words, people often fail to modify their beliefs and actions to the extent rationally justified by the new information. As a result of conservatism bias, FMPs may underreact to or fail to act on new information and continue to maintain beliefs close to those based on previous estimates and information.

As a result of conservatism bias, FMPs may do the following:

- Maintain or be slow to update a view or a forecast about an investment, even when presented with new information. For example, if an investor purchases a security of a pharmaceutical company based on the belief that the company is about to receive regulatory approval for a new drug, and then the company announces that it is experiencing problems getting the approval, the investor may cling to his initial valuation of the company and fail to respond or respond slowly to the new information. As a result, the investor may hold the security longer than a rational decision maker would.
- Decide to maintain a prior belief rather than deal with the mental stress of updating beliefs given complex data. This behavior relates to an underlying difficulty in processing new information. For example, if an investor purchases a security based on the belief that the company is entering a period of significant earnings growth, and then the company announces that its growth rate may appear lower than expected because of a number of difficult-to-interpret accounting changes, the investor may maintain the prior belief rather than attempt to decipher the fundamental impact, if any, reflected in the accounting changes. As a result, the investor may hold the security longer than a rational decision maker would.

**Confirmation Bias**    Confirmation bias is a belief perseverance bias in which people tend to look for and notice what confirms their beliefs, and to ignore or undervalue what contradicts their beliefs. This behavior encompasses aspects of selective perception and is an all-too-natural action in which people convince themselves of what they want to believe by giving more weight to evidence that supports their beliefs and ignoring or modifying evidence that conflicts with their beliefs. All FMPs—whether individual investors, analysts, investment advisors, or fund managers—may, after making an investment decision, tend to notice and consider information in a manner that supports their beliefs. They may notice and consider only confirmatory information and ignore or modify contradictory information. Most experienced private wealth advisors have dealt with a client who conducts some research and insists on adding a particular investment to his portfolio. Unfortunately, the client may have failed to consider how the investment fits into his portfolio, as well as evidence of its fundamental value. This type of client may insist on continuing to hold the investment, even when the advisor recommends otherwise, because the client's follow-up research seeks only information that confirms his belief that the investment is still a good value.

In the investment world, confirmation bias is exhibited repeatedly. As a result of confirmation bias, FMPs may do the following:

- Generally consider only positive information about an existing or proposed investment and ignore or discount negative information about the investment.
- Underdiversify portfolios, leading to excessive exposure to risk. FMPs may become convinced of the value of a single company and its stock. They ignore negative news about the company and its stock, and they gather and process only information confirming that the company is a good investment. They build a large position and eventually own a poorly diversified portfolio.

**Representativeness Bias** Representativeness bias is a belief perseverance bias in which people tend to classify new information based on past experiences and classifications. They believe their classifications are appropriate and place undue weight on them. This bias occurs because people attempting to derive meaning from their experiences tend to classify objects and thoughts into personalized categories. When confronted with new information, they use those categories even if the new information does not necessarily fit. They rely on a best-fit approximation to determine which category should provide a frame of reference from which to understand the new information. Although this perceptual framework provides an expedient tool for processing new information, it may lead to statistical and information processing errors. The new information superficially resembles or is representative of familiar elements already classified, but in reality it can be very different. In these instances, the classification reflex deceives people, producing an incorrect understanding that often persists and biases all future thinking about the information.

A wide variety of FMP behaviors indicate susceptibility to the premise of the representativeness bias. FMPs often overweight new information and small samples because they view the information or sample as representative of the population as a whole. As a result of representativeness bias, FMPs may do the following:

- Adopt a view or a forecast based almost exclusively on new information or a small sample. For example, when evaluating investment managers, FMPs may place undue emphasis on high returns during a one-, two-, or three-year period, ignoring the base probability of such a return occurring. As a result, the investor may hire an investment manager without adequately considering the likelihood of such returns continuing. This situation may also result in high investment manager turnover as the investor changes investment managers based on short-term results.

■ Update beliefs using simple classifications rather than deal with the mental stress of updating beliefs given complex data. This issue relates to an underlying difficulty (cognitive cost) in properly processing new information. For example, if an investor purchases a security based on the belief that the company is entering a period of significant earnings growth, and then the company announces that its growth rate may appear lower than expected because of a number of difficult-to-interpret accounting changes, the investor may simply reclassify the stock rather than attempt to decipher the fundamental impact, if any, reflected in the accounting changes. As a result, the investor may sell the security when fundamentals would not justify such a decision.

**Illusion of Control Bias**   Illusion of control bias is a bias in which people tend to believe that they can control or influence outcomes when, in fact, they cannot. Langer defines the illusion of control bias as the "expectancy of a personal success probability inappropriately higher than the objective probability would warrant."[1] Langer finds that choices, task familiarity, competition, and active involvement can all inflate confidence and generate such illusions. For example, Langer observed that people permitted to select their own numbers in a hypothetical lottery game were willing to pay a higher price per ticket than subjects gambling on randomly assigned numbers. Since this initial study, many other researchers have uncovered similar situations in which people perceived themselves as possessing more control than they did, inferred causal connections where none existed, or displayed surprisingly great certainty in their predictions for the outcomes of chance events.

As a result of illusion of control bias, FMPs may do the following:

■ Trade more than is prudent. Researchers have found that traders, especially online traders, believe that they have control over the outcomes of their investments. This view leads to excessive trading, which may lead to lower realized returns than a strategy where securities are held longer and traded less frequently.

■ Lead investors to inadequately diversify portfolios. Researchers have found that some investors prefer to invest in companies that they may feel they have some control over, like the companies they work for, leading them to hold concentrated positions. In fact, most investors have almost no control over the companies they work for. If the company performs poorly, the investor may experience both the loss of employment and investment losses.

**Hindsight Bias** Hindsight bias occurs when people see past events as having been predictable and reasonable to expect. People tend to remember their own predictions of the future as more accurate than they actually were because they are biased by the knowledge of what has actually happened. In other words, to alleviate discomfort associated with the unexpected occurrences, people tend to view things that have already happened as being relatively inevitable and predictable. This view is often caused by the reconstructive nature of memory. When people look back, they do not have perfect memory; they tend to fill in the gaps with what they prefer to believe. In doing so, people may prevent themselves from learning from past mistakes.

As a result of hindsight bias, FMPs may do the following:

■ Overestimate the degree to which they predicted an investment outcome, thus giving them a false sense of confidence. For example, when an investment appreciates for unforeseen reasons, FMPs may rewrite their own memories to reflect those reasons. The hindsight bias may cause FMPs to take on excessive risk, leading to future investment mistakes.
■ Cause FMPs to unfairly assess money manager or security performance. Based on their ability to look back at what has taken place in securities markets, performance is compared against what has happened as opposed to what is expected. For example, a given manager may have followed his or her strategy faithfully, and possibly even ranked near the top of the relevant peer group, but the investment results may be disappointing compared to another segment of the market or the market as a whole.

**Cognitive Dissonance Bias** When newly acquired information conflicts with preexisting understandings, people often experience mental discomfort—a psychological phenomenon known as cognitive dissonance. Cognitions, in psychology, represent attitudes, emotions, beliefs, or values; and cognitive dissonance is a state of imbalance that occurs when contradictory cognitions intersect.

The term cognitive dissonance encompasses the responses that arise when people struggle to harmonize cognitions and thereby relieve their mental discomfort. For example, a consumer might purchase a certain brand of power washer, initially believing that it is the best power washer available. However, when a new cognition that favors a substitute power washer is introduced, representing an imbalance, cognitive dissonance then occurs in an attempt to alleviate the discomfort that accompanies the notion that perhaps the buyer did not purchase the right power washer. People will go to great lengths to convince themselves that the power washer they actually bought is better than the one they just learned about, to avoid the mental discomfort associated with their initial purchase. In essence, they persist in their belief that they are correct. In this sense, cognitive dissonance bias is the basis for the all of the belief perseverance biases in this section with different variations on the same theme.

As a result of cognitive dissonance bias, FMPs may do the following:

- Cognitive dissonance can cause investors to hold losing securities positions that they otherwise would sell because they want to avoid the mental pain associated with admitting that they made a bad decision.
- Cognitive dissonance can cause investors to continue to invest in a security that they already own after it has gone down (average down) to confirm an earlier decision to invest in that security without judging the new investment with objectivity and rationality. A common phrase for this concept is "throwing good money after bad."
- Cognitive dissonance can cause investors to get caught up in herds of behavior; that is, people avoid information that counters an earlier decision (cognitive dissonance) until so much counter information is released that investors herd together and cause a deluge of behavior that is counter to that decision.
- Cognitive dissonance can cause investors to believe "it's different this time." People who purchased high-flying, hugely overvalued growth stocks in the late 1990s ignored evidence that there were no excess returns from purchasing the most expensive stocks available. In fact, many of the most high-flying companies are now far below their peaks in price.

## Information Processing Biases

The second category of cognitive errors is information processing errors or biases. Information processing biases result in information being processed and used illogically or irrationally. As opposed to clinging irrationally to one's own beliefs, these have more to do with how information is processed. The processing errors we discuss are anchoring and adjustment, mental accounting, framing, availability, self-attribution, outcome, and recency.

**Anchoring and Adjustment Bias**   Anchoring and adjustment bias is an information processing bias in which the use of psychological heuristics influences the way people estimate probabilities. When required to estimate a value with unknown magnitude, people generally begin by envisioning some initial default number—an "anchor"—which they then adjust up or down to reflect subsequent information and analysis. Regardless of how the initial anchor was chosen, people tend to adjust their anchors insufficiently and produce end approximations that are, consequently, biased. This bias is closely related to the conservatism bias. In the conservatism bias, people overweight past information compared to new information. In anchoring and adjustment, people place undue weight on the anchor. People anchor and adjust because they are generally better at estimating relative comparisons than absolute figures.

For example, FMPs exhibiting this bias are often influenced by purchase "points," or arbitrary price levels or price indexes, and tend to cling to these numbers when facing questions like, "Should I buy or sell this security?" or "Is the market overvalued or undervalued right now?" This approach is especially prevalent when the introduction of new information regarding the security further complicates the situation. Rational investors treat these new pieces of information objectively, and they do not reflect upon purchase prices or target prices in deciding how to act.

- As a result of anchoring and adjustment bias, FMPs may stick too closely to their original estimates when new information is learned. For example, if the FMP originally estimates next year's earnings for a company as $2.00 per share and the company experiences difficulties during the year, FMPs may not adequately adjust the $2.00 estimate given the difficulties. They remain anchored to the $2.00 estimate. This mindset is not limited to downside adjustments; the same phenomenon occurs when companies have upside surprises.
- In another example, FMPs may become anchored to the economic states of countries or companies. In the 1980s, Japan was viewed as a model economy, and many FMPs believed it would remain dominant for decades. It took many FMPs a significant period to revise their beliefs about Japan when its growth slowed. FMPs can similarly anchor on beliefs about companies.

**Mental Accounting Bias** Mental accounting bias is an information processing bias in which people treat one sum of money differently from another equal-sized sum based on which mental account the money is assigned to. Richard Thaler describes mental accounting as a process in which people code, categorize, and evaluate economic outcomes by grouping their assets into any number of non-fungible (non-interchangeable) mental accounts.[2] This method contradicts rational economic thought because money is inherently fungible. Mental accounts are based on such arbitrary classifications as the source of the money (e.g., salary, bonus, inheritance, gambling) or the planned use of the money (e.g., leisure, necessities). According to traditional finance theory, FMPs should consider portfolios holistically in a risk/return context.

A potentially serious problem that mental accounting creates is the placement of investments into discrete "buckets" without regard for the correlations among these assets. Meir Statman contends that the difficulty individuals have in addressing the interaction of different investments leads investors to construct portfolios in a layered pyramid format.[3] As a result of mental accounting bias, FMPs may do the following:

- Neglect opportunities to reduce risk by combining assets with low correlations. Inefficient investing may result from offsetting positions in the various layers.[4] This approach can lead to suboptimal aggregate portfolio performance.[5]
- Irrationally distinguish between returns derived from income and those derived from capital appreciation. Although many people feel the need to preserve capital appreciation (principal), they focus on the idea of spending income that the principal generates. As a result, many FMPs chase income streams, such as through the purchase of a high-yield or junk bond that pays a high dividend but can suffer significant loss of principal if the company issuing the bond experiences financial difficulties, unwittingly eroding principal in the process.

**Framing Bias**   Framing bias is an information processing bias in which a person answers a question differently based on the way in which it is asked (framed). The frame that a decision maker adopts is controlled partly by the formulation of the problem and partly by the norms, habits, and personal characteristics of the decision maker. A framing effect results in a change of preferences between options as a function of the variation of frames, perhaps through variation of the formulation of the decision context. For example, a decision may be presented within a gain context (20 percent of the people with disease X given injection Z will survive), or within a loss context (80 percent of the people with disease X will die even if given injection Z). In the first presentation, people with disease X tend to adopt a positive outlook based on a gain frame of reference and are generally less likely to engage in risky behavior; they are risk-averse because they view themselves as having a potential to gain (survive in this case). In the second presentation, people with disease X tend to adopt a negative outlook based on a loss frame of reference; they may seek risk because they view themselves as having nothing to lose (likely to die in this case).

FMPs' willingness to accept risk can be influenced by how situations are presented or framed. A common framing problem occurs when investment questions are posed positively or negatively. For example, suppose Mr. Ing has a choice of Portfolio A or Portfolio B, which are identical in terms of expected risk and return. Mr. Ing is told that Portfolio A offers a 70 percent chance of attaining his financial goals, and Portfolio B offers a 30 percent chance of falling short of his financial goals. Mr. Ing is likely to choose Portfolio A because of the positive way the question was framed.

As a result of framing bias, FMPs may do the following:

- Misidentify risk tolerances because of how questions about risk tolerance were framed; may become more risk-averse when presented with a gain frame of reference and more risk-seeking when presented with a loss frame of reference. This may result in suboptimal portfolios.
- Choose suboptimal investments, even with properly identified risk tolerances, based on how information about the specific investments is framed.

**Availability Bias**   Availability bias is an information processing bias in which people take a heuristic (also known as a rule of thumb or a mental shortcut) approach to estimating the probability of an outcome based on how easily the outcome comes to mind. Easily recalled outcomes are often perceived as being more likely than those that are harder to recall or understand. People often unconsciously decide the probability of an event by how easily they can recall a memory of the event. The fundamental issue is that many people are biased in their memories. For instance, recent events are much more easily remembered and available.

FMPs' investment choices may be influenced by how easily information is recalled. As a result of availability bias, FMPs may do the following:

- Choose an investment, investment advisor, or mutual fund based on advertising rather than on a thorough analysis of the options. For instance, when asked to name potential mutual fund companies to invest with, many people will name only the funds that do extensive advertising. In reality, many mutual fund companies do little or no advertising.
- Limit their investment opportunity set. This may be because they use familiar classification schemes. They may restrict investments to stocks and bonds of one country or may fail to consider alternative investments when appropriate.

**Self-Attribution Bias**   Self-attribution bias (or self-serving attribution bias) refers to the tendency of individuals to ascribe their successes to innate aspects, such as talent or foresight, while more often blaming failures on outside influences, such as bad luck. Students faring well on an exam, for example, might credit their own intelligence or work ethic, while those failing might cite unfair grading. Research has shown that if people intend to succeed, then outcomes in accordance with that intention—successes—will be perceived as the result of people acting to achieve what they've originally intended. Individuals, then, will naturally accept more credit for successes than failures, since they intend to succeed rather than to fail.

Four key consequences of self-attribution bias are:

1. Self-attribution investors can, after a period of successful investing (such as one quarter or one year) believe that their success is due to their acumen as investors rather than to factors out of their control. This behavior can lead to taking on too much risk, as the investors become too confident in their behavior.
2. Self-attribution bias often leads investors to trade much more than is prudent. As investors believe that successful investing (trading) is attributed to skill versus luck, they begin to trade too much, which has been shown to be "hazardous to your wealth."
3. Self-attribution bias leads investors to "hear what they want to hear." That is, when investors are presented with information that confirms a decision that they made to make an investment, they will ascribe brilliance to themselves. This may lead to investors that make a purchase or hold an investment that they should not.
4. Self-attribution bias can cause investors to hold underdiversified portfolios, especially among investors that attribute the success of a company's performance to their own contribution, such as corporate executives, board members, and so on. Often the performance of a stock is not attributed to the skill of an individual person, but rather many factors, including chance; thus, holding a concentrated stock position can be associated with self-attribution and should be avoided.

**Outcome Bias**   Outcome bias refers to the tendency of individuals to decide to do something—such as make an investment in a mutual fund—based on the outcome of past events (such as returns of the past five years) rather than by observing the process by which the outcome came about (the investment process used by the mutual fund manager over the past five years). An investor might think: "This manager had a fantastic five years, I am going to invest with her," rather than understanding how such great returns were generated or why the returns generated by other managers might not have had good results over the past five years.

Three key consequences of outcome bias are:

1. Investors may invest in funds that they should not because they are focused on the outcome of a prior action, such as the performance

record of the manager, rather than on the process by which the manager achieved the results. This may cause investors to subject themselves to excessive risk if the source of the performance was a risky strategy.

2. Investors may avoid investing in funds that they should not because they are focused on the outcome of a prior action, such as the performance record of the manager, rather than on the process by which the manager achieved the results. Investors may avoid a manager based on a bad outcome while ignoring the potentially sound process by which the manager made the decision.

3. Investors may invest in overvalued asset classes based on recent outcomes, such as strong performance in gold or housing prices, and not pay heed to valuations or past price history of the asset class in question, thereby exposing them to the risk that the asset class may be peaking, which can be "hazardous to one's wealth."

**Recency Bias** Recency bias is a cognitive predisposition that causes people to more prominently recall and emphasize recent events and observations than those that occurred in the near or distant past. Suppose, for example, that a cruise passenger peering off the observation deck of a ship spots precisely equal numbers of green boats and blue boats over the duration of the trip. However, if the green boats pass by more frequently toward the end of the cruise, with the passing of blue boats dispersed evenly or concentrated toward the beginning, then recency bias would influence the passenger to recall, following the cruise, that more green than blue boats sailed by.

Four key consequences of recency bias are:

1. Recency bias can cause investors to extrapolate patterns and make projections based on historical data samples that are too small to ensure accuracy. Investors who forecast future returns based too extensively on only a recent sample of prior returns are vulnerable to purchasing at price peaks. These investors tend to enter asset classes at the wrong times and end up experiencing losses.

2. Recency bias can cause investors to ignore fundamental value and to focus only on recent upward price performance. When a return cycle peaks and recent performance figures are most attractive, human nature is to chase promise of a profit. Asset classes can and do become overvalued. By focusing only on price performance and not on valuation, investors risk principal loss when these investments revert to their mean or long-term averages.

3. Recency bias can cause investors to utter the words that many market veterans consider the most deceptive and damning of all: "It's different

this time." In 1998 and 1999, for example, the short-term memory of recent gains influenced some investors so strongly as to overrule, in their minds, historical facts regarding rational valuations and the bubbles, peaks, and valleys that naturally occur. If your client ever seems to be yielding to this rationale, then it is time for a reality check.

4. Recency bias can cause investors to ignore proper asset allocation. Professional investors know the value of proper asset allocation, and they rebalance when necessary in order to maintain proper allocations. Recency bias can cause investors to become infatuated with a given asset class that, for example, appears in vogue. They often concentrate their holdings accordingly. Proper asset allocation is crucial to long-term investment success.

## EMOTIONAL BIASES

We will now review seven emotional biases and their implications for investment decision making. Emotion has no single universally accepted definition; however, an emotion may be thought of as a mental state that arises spontaneously rather than through conscious effort. Emotions may be undesired to the individuals feeling them; although they may wish to control the emotion and their response to it, they often cannot. Emotional biases are harder to correct for than cognitive errors because they originate from impulse or intuition rather than conscious calculations. In the case of emotional biases, it may only be possible to recognize the bias and adapt to it rather than correct for it.

Emotional biases can cause investors to make suboptimal decisions. Because emotions are rarely identified and recorded in the decision making process—they have to do with how people feel rather than what and how they think—fewer emotional biases have been identified. The seven emotional biases discussed are loss aversion, overconfidence, self-control, status quo, endowment, regret aversion, and affinity.

### Loss-Aversion Bias

Loss-aversion bias was identified by Daniel Kahneman and Amos Tversky in 1979 while they were working on developing the seminal work in modern behavioral finance, prospect theory.[6] In prospect theory, loss-aversion occurs when people tend to strongly prefer avoiding losses as opposed to achieving gains. A number of studies suggest that, psychologically, losses are significantly more powerful than gains. Some of these studies estimate that avoiding losses is two times as powerful a motivator as gains.

Rational FMPs should accept more risk to increase gains, not to mitigate losses. However, paradoxically, they tend to accept more risk to avoid losses than to achieve gains. Loss aversion leads people to hold their losers even if an investment has little or no chance of going back up. Similarly, loss-aversion bias leads to risk avoidance when people evaluate a potential gain. Given the possibility of giving back gains already realized, FMPs lock in profits, thus limiting their upside profits.

As a result of loss-aversion bias, FMPs may do the following:

- Hold investments in a loss position longer than justified by fundamental analysis. FMPs hold losing investments in the hope that they will return to break even.
- Sell investments in a gain position earlier than justified by fundamental analysis. FMPs sell winning investments because they fear that their profit will erode.
- Hold riskier portfolios than is acceptable based on the risk/return objectives of the FMP. This is caused by the sale of investments that are winners and the retention of investments that are losers. FMPs may accept more risk in their portfolios than they would if they had based their decision on risk/return objectives and fundamental analysis.

## Overconfidence Bias

Overconfidence bias is a bias in which people demonstrate unwarranted faith in their own intuitive reasoning, judgments, and/or cognitive abilities. This overconfidence may be the result of overestimating knowledge levels, abilities, and access to information. For example, people generally do a poor job of estimating probabilities; still, they believe they do it well because they believe that they are smarter and more informed than they actually are. Overconfidence bias has aspects of both cognitive and emotional errors but is classified as emotional because the bias is primarily the result of emotion. It is difficult to correct for because it is difficult for people to revise self-perceptions of their knowledge and abilities. The concept of overconfidence has been derived from a large number of psychological experiments and surveys in which subjects overestimate both their own predictive abilities as well as the precision of the information they have been given.

As a result of overconfidence bias, FMPs may do the following:

- Underestimate risks and overestimate expected returns.
- Hold poorly diversified portfolios.
- Trade excessively.
- Experience lower returns than those of the market.

### Self-Control Bias

Self-control bias is a bias in which people fail to act in pursuit of their long-term, overarching goals because of a lack of self-discipline. There is an inherent conflict between short-term satisfaction and achievement of some long-term goals. Money is an area in which people are notorious for displaying a lack of self-control, but it is not the only one. Attitudes toward weight loss provide an example. A person who is 100 pounds overweight is told by a doctor that weight loss is essential to long-term good health. Despite this knowledge, the individual may fail to cut back on food consumption. The short-term satisfaction of eating conflicts with the long-term goal of good health. Rational behavior would suggest that people would do whatever was necessary to achieve their long-term goals, but it often does not happen.

When it comes to money, people may know they need to save for retirement, but they often have difficulty sacrificing present consumption because of the human tendency to prefer small payoffs now compared to larger payoffs in the future. Sacrifices in the present require much greater payoffs in the future. People spend today rather than save for tomorrow. This behavior can lead to high short-term utility and disastrous long-term utility.

As a result of self-control bias, FMPs may do the following:

- Save insufficiently for the future. And upon realizing that their savings are insufficient, FMPs may accept too much risk in their portfolios in an attempt to generate higher returns. In this attempt to make up for less than adequate savings, the capital base is put at risk.
- Cause asset allocation imbalance problems. For example, some FMPs prefer income-producing assets in order to have income to spend. This behavior can be hazardous to long-term wealth because income-producing assets may offer less total return potential, particularly when the income is not reinvested, which may inhibit a portfolio's ability to maintain spending power after inflation.

### Status Quo Bias

Status quo bias, coined by Samuelson and Zeckhauser, is an emotional bias in which people do nothing (maintain the status quo) instead of making a change.[7] People are generally more emotionally comfortable keeping things the same than they are with change, and thus do not necessarily look for opportunities where change is beneficial. Given no apparent problem requiring a decision, the status quo is maintained. Further, if given a situation where one choice is the default choice, people will frequently let that choice stand rather than opt out of it and make another choice. Thus, the process in presenting choices can influence decisions.

As a result of status quo bias, FMPs may do the following:

- Unknowingly maintain portfolios with risk characteristics that are inappropriate for their circumstances.
- Fail to explore other opportunities.

## Endowment Bias

Endowment bias is an emotional bias in which people value an asset more when they hold rights to it than when they do not. Endowment bias is inconsistent with standard economic theory, because the price a person is willing to pay for a good should equal the price at which that person would be willing to sell the same good. However, psychologists have found that when asked, people tend to state minimum selling prices for a good they own but exceed maximum purchase prices that they are willing to pay for the same good. Effectively, ownership "endows" the asset with added value.

As is the case with status quo bias, endowment bias may lead FMPs to do the following:

- Fail to sell off certain assets and replace them with other assets. For example, a child or grandchild may hold an outsized inherited stock position because of an emotional attachment, despite the risk of a sizable loss if the stock stumbles. These investors are often resistant to selling even in the face of poor prospects.
- Continue to hold classes of assets with which they are familiar. FMPs may believe they understand the characteristics of the investments they already own and may be reluctant to purchase assets with which they have less experience. Familiarity adds to owners' perceived value of a security.

## Regret-Aversion Bias

Regret-aversion bias is an emotional bias in which people tend to avoid making decisions that will result in action out of fear that the decision will turn out poorly. Simply put, people try to avoid the pain of regret associated with bad decisions. This tendency is especially prevalent in investment decision making. Regret aversion can cause FMPs to hold onto positions too long. They are reluctant to sell because they fear that the position will increase in value and then they will regret having sold it.

Regret aversion can also keep FMPs out of a market that has recently generated sharp losses or gains. Having experienced losses, our instincts tell us that to continue investing is not prudent. Yet periods of depressed prices may present great buying opportunities. Regret aversion can persuade us to stay out of the stock market just when the time is right for investing. On the upside, fear of getting in at the high can restrict new investments from taking place.

As a result of regret-aversion bias, FMPs may do the following:

- Be too conservative in their investment choices as a result of poor outcomes on risky investments in the past. FMPs may wish to avoid the regret of making another bad investment and decide that low-risk instruments are better. This behavior can lead to long-term under-performance and potential failure to reach investment goals.
- Engage in herding behavior. FMPs may feel safer in popular investments in order to limit potential future regret. It seems safe to be with the crowd, and a reduction in potential emotional pain is perceived. Regret aversion may lead to preference for stocks of well-known companies even in the face of equal risk and return expectations. Choosing the stocks of less familiar companies is perceived as riskier and involves more personal responsibility and greater potential for regret.

## Affinity Bias

Affinity bias refers to an individual's tendency to make irrationally un-economical consumer choices or investment decisions based on how they believe a certain product or service will reflect their values. This idea focuses on the expressive benefits of a product rather than on what the product or service actually does for someone (the utilitarian benefits). A common example of this behavior in the consumer product realm is when one pur-chases wine. A consumer may purchase a fine bottle of well-known wine in a restaurant or wine shop for hundreds of dollars to impress their dinner guests, while a bottle that costs much less could be equally delicious but would not convey the same status. Similarly, in the investment realm, in-vestors might invest in certain companies, such as those that produce Range Rovers, because they feel that this company reflects their values or self-image. This behavior may lead to suboptimal investment results if the com-pany producing the product or service is poorly managed or has financial or business-related problems.

Four key consequences of affinity bias are:

1. Investors subject to affinity bias can make investments in companies that make products or deliver services that they like, but they don't examine carefully enough the soundness of the investment characteristics of those companies.
2. Investors subject to affinity bias can invest in companies that reflect their environmental, social, or governance values but don't carefully examine the soundness of the investment characteristics of those companies.
3. Investors subject to affinity bias can invest in their home countries at the expense of investing in foreign countries due to home country bias.
4. Investors subject to affinity bias can sometimes invest in "sophisticated" investment products that convey status, only to find they have invested in something they don't understand, which can be "hazardous to your wealth."

## SUMMARY

In conclusion, cognitive errors are statistical, information processing, or memory errors that result in faulty reasoning and analysis. The individual may attempt to follow a rational decision making process but fail to do so because of cognitive errors. For example, the person may fail to update probabilities correctly, properly weigh and consider information, or gather information. If these errors are drawn to the attention of an individual attempting to follow a rational decision making process, he or she is likely to be receptive to correcting the errors.

Individuals are less likely to make cognitive errors if they remain vigilant to the possibility of their occurrence. A systematic process to describe problems and objectives; to gather, record, and synthesize information; to document decisions and the reasoning behind them; and to compare the actual outcomes with expected results will help reduce cognitive errors.

Emotional biases, however, stem from impulse, intuition, and feelings and may result in personal and unreasonable decisions. When possible, focusing on cognitive aspects of the biases may be more effective than trying to alter an emotional response. Also, educating about the investment decision making process and portfolio theory can be helpful in moving the decision making from an emotional basis to a cognitive basis. When biases are emotional in nature, drawing these to the attention of an individual making the decision is unlikely to lead to positive outcomes; the individual is likely to become defensive rather than receptive to considering alternatives. Thinking of the appropriate questions to ask to potentially alter the decision making process is likely to be most effective.

## NOTES

1. Ellen Langer, *Psychology of Control* (Beverly Hills, CA: Sage, 1983).
2. Richard Thaler, "Towards a Positive Theory of Consumer Choice," *Journal of Economic Behavior and Organization* 1 (1980): 39–60.
3. "Behavioral Finance: Past Battles and Future Engagements," *Financial Analysts Journal*, November/December 1999.
4. Hersh Shefrin and Meir Statman, *The Journal of Financial and Quantitative Analysis* 35, no. 2 (June 2000): 127–151.
5. Y. Kroll, H. Levy, and A. Rapoport, "Experimental Tests of the Mean-Variance Model for Portfolio Selection," *Organizational Behavior and Human Decision Processes* 42 (1988): 388–410.
6. D. Kahneman, and A. Tversky, "Prospect Theory: An Analysis of Decisions Under Risk," *Econometrica* 47 (1979): 313–327.
7. W. Samuelson, and R. Zeckhauser, "Status Quo Bias in Decision Making," *Journal of Risk and Uncertainty* 1 (1988): 7–59.

# Two

# Personality Theory

With a solid background in understanding why financial goals are difficult to reach, a background in the subject of behavioral finance, as well as an introduction to twenty specific behavioral biases under your belt, we are now in a position to explore Part II of the book which involves personality history and theory, personality testing, and behavioral investor type (BIT) theory. We start with an introduction to personality theory in Chapter 4, and then move to the history of personality testing in Chapter 5. In Chapter 6, the behavioral investor type framework is introduced and in Chapter 7, behavioral investor type diagnostic testing is reviewed.

# Introduction to
# Personality Theory

**A**fter completing Part One of the book, readers should have a basic understanding of why self-defeating behavior in general is important and, in particular, why understanding behavioral finance is crucial to making good financial decisions. Before we move into the details of each behavioral investor type in Chapters 8 through 11, we will spend the next three chapters learning about the history of personality and personality theory, the history of personality type testing, as well as the framework for the creation of behavioral investor types. Armed with this knowledge, learning about each BIT will be easier and you will take more away from it. In addition, you will get a better feel for why the questions asked in Chapter 7, the BIT quiz, are asked the way they are, and what information we are looking for to make a BIT assessment.

The fact is that if we are to fully understand how we as individuals make decisions about investments and create profiles of various types of investors, we need to take a step back and understand how the study of human characteristics and traits has evolved over the years. This chapter aims to introduce the reader to the rich history of thought and research in the field of personality psychology. Along the way you will learn about some of the techniques used in this sub-discipline of psychology, as well as some interesting facts about the psychologists whose theories will be reviewed and compared below. Additionally, you will be introduced to the philosophical foundations of the relatively young discipline of psychology.

It will probably not be a surprise to any of you that the study of personality is not an exact science (but you already knew that!). People are people and hence are unpredictable, varied, and have a mix of traits that don't always provide us with a full understanding of why people make the behavioral decisions that they make generally and how financial decisions are made, in particular. It is therefore incumbent upon us to realize the limitations of the ideas presented in this book. A good portion of these ideas is based on my own experience in dealing with clients over a more than 20-year career, surveys I have given to investors who may or may not give a complete picture of their behavior and/or may not fully understand their own behavior consistently, and research of others that demonstrates that investor behavior cannot be understood with precision. With that as a backdrop, we will delve into the history of personality and some theories of personality.

## HISTORY OF PERSONALITY THEORY

Whether we realize it or not, we describe and assess the personalities of the people around us on a daily basis. These daily musings about how and why people behave as they do are similar to what personality psychologists do. While our informal assessments of personality tend to focus more on individuals, personality psychologists instead use well-developed conceptions of personality that can apply to everyone. Personality research has led to the development of a number of theories that help explain how and why people act the way they do and why certain personality traits develop.

While there are many different theories of personality, the first step is to understand exactly what is meant by the term *personality*. A brief definition is that personality is made up of the characteristic patterns of thoughts, feelings, and behaviors that make a person unique. In addition to this, personality arises from within the individual and remains fairly consistent throughout life.

Some of the fundamental characteristics of personality include:

- Consistency: There is generally a recognizable order and regularity to behaviors. Essentially, people act in the same ways or similar ways in a variety of situations.
- Psychological and physiological traits: Personality is a psychological construct, but research suggests that it is also influenced by biological processes and needs.
- Impact on behaviors and actions: Personality does not just influence how we move and respond in our environment; it also causes us to act in certain ways.
- Multiple expressions: Personality is displayed in more than just behavior. It can also be seen in our thoughts, feelings, close relationships, and other social interactions.

Now that we've described the basic components of personality known today, let's discuss the very beginnings of the study of personality and take a brief look at the discipline's first practitioners and their contributions to the more modern theorists. This takes us all the way back to Ancient Greece, around 400 B.C., to the work of Hippocrates. The great physician believed that people could be "typed" into four distinct categories named Melancholic, Sanguine, Choleric, and Phlegmatic, after the various bodily fluids that were then thought to influence personality. Each category was also linked to one of the four elements: fire, air, water, and earth, collectively referred to as the "humors." Today, Hippocrates's personality types are called: Guardians, Artisans, Idealists, and Rationalists. Below is a brief description of these humors, which are quite vague and simplistic when compared with today's personality theories.

- Guardians: Fact-oriented
- Artisans: Action-oriented
- Idealists: Ideal-oriented
- Rationalists: Theory-oriented

As you can see, these humors encompass the most basic, underlying characteristics of what we today refer to as "personality," but it is clear that no one's actions are entirely "rational" or "theory-based," and that no one is solely "action-oriented," but rather that most people are a combination of many of these humors, but in varying proportions. For example, your wife may be a "rationalist" and you may be more "action-oriented," but obviously neither of these characteristics comprises your entire personality.

In addition to Hippocrates, another ancient thinker, Plato, had his own vision of personality. Plato is one of the notable figures in the Pythagorean tradition who developed simple ideas to explain human behavior. Plato's theory of the three parts of the soul closely parallels Freud's three parts of our personalities, which we will soon discuss. In Plato's view, the soul has an appetitive part, a spirited part, and a rational part. The appetitive part controls desires for the most basic needs of the body, such as food and drink. The rational or thinking part of the soul controls our capacity for rational calculation and problem solving. The rational part tries to keep the appetitive part in check. The spirited part disciplines either the appetitive or rational part when one of the two gets the better of the other. For example, if our appetite for something is so strong that even reason cannot keep that appetite in check, the spirited part punishes the soul with feelings of guilt. Conversely, the spirited part can reward us with feelings of righteousness when we properly keep our appetites in check and thus reinforce such righteous behavior.

Plato also had some interesting thoughts about the unconscious. Plato thought that the soul is a part of us that never dies, although it is unclear whether or not he believed in reincarnation. The soul, according to Plato, is born with information that can be forgotten with time. In one of his Socratic dialogues, the *Meno*, Socrates (the main character in most of Plato's dialogues) asks a young uneducated boy to solve a geometrical problem. At first the boy answers incorrectly, and then Socrates begins questioning him in the "Socratic method." After the bout of questioning, the boy arrives at the correct answer. Socrates never gave the boy information, but only asked him simple questions in a logical manner. Socrates concludes to his friend Meno that the boy must have been recollecting something that he already knew, but had forgotten. The answer to the question was in the boy's unconscious!

## FOUR MAIN PERSONALITY THEORIES

Now that I've provided a historical basis for the development of personality theory, I will discuss the major theories known and used today. There are a number of different theories about how personality develops. Different schools of thought in psychology influence many of these theories, and some of these major perspectives on personality include: *trait theories, behavioral theories, humanist theories,* and *psychodynamic theories.* Keep in mind that this is not an exhaustive list of the theories, but these four will serve our purposes in this book. Sigmund Freud, possibly the most influential psychologist in the world, belonged to the psychodynamic school of study. We will discuss the other theories and their main contributors before we discuss psychodynamic theory, as it provides the basis for most of our understanding of personality today, and thus will be the most thorough section.

### Trait-Based Theory

Psychologists have made heavy use of factor analysis in theorizing about personality. Factor analysis is a statistical method used by psychologists to isolate and verify the existence of personality traits. The following is a quick and easy-to-understand example of how factor analysis works.

Suppose we gave tests to 100 fourth graders in the following six areas: spelling, vocabulary, grammar, addition, subtraction, and multiplication. After tabulating the results, we would create a table of correlation coefficients, or $r$-values (Table 4.1).

The $r$-value is a statistic first used by Karl Pearson, but Francis Galton used a similar idea as early as the 1880s. The statistic measures the degree to which a change in one variable predicts a change in another variable. The different subjects in our example represent variables. We can see that the

**TABLE 4.1** Correlation Coefficients

| Subject | Spelling | Vocabulary | Grammar | Addition | Subtraction | Multiplication |
|---|---|---|---|---|---|---|
| Spelling | – | 0.65 | 0.43 | 0.09 | 0.11 | 0.10 |
| Vocabulary | | – | 0.39 | 0.12 | 0.08 | 0.10 |
| Grammar | | | – | 0.07 | 0.06 | 0.10 |
| Addition | | | | – | 0.68 | 0.72 |
| Subtraction | | | | | – | 0.59 |
| Multiplication | | | | | | – |

six subjects divide naturally into two groups. A student's score in spelling is a good predictor of his vocabulary and grammar scores, but not a good predictor of his addition, subtraction, or multiplication skills. So out of the six initial testing areas we can form two "higher order" factors: Verbal and Quantitative (or whatever you want to call them). The same method outlined above was the primary research method of choice for both Cattell and Eysenck.

**Cattell: The Hierarchy of Traits**   Raymond Cattell defines personality as "that which tells what a [person] will do when placed in a particular situation."[1] He even has a formula for expressing this position: $R = f(S \times P)$. In this equation, $R$ is the "nature and magnitude of a person's behavioral response . . . what he [or she] says, thinks, or does" and is a function of both $S$, the "stimulus situation in which [the person] is placed" and $P$, which stands for the nature of the person's personality.[2] Cattell is well known and often criticized for his belief that most human characteristics, especially intelligence, are determined by genetic factors. As we have already seen from the equation above, however, Cattell does think that the environment plays a significant role in human behavior. Cattell developed the Econetic model, which is a framework that integrates environmental and person-based factors into a theory of human behavior. As various personality traits were uncovered, Cattell would indicate based on his research whether or not the trait was determined genetically or by the environment. For example, Cattell thought that the trait "self-sentiment" was genetically determined, but the trait "superego strength" was a function of a person's environment.[3]

This brings us to a discussion of what exactly a trait is according to Cattell. Cattell thought that a personality trait is "a permanent entity that does not fade in and out like a state; it is inborn or develops during the life course and regularly directs behavior."[4] Cattell developed a hierarchy of personality traits, whereby some more specific traits are subsumed by broader traits. This idea is called subsidiation, and was borrowed from the noted psychologist Henry A. Murray. Cattell's hierarchy of traits situates the most general and least in number residing at the top and gradually descends to the more specific and greater in number. A common trait is "A trait which can be measured for all people by the same battery [of tests] and on which [the people] differ in degree rather than in form." A good example of this is the trait dimension extraversion-introversion. Everyone's personality resides on a continuum between extraversion and introversion. Most people lie somewhere in the middle and have some introverted traits and some extraverted traits. The opposite of a common trait is a unique trait. A unique trait is "so specific to an individual that no one else could be scored on its dimension."[5]

Second-order traits are at the top of the hierarchy. In Cattell's terminology these are also known as superfactors. Two of these traits are introversion-extraversion, and anxiety. Other second order traits often considered in Cattell's factor analytic studies are a measure of intelligence as well as "an index of good upbringing,"[6] which is akin to having good manners.

Below superfactors on the hierarchy lie source traits. A source trait is "a [primary] factor-dimension, stressing the proposition that variations along it are determined by a single unitary influence or source."[7] Cattell believed that these traits could only be determined through factor analysis.[8] An example of a source trait is emotionality, which is a sort of umbrella term for such behaviors as calmness on one end of the spectrum and jitteriness on the other end.[9] Source traits break down into three distinct categories: ability traits, temperament traits, and dynamic traits. Ability traits fall mostly under the domain of one's intelligence, and not personality, so we will not investigate them further. Temperament traits are general personality traits that explain a wide variety of responses and generally cover the "tempo and persistence" of those responses.[10] The emotionality trait alluded to above is a good example of a temperament trait. Cattell places more emphasis on dynamic traits. A dynamic trait refers to one's motivations and interests. They are similar to Maslow's needs in that they are goal directed.[11] Dynamic traits consist of three interrelated subcategories: ergs, attitudes, and sentiments. These three subcategories combine to form a dynamic lattice, which are described next.

The erg is the most basic of the components of the dynamic lattice. Ergs are essentially motives, with the added stipulation that they are mostly hereditary. General patterns of behavior are what Cattell refers to as sentiments, and more specific tendencies are expressed as attitudes. The object of sentiments and attitudes is to reduce the ergic drives.[12] This all becomes a lot clearer when we take an example of a specific erg and relate it to its corresponding attitudes and sentiments. For example, Cattell recognizes an

**FIGURE 4.1** Lattice

erg for "security-seeking" (not unlike Maslow's safety needs). An attitude expressing this erg might be the act of voting for a presidential candidate who promises to beef up our armed forces. The corresponding sentiment for this erg might be something like patriotism. The lattice looks like Figure 4.1 and is referred to as a subsidiation chain.[13]

A major part of Cattell's research program was cataloging human ergs by investigating numerous attitudes. He collected three different types of attitude data. He gathered L data by general observation of everyday human behavior. T data was gathered by issuing written tests to research subjects. And Q data was gathered by administering questionnaires. Cattell factor analyzed the T and Q data to come up with his 16 human ergs.

Cattell's unorthodox research methods distinguish him from the other psychologists in this chapter. Rather than begin by hypothesizing ideas from "off the top of his head," Cattell insisted on gathering data and analyzing it before he made his hypotheses. He made use of what is termed the inductive-hypothetical-deductive spiral. He used inductive reasoning based on preliminary data to arrive at plausible hypotheses. From these hypotheses he carried out experiments and based on the results of the experiments he used deductive logic to either falsify or verify the original hypothesis.[14]

**Eysenck: "Off the Top of the Head" Theorizing**   Hans Eysenck, the next personality theorist that we discuss, also made extensive use of this type of rigid experimental method and eschewed "off the top of the head" theorizing. As quoted in Allen's book, Eysenck advocated a slightly different research program than Cattell:

> *Thus, Cattell starts from the generation of hypotheses [from factor analysis] about the major factors involved, stays [with] factor analysis ... and assigns ... low importance to the fact that his primary factors are intercorrelated, and give rise to superfactors. ... At each*

*stage I follow exactly the opposite line. Starting out with a theo-*
*retical model. . . . I use factor analysis to test theories rather than to*
*originate them. I tried to use [theory] from psychology and physiol-*
*ogy to link the factors . . . with causal hypotheses which led outside*
*factor analysis altogether.*

Traits, as defined by Eysenck, are: "theoretical constructs based on observed intercorrelations between a number of different habitual responses." Eysenck developed three dimensions of personality: extraversion-introversion, neuroticism, and psychoticism. He called these types rather than traits and they are analogous to Cattell's second order factors. Much like the way Cattell did not think that a specific trait is 100 percent environmentally determined, Eysenck did not think that anyone is 100 percent introverted, for example. Most people's personalities fall within an average range of the three type measurements, with only a mild deviation one way or another. For example, suppose that you are only slightly introverted and your partner is only slightly extraverted. Despite the fact that the two of you fall within the normal range, you both perceive a great distance between your personalities on this dimension. In this way Eysenck explains and allows for subjective judgments in his theory of personality.

Contrary to Cattell's beliefs, Eysenck thought that personality was more determined by genetic factors than by environmental factors. Eysenck writes on the subject: "Personality is determined to a large extent by a person's genes; . . . while environment can do something to redress the balance, its influence is severely limited. [For] Personality [and] intelligence . . . genetic influence is overwhelmingly strong, and the role of environment . . . is reduced to effecting slight changes." Eysenck even tied the E-I personality dimension to particular physiological differences. According to him, extraversion is linked with the brain's ascending reticular activating system (ARAS). In layman's terms the ARAS's function is to process sensory inputs and send messages via nerve fibers to the cerebral cortex. Since the cerebral cortex is responsible for coordinating other brain areas, the entire organism is stimulated. If the stimulus is associated with a favorable survival-promoting environment, then the cerebral cortex will signal the ARAS to continue seeking that stimulus. The theory is that introverts' ARAS are more prone to stimulate the nervous system without as much external input. Extraverts' ARAS need more input from the environment in order to send messages to the cerebral cortex. Thus, introverts do not need as much arousal and this explains their socially withdrawn behavior. Conversely, extraverts need more arousal from their environments and this explains their tendency to interact more with their surroundings. The link between E-I and ARAS is Eysenck's most profound experimental contribution to personality science.

## Behavioral Theory

Behavioral theories suggest that personality is the result of interaction between the individual and the environment. Behavioral theorists study observable and measurable behaviors, rejecting theories that take internal thoughts and feelings into account. Two very important behavioral theorists were B. F. Skinner and Albert Bandura, both of whom we discuss in this section.

The philosophical forerunner of behavioral psychology was called Positivism. Positivists held the view that science must be grounded in the evidence provided by our senses. The influence of positivist thought took hold on psychology throughout the first half of the twentieth century. Behavioral psychologists abandoned the hypothetical constructs of the psychoanalysts in favor of a "rigorously empirical, and preferably experimental, study of behavior."[15] Behaviorists severely deemphasize the role inner or mental states play in determining behavior. They did not, however, go so far as to say they do not exist, and the general position among behaviorists is that a causal analysis of behavior involves three parts. The first part is some action or state of the environment of which the individual is aware. For example, an individual might find himself in a hot and dry environment with no readily available source of water. To continue the example, the second link would be an inner state consisting of thirst. Lastly, the individual performs a behavior (called an operant), which in this case would be searching for water and then drinking it. Now let's move on to discussing our first behaviorist, B. F. Skinner.

**B. F. Skinner** B. F. Skinner believes that we have freedom only by way of the capacity to arrange our own circumstances. He once said: "We can arrange our environment so that the consequences we desire become likely, but having done so, we are under the control of our own creation."[16] He is best known for his experiments in operant conditioning (explained further on) and his beliefs about the implications of conditioned behaviors to society as a whole. Skinner was influenced by Pavlov's experiments, which demonstrated "classical conditioning." Pavlov's famously demonstrated classical conditioning in what is popularly known today as the "Pavlov's dog" experiment. Most of you have no doubt at least heard of this experiment and probably know how it works. It is worth retelling the story in order to contrast classical and operant conditioning. Pavlov used to ring a bell before he fed his dogs, and over time the dogs would begin to salivate when they heard the bell even if there was no food present. Thus the salivation of the dogs is contingent upon their being fed in the presence of a ringing bell. Skinner had the idea of reversing the order of contingency. Skinner's conditioning involves a behavior that produces consequences, which in turn influence the probability of the same or similar behavior occurring again. Skinner used to put a pigeon inside a box (Skinner's Box) with a feeder that would dispense food only when the pigeon would peck at a disk hanging on the wall of the box. The pigeon would peck around the box at random until it happened to peck the disk and receive food. Eventually the fraction of pecks at the disk to total pecks would approach 1, at which point the bird was "conditioned" to peck the disk.

At this point you might be asking yourself what any of this has to do with personality. Don't worry; I thought the same thing when doing research for this chapter led me repeatedly to Skinner and his ideas. The importance of Skinner's approach to personality psychology emerges when we apply the principles of operant conditioning outside the laboratory, in our everyday lives. Instead of trying to overcome external influences, Skinner recommends that we embrace the "fact" that our environment determines our behaviors. When we ignore the effects of outside agencies, such as governments and corporations, we only increase their control over us. What we should instead do is seek to actively manipulate our circumstances so that desirable behaviors are reinforced and unwanted behaviors are punished. We have to remember that we are part of the collective environment and have the potential to shape the behavior of others, just as they have the potential to shape our behavior. For example, instead of faking interest in a conversation with a rambler by making eye contact or smiling politely, make an effort to change the subject whenever possible. By feigning interest we only reinforce the very behavior we want to change. Conversely, by changing the topic of discussion to something you are interested in, you shape your friend's behavior by negatively reinforcing a one-way style of conversation and positively reinforcing that topic for future discussions.

Another common notion Skinner entices us to reconsider is dignity. Oftentimes people act irrationally or in ways that do not seem congruent with their circumstances. An example is that of an anonymous charitable donation.[17] The donor could not have been seeking recognition or admiration, thus we commonly associate such selfless acts with the concept of altruism. We associate this type of behavior with an inner quality of the individual, perhaps dignity or altruism. But in doing so we are ignoring the true cause of the act, which must have been some prior conditions that reinforced altruistic behaviors. Consequently, we miss out on an opportunity to try to replicate those conditions in our own household or community. We now move on to our second behaviorist and contemporary of Skinner's, Albert Bandura.

**Bandura: Social Cognitive Theory and Self-Efficacy**   Albert Bandura was a contemporary of Skinner's and firmly entrenched in the behaviorist camp.

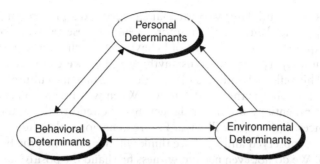

**FIGURE 4.2**   The Reciprocal Relationship of Behavioral, Personal and Environmental Factors

He did not share Skinner's extreme view about mental states as discussed above. By contrast, Bandura thought that we have free will to a significant degree by way of selecting the environments and situations in which we choose to participate.

Bandura traced human behavior to both environmental factors as well as "person factors" such as cognition and other internal processes. His theory revolves around the idea that behavioral, internal, and external factors have a reciprocal relationship with each other. This is to say that each individual factor both causes and is caused by the other two factors (see Figure 4.2).

We already know about the relationship between behavior and environment from the Skinner section. Behavior affects our psychic states when we reflect positively or negatively on our experiences. If we do something well the first time we try, it is likely that our thinking about that activity will change in a positive way.[18] Consider a high school student studying geometry for the first time. If he cannot understand the material and performs poorly at first, he will likely think negatively about his ability to perform any geometrical calculation in the future, no matter how simple it may be. Fast-forward three years, and suppose this student is taking the SAT soon. He knows he needs to focus his preparation on the quantitative reasoning section, and studies very hard in this area. However, going into the test all he can think about is that first geometry test he failed. Because of this memory he believes that he will not do well on the test. According to Bandura this mere negative belief can actually increase the odds that he will perform poorly on the test, despite his preparations.

Bandura thinks that the environment can induce behavior directly, without any conditioning involved at all. This process is detailed in his social cognitive theory. According to Bandura, humans can acquire novel patterns of behavior simply by observation. For example we might observe that a colleague always comes into work an hour early and takes her lunch break at her desk. A month later we hear that she received a promotion. Without having experienced any positive reinforcement for these behaviors ourselves, we can acquire this novel pattern of behavior. Note that our colleague was not intentionally trying to teach us anything and we were not actively trying to learn. This reflects Bandura's observation that in some cultures the word "teach" is the same as the word "show." When we observe someone doing something potentially useful (or dangerous), we tend to think about what consequences that action will have. Future behavior is then adjusted based on what was observed and what we think will happen when the behavior is replicated. We do not even need to witness firsthand the positive or negative consequences of the observed behavior. We can think of the personal factors in Bandura's learning theory as the analogue of conditioning in Skinner's.

In addition to being selective about the situations we face, Bandura thinks that we can exert significant control over our lives through self-influence. Goals are significant determinants of behavior if the goal-setter receives feedback on his progress.[19] Still, merely setting a goal is not enough to guarantee that we will increase our output. We also must put to use what Bandura terms "self-regulatory processes." These are internal, cognitive functions that include self-persuasion and self-praise or self-criticism. We even adjust our personal standards according to our own evaluation about how those standards are affecting our performance.[20]

## Humanist Theory

Humanist theories emphasize the importance of free will and individual experience in the development of personality. Humanist theorists include Carl Rogers and Abraham Maslow. Humanistic psychology "emphasizes the present experience and essential worth of the whole person, promotes creativity, intentionalism, free choice, and spontaneity, and fosters the belief that people can solve their own psychological problems."[21] The personality psychology of Rogers and Maslow marks a dramatic shift from the pessimistic views of Freud and others in the psychoanalytic tradition. Humanists thought that the best way to understand human nature is to "begin by studying individuals who are healthy, productive, creative, and to all appearances, happy and optimistic."[22] They thought that the goal of our lives is to fully realize our innate potential, no matter if that potential is modest, extraordinary, or somewhere in between. Maslow summarizes the overall project of the Humanist psychologists in this statement: "Freud supplied us with the sick half of psychology, we must now fill it out with the healthy half."[23] Humanists believed in the concept of self-actualization, which is the process of creating a conscious vision of the self through life experiences and then fulfilling the potential of the self.

**Rogers** Rogers defines the "one central source of energy in the human organism"[24] as "the inherent tendency of the organism to develop all its capacities in ways which serve to maintain or enhance the organism."[25] This tendency serves as the basic motivation for all human activity and is called the actualization tendency. The actualizing tendency has four basic characteristics:

1. It is a biological predisposition and so exists as part of the inherent nature of humans.
2. It is an active rather than passive process. The actualizing tendency is at work in exploring, manipulating the environment, and even the creative process.
3. It is directional as opposed to random. It inclines us to grow into our own person and become independent from the control of other people.
4. It is a selective tendency, which means that not all of our inherent potentialities are realized.

Self-actualization refers to the lifelong process of enhancing our functioning in three specific ways:

1. Increasing our openness to experience. Experience comprises the mental activity at any one time of which we are conscious. The ability to accept all experiences into our awareness, without distortion one way or another, is the foundation of self-actualization.
2. Developing the capacity to live in the present. The self-actualized individual does not let past preconceptions interfere with her present actions. Similarly, she does not obsess over the need to control future outcomes. She "goes with the flow."
3. Lastly, the self-actualized individual learns to trust his own intuitions, regardless of social conventions. He believes in the inherent trustworthiness of his fellow man and has great appreciation for the act of free choice.

Unconditional positive regard is a precondition for becoming self-actualized. Unconditional positive regard from others, such as our family and friends, means that they accept all of our feelings and actions without judgment. However, it is a good thing when someone close to us lets us know that our behavior ought to change in one way or another. When we have unconditional positive self-regard we accept ourselves in a positive way in the absence of any external influence on the way we think of ourselves. The "locus of evaluation" must lie within us entirely if we are to become truly self-actualized.

**Maslow: Basic Human Nature and Hierarchy of Needs**   For the most part Maslow shared Roger's optimistic views of the basic nature of human beings. Both contributed to the theory of self-actualization and believed that on the whole human actions are a manifestation of the actualizing tendency. Maslow distinguished between deficiency motives (D-motives) and growth or being motives (B-motives). Deficiency motives are instinctive impulses to reduce such drives as hunger, thirst, security, and obtaining esteem from others.[26] Every human has these motives. Appropriate external objects or people (water, siblings, etc.) are the objects of D-motives.

B-motives, unlike D-motives, are independent of environmental factors and are unique to each individual. Also, B-motives are not reduced when their objects have been reached; rather, B-drives increase in intensity as they are fulfilled. B-motives "tend to represent a more pleasurable, higher, and healthier level of functioning."[27] Maslow thought that, "satisfying deficiencies avoids illness; growth satisfactions produce positive health...like the difference between fending off threat or attack, and positive triumph and achievement."[28]

Maslow thought that human motives are extremely complex and interrelated. Some needs often go unnoticed until other needs have been fulfilled. Additionally, the same behavior can often be attributed to vastly different motives. It is for these reasons that Maslow developed a hierarchical structure of human needs. There are five levels of human needs in Maslow's hierarchy:

1. The lowest level needs are physiological needs. Most of these needs are deficiencies and governed by D-motives such as the need for food to eat, water to drink, oxygen to breathe, and so on. Remember that the drive for deficiency needs decreases as the needs are fulfilled.
2. After physiological needs have been satisfied the need for safety begins to emerge. Things such as a stable and predictable environment constitute the need for safety. Activities such as securing a steady source of income and saving money in case of future catastrophe fulfill these latter needs.
3. Next to emerge as primary motivators are the needs for belongingness and love. This could take the form of close friends, a spouse, or offspring. Maslow distinguishes between two kinds of love. D-love is a possessive and selfish desire that often involves, "anxious and manipulative efforts to win the loved one's affection."[29] This kind of love is needed, however, in order to develop B-love. B-love is unconditional and nonpossessive and overall more enjoyable than D-love. With B-love we can be truly honest about ourselves and not feel afraid to reveal our weaknesses as well as our strengths.

4. There are two kinds of esteem needs, one that is focused on personal desires and another that is focused on the desire for the respect of others. Overall competence, the mastery of a skill, and independence fulfill our need for personal esteem (self-esteem). We will never achieve our full potential without actual competence and achievement, no matter how much respect others have for us.
5. Self-actualization needs consist of discovering and eventually fulfilling our innate potential. It is at the self-actualizing level where people's needs begin to differ, because each person has his own potential and unique nature. "What a man *can* be, he *must* be."[30]

   These needs are not always met in this order, but the overall hierarchy is meant to apply generally to all humans. For example, people sometimes choose to deny themselves basic physiological needs in order to fulfill a higher-order need. The most typical reversal of needs is pursuing esteem before love and belongingness. The result is the misguided conviction that those who are highly regarded will automatically be loved.[31]

## Psychodynamic Theory

Psychodynamic theories of personality are heavily influenced by the work of Sigmund Freud, and emphasize the influence of the unconscious on one's personality. Psychodynamic theories include Sigmund Freud's psychosexual stage theory, the work of Carl Jung, and Erik Erikson's stages of psychosocial development. Personality theory as a somewhat scientific discipline begins with the work of the early twentieth century psychologists Sigmund Freud and Carl Jung. Before we can begin to understand their work we need to know a little bit about their educational and personal backgrounds. Both men were well versed in the romantic tradition and nature philosophy, which essentially represents the humanistic, as opposed to the scientific, thought that emerged around the period of the Enlightenment. Both of these scholars studied the work of German writer Goethe extensively, and as a consequence of studying the tragic figures in his books so heavily before going on to become physicians, the theories these men would eventually develop focus on explaining what goes wrong when someone becomes afflicted with some neurosis or psychosis.

### Freud: Psychosexual Development and the Structure of Personality

Freud's main contributions to psychoanalysis (and personality psychology in general) were his theories of psychosexual development and the structure of personality. He thought that human behavior could be best explained by the tension created between our most basic instincts and our attempts to control those instincts. The two most important instincts in Freud's work are sexual instincts and destructive instincts.[32] Ewen provides a brief summary of Freud's view of the basic nature of human beings, saying, "Our inherent nature is murderous, incestuous, and cannibalistic; so to enjoy the benefits of civilized society, we must accept some of the frustration and subliminate our true illicit desires into socially acceptable outlets."[33]

Though this view may seem quite jarring and hedonistic, we must view it in the context of what can "go wrong" with one's personality; that is, his theories are negative because they discuss the bad aspects of human personality. It is important because some of Freud's theories provide the basis for our modern understanding of personality theory. Furthermore, Freud believed that all of our mental activity is governed by psychic energy. He devised a tripartite structure of the human psyche that explains how these processes of drive and drive reduction are played out. These parts will become important later in the book when we are discussing what drives some of the seemingly irrational financial decisions that people make every day. The three parts are as follows:

1. *Id:* The id is a representation of the psyche as it is at birth. Thus, it represents the totality of one's psychic energy. It is "the dark, inaccessible part of our personality . . . a chaos"[34] and is entirely unconscious, and thus does not change or develop as we age. The id lacks a sense of time, morality, and rationality and is the biological side of personality (i.e., you're born with it and there's nothing you can do to alter it). It is easiest to think of the id as a newborn child—it does nothing for anyone else intentionally, and has absolutely no concept of the consequences of its actions.

2. *Ego:* The ego emerges around six to eight months of age, is directed toward the outside world, spans the conscious and unconscious realms, and functions according to the "reality principle." Instead of seizing every opportunity for pleasure, the ego functions in a way that maximizes overall pleasure via problem solving. It is concerned with self-preservation, which is in direct conflict with the motivations of the impulsive id. The ego determines which actions of the id are dangerous to the self and checks these actions when necessary.

3. *Superego:* The superego spans the conscious and the unconscious. It develops out of the ego in the third to fifth years of life. It incorporates the social norms of the individual's surroundings, and functions according to the codes of conduct of the society in which the individual lives. It is easiest to think of the superego as one's conscience, as it rewards us with a feeling of self-virtue when we do not act impulsively or immorally and punishes us with feelings of guilt when we do wrong.

So, in a nutshell, Freud believed that the interaction of the id, ego, and the superego form our personalities, but this only describes the formation of personality. Freud's other great work surrounds the idea of psychosexual development, and he firmly believed that our personality was developed fully by age six. While I'd like to think that my personality has developed since my childhood, it is an interesting perspective and provides some explanation for adult irrationality and impulsivity, which we apply later to investors' financial decisions.

**Carl Jung: Structure of Personality and Character Typology** Jung was a colleague of Freud's. In some ways he carried on the psychoanalytic tradition, but he also had many original ideas and doubted many of Freud's ideas and constructs, especially the existence of the Oedipus Complex. Jung called his theory analytic psychology. Though some of the constructs are the same, Jung's theory is an entity distinct from Freud's psychoanalytic theory.

Jung believed that life itself consists in a set of opposites (the principle of opposites): day and night, birth and death, happiness and misery, introversion and extroversion, conscious and unconscious, thinking and feeling, love and hate, cynicism and belief, and haughtiness and inferiority.[35] These contradictory ideas existing in one psyche produce tension and are the wellspring of our psychic energy. Jung believed that the psyche is a self-regulating system. Psychic energy (libido) flows from the libido-rich component to the libido-poor component in the same way that heat flows from hot to cold. Over time a libido-rich component will unconsciously pass psychic energy to the libido-poor component in order to create a balanced system. Jung calls this phenomenon *enantiodromia*. Together these two principles imply that no personality is ever truly dominated by one or another opposite. Someone who during her younger years was very introverted may over time become more extraverted and vice-versa. The culmination of a well-adjusted personality consists in the unity of all the opposites into a "middle path." This idea is common in Eastern cultures but the West did not have a term for it; Jung called it the transcendent function.

According to Jung, personality can be divided into three parts: Conscious, Personal Unconscious, and Collective Unconscious. The realm of the conscious consists of the ego and the persona. The ego according to Jung is the center of one's awareness. The ego grows by experiences and bodily sensations that serve to differentiate between "I" and "not I."[36] The ego is weak compared to the other components.

The persona is our outward appearance that we put on in order to satisfy the demands of society. Additionally the persona reflects an individual's inner desires and fantasies. This side of the persona helps to explain why not everyone actually puts on a persona that is socially acceptable. The development of the persona, like the ego, is guided by conscious experience.

Jung's views of the unconscious were markedly different from Freud's in some respects. Jung thought that the unconscious is an autonomous entity, and that we are actually capable of carrying on a conversation with our unconscious. Unlike Freud, Jung thought that the unconscious could be a source of creativity and suggest solutions to problems when our conscious mind stalls. "[The unconscious] has at its disposal ... all those things which have been forgotten or overlooked, as well as the wisdom and experience of uncounted centuries.[37]

The personal unconscious forms at birth and is comprised of information based on personal experience that is beyond the level of conscious awareness. This could be because the individual is simply too young to understand his experiences, or because the stimuli are too subtle for conscious comprehension. The shadow is the primitive side of our personality, not unlike Freud's id, derived from our animal forebears. This personality construct contains material repressed from consciousness because of its unpleasant nature. Jung did not think that we repress unpleasant experiences on purpose, and that because of this it is possible to examine our shadow directly (remember that Freud thought the id was completely unconscious). The tendency to see the worst in people is really a denial of our own shadow. Instead of embracing that some of our nature is unpleasant, we project our own shortcomings and inferiorities onto other people. Jung believed this could cause a snowball effect resulting in the completely disordered social relationships characterizing a neurotic individual.

The collective unconscious consists of archetypes. An archetype is something that is innate in each of us and is due exclusively to heredity. Jung describes archetypes as, "preexistent forms that ... represent psychic predispositions that lead people to apprehend, experience, and respond to the world in certain ways."[38]

Jung denies the existence of any formal stages of development, and thus does not attribute individual differences in personality to an individual's development. Instead, Jung explains that personalities differ according to the ways that people typically process internal and external stimuli, and "the characteristic direction (inward or outward) of libido movement."[39] Those who tend to focus their energy inward are introverts and those who focus their energy on the external world are extraverts. These are the two fundamental attitudes.

Along with these two attitudes Jung hypothesizes four functions: sensation, thinking, feeling, and intuition. "Sensation tells you that something exists; thinking tells you what it is; feeling tells you whether it is agreeable or not, and intuition tells you whence it comes and where it is going."[40]

Thinking and feeling are opposed to each other just like introversion and extraversion. This makes eight possible permutations in Jung's personality typology. Intuition and sensing make another pair of opposites. Thinking and feeling are called the "rational" functions. Sensation and intuition are called the "irrational" functions. Everyone possesses the ability to use all four functions, but in everyone one function will become dominant over the others. The "dominant" function serves as a basis for organizing one's personality as well as the major mode of experience.[41] Inferior function is the opposite of the dominant function. The inferior attitude is the opposite of the dominant attitude. For example, let's consider an extravert whose dominant function is thinking. His inferior attitude is introversion and his inferior function is feeling. These inferior processes are thought to be repressed in the unconscious. In this way the unconscious compensates for the superior function and attitude. The two functions that are neither dominant nor inferior "waver between consciousness and unconsciousness, and serve as potential auxiliaries to the dominant function."[42]

## NOTES

1. Bem P. Allen, *Personality Theories: Development, Growth, and Diversity.* 3rd ed. (Boston: Pearson/Allyn & Bacon, 2006), 376.
2. Ibid., 376.
3. Ibid., 376 (Cattell, Rao, and Schuerger quoted in Allen).
4. Ibid., 377.
5. Ibid., 378 (Cattell quoted in Allen).
6. Ibid., 378.
7. Ibid., 378 (Cattell quoted in Allen).
8. Robert B. Ewen, *An Introduction to Theories of Personality*, 4th ed. (Hillsdale, NJ: Lawrence Erlbaum Associates, 1993), 321.
9. Allen, *Personality Theories*, 378.
10. Ibid., 378.
11. Ibid., 378.
12. Ewen, *Theories of Personality*, 321.
13. Allen, *Personality Theories*, 322.
14. Ibid, 375.
15. Frank Dumont, *A History of Personality Psychology: Theory, Science, and Research from Hellenism to the Twenty-First Century* (Leiden: Cambridge University Press, 2010), 185.
16. Allen, *Personality Theories*, 328.
17. Ibid.
18. Ibid., 285.
19. Ibid., 300.
20. Ibid., 305.

21. Ibid., 205.
22. Allen, *Personality Theories*, 198.
23. Dumont, *History of Personality*, 65.
24. Allen, *Personality Theories*, 202.
25. Ibid., 202.
26. Ewen, *Theories of Personality*, 400.
27. Ibid., 401.
28. Ibid., 401.
29. Ibid., 403.
30. Ibid., 404.
31. Allen, *Personality Theories*, 229.
32. Ewen, *Theories of Personality*, 73.
33. Ibid., 74.
34. Ibid., 27.
35. Allen, *Personality Theories*, 28.
36. Ibid., 87.
37. Ibid., 90.
38. Ibid.
39. Ewen, *Theories of Personality*, 100.
40. Ibid., 100 (Jung quoted in Ewen).
41. Ibid.
42. Ibid., 101.

Chapter **5**

# The History of
# Personality Testing

I n the last chapter we reviewed the history of personality theory. We are now moving to the practical realm of how to test for personality traits. This chapter provides background on personality testing to give you a sense of how personality tests have developed over the years and how we can think about how to assess an investor's personality traits. In the next chapter there will be a test for Behavioral Investor Types and individual biases that will be based in part on the techniques and concepts presented in this chapter. What is important to keep in mind is that initially we are trying to determine what orientation a given investor has and then test for what biases that orientation is likely to have. As has been repeated several times—intentionally—we need to correct for the biases that may cause serious problems in terms of sticking to an investment plan over the long term.

## TYPES OF PERSONALITY TESTS

There are two basic kinds of personality tests: objective and projective tests. An objective test is usually a pencil and paper questionnaire. Answers to each item are either true/false or multiple choice. These tests are considered highly structured because of the limited amount of freedom the subject has in terms of his available responses to the test's questions. Objective tests are scored in a straightforward manner. In the next chapter you will see that we are using an objective test rather than a projective test.

As mentioned, objective tests are scored in a straightforward manner. Each response is assigned a numerical value relative to some dimension of personality (extraversion, for example). Objective tests usually measure personality along many different dimensions, as we will see with the Myers-Briggs Type Indicator and the Big 5 Factor model. Because these tests can be scored in an objective, nonarbitrary fashion, they show high reliability compared to projective tests.[1] Projective tests present people with arbitrary, open-ended test items. Not only are the items of this kind of test arbitrary, but also the tests themselves are unstructured by design. This allows subjects to "project" themselves onto the "blank screens" that are the test items themselves.[2] Scoring of these tests is consequently very difficult to do in an objective manner, because it is often up to the interpretation of one particular psychologist. To make matters worse, test administrators are often unaware of the subtle cues they give to subjects.

## Woodsworth Personal Data Sheet

The historical precursor to all personality tests was the Woodsworth Personal Data Sheet. R. S. Woodsworth devised the instrument during World War I in order to screen for individuals who were likely to be susceptible to shell shock. At the time, shell shock (or "war neurosis") was thought to be as much a hindrance to the efficiency of a military unit as low intelligence. Here are two sample items that showed much differentiation between those susceptible to shell shock and those who were not: Do you feel sad or low-spirited most of the time? Are you ever bothered with the feeling that people are reading your thoughts?[3]

## Edwards Personality Inventory

The Edwards Personality Inventory is a deductive, theory-based approach and makes use of factor analysis. It is a pretty simple test. For example, an item measuring sensitivity is: "Am I sensitive and easily hurt by others?" All together there were 2,824 items, which were sorted by factor-analytic methods into 216 categories thought to represent various personality traits. Further factor analysis reduced the number of categories to 18 traits that seem to "enable the assessment of examinees' interpersonal-relations skills, personality traits, interests, and values."[4]

## Myers-Briggs Type Indicator

The idea for this test came from Carl Jung's theory of personality types, which we discussed in Chapter 4. The MBTI measures personality along four bipolar scales: introversion-extroversion, sensing-intuition, thinking-feeling, and judging-perceiving.

According to Allen, "The essence of the theory is that much seemingly random variation in the behavior is actually quite orderly and consistent, being due to basic differences in the ways individuals prefer to use their perception and judgment."[5]

The idea for this test came from Carl Jung's theory of personality types. He introduced the idea of a personality type in the 1920s. Jung thought that individual differences in personality could be attributed to two overarching dimensions. The first dimension is responsible for the apprehension of external stimuli and is governed by two sets of opposites that are together known as the four functions: thinking (T)-feeling (F) and sensing (S)-intuiting (N). The second dimension consists of two attitudes, extraversion (E) and introversion (I). The MBTI added another set of opposites to Jung's four: They are judging (J) and perceiving (P). All in all, MBTI measures personality along four bipolar scales: introversion-extroversion, sensing-intuition, thinking-feeling, and judging-perceiving. There are 16 possible combinations, and all are considered "equal," that is to say, there is no one type that is objectively preferable in any way to another. The MBTI instrument was developed in the 1940s by Isabel Briggs Myers and original research was done in the 1940s and 50s. Over the past 40 years the test has been proven to have a high degree of content validity (the test measures what it says it measures) and reliability (the results are reproducible). Although the MBTI is derived from Jung's theory, the MBTI makes use of factor-analytic techniques Eysenck used to create his EPI.

## THE 16 MBTI TYPES

1. ISTJ: Quiet, serious, earn success by thoroughness and dependability. Practical, matter-of-fact, realistic, and responsible. Decide logically what should be done and work toward it steadily, regardless of distractions. Take pleasure in making everything orderly and organized—their work, their home, their life. Value traditions and loyalty.
2. ISFJ: Quiet, friendly, responsible, and conscientious. Committed and steady in meeting their obligations. Thorough, painstaking, and accurate. Loyal, considerate, notice and remember specifics about people who are important to them, concerned with how others feel. Strive to create an orderly and harmonious environment at work and at home.
3. INFJ: Seek meaning and connection in ideas, relationships, and material possessions. Want to understand what motivates people and are insightful about others. Conscientious and committed to

*(Continued)*

their firm values. Develop a clear vision about how best to serve the common good. Organized and decisive in implementing their vision.

4. INTJ: Have original minds and great drive for implementing their ideas and achieving their goals. Quickly see patterns in external events and develop long-range explanatory perspectives. When committed, organize a job and carry it through. Skeptical and independent, have high standards of competence and performance, for themselves and others.

5. ISTP: Tolerant and flexible, quiet observers until a problem appears, then act quickly to find workable solutions. Analyze what makes things work and readily get through large amounts of data to isolate the core of practical problems. Interested in cause and effect, organize facts using logical principles, value efficiency.

6. ISFP: Quiet, friendly, sensitive, and kind. Enjoy the present moment, what's going on around them. Like to have their own space and to work within their own time frame. Loyal and committed to their values and to people who are important to them. Dislike disagreements and conflicts, do not force their opinions or values on others.

7. INFP: Idealistic, loyal to their values and to people who are important to them. Want an external life that is congruent with their values. Curious, quick to see possibilities, can be catalysts for implementing ideas. Seek to understand people and to help them fulfill their potential. Adaptable, flexible, and accepting unless a value is threatened.

8. INTP: Seek to develop logical explanations for everything that interests them. Theoretical and abstract, interested more in ideas than in social interaction. Quiet, contained, flexible, and adaptable. Have unusual ability to focus in depth to solve problems in their area of interest. Skeptical, sometimes critical, always analytical.

9. ESTP: Flexible and tolerant, they take a pragmatic approach focused on immediate results. Theories and conceptual explanations bore them; they want to act energetically to solve the problem. Focus on the here-and-now, spontaneous, enjoy each moment that they can be active with others. Enjoy material comforts and style. Learn best through doing.

10. ESFP: Outgoing, friendly, and accepting. Exuberant lovers of life, people, and material comforts. Enjoy working with others to make

things happen. Bring common sense and a realistic approach to their work, and make work fun. Flexible and spontaneous, adapt readily to new people and environments. Learn best by trying a new skill with other people.

11. ENFP: Warmly enthusiastic and imaginative. See life as full of possibilities. Make connections between events and information very quickly, and confidently proceed based on the patterns they see. Want a lot of affirmation from others, and readily give appreciation and support. Spontaneous and flexible, often rely on their ability to improvise and their verbal fluency.

12. ENTP: Quick, ingenious, stimulating, alert, and outspoken. Resourceful in solving new and challenging problems. Adept at generating conceptual possibilities and then analyzing them strategically. Good at reading other people. Bored by routine, will seldom do the same thing the same way, apt to turn to one new interest after another.

13. ESTJ: Practical, realistic, matter-of-fact. Decisive, quickly move to implement decisions. Organize projects and people to get things done, focus on getting results in the most efficient way possible. Take care of routine details. Have a clear set of logical standards, systematically follow them and want others to also. Forceful in implementing their plans.

14. ESFJ: Warmhearted, conscientious, and cooperative. Want harmony in their environment, work with determination to establish it. Like to work with others to complete tasks accurately and on time. Loyal, follow through even in small matters. Notice what others need in their day-by-day lives and try to provide it. Want to be appreciated for who they are and for what they contribute.

15. ENFJ: Warm, empathetic, responsive, and responsible. Highly attuned to the emotions, needs, and motivations of others. Find potential in everyone, want to help others fulfill their potential. May act as catalysts for individual and group growth. Loyal, responsive to praise and criticism. Sociable, facilitate others in a group, and provide inspiring leadership.

16. ENTJ: Frank, decisive, assume leadership readily. Quickly see illogical and inefficient procedures and policies, develop and implement comprehensive systems to solve organizational problems.

*(Continued)*

Enjoy long-term planning and goal setting. Usually well informed, well read, enjoy expanding their knowledge and passing it on to others. Forceful in presenting their ideas.

*Source:* www.myersbriggs.org/my-mbti-personality-type/mbti-basics/the-16-mbti-types.asp#ISTJ.

## Eysenck Personality Questionnaire

Hans Eysenck's questionnaire measured personality traits along three dimensions: E (introversion-extraversion), N (neuroticism), and P (psychoticism). The EPQ developed out of two prior instruments: The Maudsley Medical Questionnaire (MMQ) and the Maudsley Personality Inventory (MPI). The MMQ introduced the concept of neuroticism, and the MPI included a measurement of introversion-extraversion. Eysenck added items to test for psychoticism around the year 1952. The following chart lists the characteristics that are associated with the scores:

E Scores:
- Subjects with a high E score tend to be more sociable, popular, easy-going, talkative, impulsive, risk-taking, and unreliable.
- Subjects with a low E score tend to be more introspective, quiet, distant (except to close friends), serious, organized, and reliable.
- E scores tend to be higher for men, to decrease with age, and to be uncorrelated with socioeconomic class.[6]

N Scores:
- Subjects with high N scores tend to be moody, restless, touchy, emotionally over-reactive, and anxious.
- Low N scorers are calm, carefree, even tempered, and reliable.
- N scores tend to decrease with age and be higher for women and for people of lower socioeconomic class.[7]

In considering whether or not to add P to the EPQ, Eysenck considered whether there was a clear-cut difference between psychotic people and normal (nonpsychotic) people. He came to the conclusion that most people have at least a small psychotic tendency.

- Subjects with high P scores are solitary, uncooperative, hostile, cruel, socially withdrawn, delusional, and creative.

■ P scores tend to be higher for men, lower for middle-class individuals, and to decrease with age.[8]

Eysenck found that this schema meshed well with Jung's personality typology as well as the typology of the ancient thinkers Hippocrates and Galen. For example, combining the two type dimensions E and N resulted in the four temperaments hypothesized by Hippocrates: sanguine, choleric, melancholic, and phlegmatic. "Thus, the [emotionally] stable extravert is sanguine, the unstable extravert is melancholic, and the stable introvert is phlegmatic."[9] Likewise, Eysenck's model resembles Jung's character typology. Both have the extraversion-introversion dimension. Jung postulates a feeling-intuiting dimension as well as a thinking-sensing dimension. We can see that both models yield eight possible permutations.

## Minnesota Multiphasic Personality Inventory

This test was originally developed in the 1930s by Starke R. Hathaway and J. C. McKinley[10] in order to diagnose mental disorders. Since then it has been updated twice and has expanded its scope to assess "normal" individuals for such purposes as career guidance, military aptitude, and marriage counseling. The test is formulated to accurately assess what people think is going on in their lives, not what is actually going on in their lives. Accordingly subjects are asked to respond to such true or false items as "I believe I am being plotted against" and "I am sure I am being talked about."[11] Over the years the MMPI began to reflect a lifestyle that was rapidly disappearing. An upgraded inventory included such issues as political and social attitudes, career and educational interests, marital issues and family dynamics.[12] Even the updated versions of this test have been criticized for underrepresenting increasingly growing Asian-American and Hispanic populations. Additionally, later versions of the MMPI included several "validity scales" designed to determine, for example, whether the subject is merely selecting the most socially acceptable response to each item. This has become commonplace in interviews for highly competitive jobs, where applicants have a strong incentive to not represent themselves truly.

## Cattell's 16PF

The final outcome of Raymond Cattell's factor analysis of personality traits was his 16 Personality Factors test. He began with a 4,500-word list of all traits applying to human personality. Cattell and his colleague Odbert reduced the list to 160 synonym groups called "surface clusters." Then the surface clusters were reduced to 171 "trait elements" by again eliminating synonyms. The 171 elements were intercorrelated into 36 clusters. These clusters were called surface traits. Ten more surface traits were added and then the 46 traits were used to isolate Cattell's 16 primary factors.

The 16PF is still used widely in business and education. It has served businesses as an aid to decision making regarding employee selection, efficiency, and promotion. In schools it has helped teachers develop individualized plans for students as well as predict the future success of a school. The 1970 handbook for the 16PF described the ideal trait profiles for 125 different jobs. In clinical settings, it has helped couples in marriage/couples therapy as well as individuals suffering from anxiety, neurosis, alcoholism, and drug addiction.[13] The 16 factors are listed in Tables 5.1 and 5.2 along with the characteristics of both extremes.

**TABLE 5.1**   Cattell's 16 Primary Factor Descriptions

| Factor | "Left" Extreme | "Right" Extreme |
|---|---|---|
| Warmth | Reserved, impersonal, distant | Warm, outgoing, attentive to others |
| Reasoning | Concrete | Abstract |
| Emotional Stability | Reactive, emotionally changeable | Emotionally stable, adaptive, mature |
| Dominance | Deferential, cooperative, avoids conflict | Dominant, forceful, assertive |
| Liveliness | Serious, restrained, careful | Lively, animated, spontaneous |
| Rule-consciousness | Expedient, nonconforming | Rule-conscious, dutiful |
| Social boldness | Sly, threat-sensitive, timid | Socially bold, venturesome, thick-skinned |
| Sensitivity | Utilitarian, objective, unsentimental | Sensitive, aesthetic, sentimental |
| Vigilance | Trusting, unsuspecting, accepting | Vigilant, suspicious, skeptical, wary |
| Abstractedness | Grounded, practical, solution-oriented | Abstracted, imaginative, idea-oriented |
| Privateness | Forthright, genuine, artless | Private, discreet, nondisclosing |
| Apprehension | Self-assured, unworried, complacent | Apprehensive, self-doubting, worried |
| Openness to change | Traditional, attached to familiar objects | Open to change, experimenting |
| Self-reliance | Group-oriented, affiliative | Self-reliant, solitary, individualistic |
| Perfectionism | Tolerates disorder, unexacting, flexible | Perfectionistic, organized, self-disciplined |
| Tension | Relaxed, placid, patient | Tense, high energy, impatient, driven |

**TABLE 5.2**   Five Global Factor Descriptions

| Factor | "Left" Extreme | "Right" Extreme |
|---|---|---|
| Extraversion | Introverted, socially inhibited | Extraverted, socially participating |
| Anxiety | Low anxiety, unperturbed | High anxiety, perturbable |
| Tough-mindedness | Receptive, open-minded, intuitive | Tough-minded, resolute, unempathetic |
| Independence | Accommodating, agreeable, selfless | Independent, persuasive, willfull |
| Self-control | Unrestrained, follows urges | Self-controlled, inhibits urges |

*Source: The 16PF Fifth Edition Administrator's Manual.*

## The Five-Factor Model and the Revised NEO Personality Inventory

There is a history of the Five Factor Model (often referred to as the Big Five) dating back to the early 1930s. According to many notable historians, Raymond Cattell deserves credit for the discovery of five basic personality factors, although he denies credit for the discovery. Over the years, depending on the way researchers do their factor analyses, five factors have often emerged as the least number of factors to which a set of data reduces. The most recent five-factor model comes from psychologists Robert McCrae and Paul Costa. They are also the authors of the Revised NEO Personality Inventory. This inventory measures personality traits along five dimensions: Neuroticism, Extraversion, Openness to experience, Agreeableness, and Conscientiousness (Table 5.3).

McCrae and Costa make four philosophical assumptions about human nature.

1. First, they think that there is a certain lawfulness in human behavior such that it is possible to come to know and detect its regularities. This is tantamount to saying that the traits that all humans share are more important than the idiosyncratic traits of individual people.
2. Second, they posit that humans as a species are capable of delivering an objective report of their own as well as others' behavior. This is important as their research often uses self-reports and the observations that one spouse makes of another.
3. Third, they allow that the scales of the five factors can vary widely to accommodate those of us who do not fall within the average ranges. This assumption is a nod to the humanistic psychologists Carl Rogers and Abraham Maslow, who emphasize and cherish individual differences in personality.

**TABLE 5.3** Five Dimensions of Measuring Personality Traits

| Factor | Low Scorer Characteristics | Factor Measures... | High Scorer Characteristics |
|---|---|---|---|
| (N) Neuroticism | Worrying, nervous, emotional, insecure. | adjustment versus emotional instability. Identifies individuals prone to psychological distress, unrealistic ideas, and maladaptive coping mechanisms. | Calm, relaxed, unemotional, hearty, self-satisfied. |
| (E) Extraversion | Sociable, active, talkative, person-oriented, optimistic, fun-loving. | the quantity and intensity of interpersonal interaction, activity level, need for stimulation, and capacity for joy. | Reserved, sober, unexuberant, aloof, task-oriented, quiet. |
| (O) Openness to experience | Curious, broad interests, creative, original. | amount of proactive-seeking, and appreciation of experience for its own sake, toleration for and exploration of the unfamiliar. | Conventional, down-to-earth, narrow interests, unartistic, unanalytical. |
| (A) Agreeableness | Soft-hearted, good-natured, trusting, helpful, gullible, straightforward. | the quality of one's interpersonal orientation along a continuum from compassion to antagonism in thoughts, feelings and actions. | Cynical, rude, suspicious, uncooperative, ruthless, irritable, and manipulative. |
| (C) Conscientiousness | Organized, reliable, hard-working, punctual, neat, and persevering. | the individual's degree of organization persistence, and motivation and goal-directed behavior. Contrasts dependable, fastidious people with those who are lackadaisical. | Aimless, unreliable, lazy, careless, negligent, weak-willed. |

*Source: The NEO Personality Inventory Manual.*

4. Lastly, they reject the determinism that is present in most of the theories we have discussed. Dumont puts their position this way: "In spite of the dispositional and longstanding character of our orientation to the myriad stimulus fields with which we are presented, there is a spontaneous element to much of human behavior."[14]

## SUMMARY

As you can see, there are a number of ways in which practitioners involved in assessing human personality have developed and used their tests. There is no one right way to assess personality. The purpose of this chapter was to introduce the concept of personality testing so that readers can begin to think about themselves and their clients in terms of an investor personality type. When reading the next two chapters this chapter should give perspective on how behavioral investor types were developed, vis-à-vis nonfinancial personality assessments that have been developed. We now move to the Behavioral Investor Type framework in Chapter 6.

## NOTES

1. Bem P. Allen, *Personality Theories: Development, Growth, and Diversity.* 3rd ed. (Boston: Pearson/Allyn & Bacon, 2006), 11.
2. Ibid., 9.
3. Philip H. DuBois, *The History of Psychological Testing* (Boston: Allyn & Bacon, 1970), 95–96.
4. Frank Dumont, *A History of Personality Psychology: Theory, Science, and Research from Hellenism to the Twenty-First Century.* (Leiden: Cambridge University Press, 2010), 353.
5. Allen, *Personality Theories*, 395.
6. Ibid.
7. Ibid., 396–397.
8. DuBois, *History of Psychological Testing*, 99.
9. Dumont, *History of Personality Psychology*, 175 (Clark and Watson quoted in Dumont).
10. Ibid., 354.
11. Ibid.
12. Allen, *Personality Theories*, 381.
13. Ibid.
14. Ibid., 179.

# Chapter 6

# The Behavioral Investor Type Framework

In the last two chapters we reviewed the history of personality theories and personality testing. I hope you now have a perspective on this subject that will provide a frame of reference for the next two chapters, which are the "meat and potatoes" of the book. In this chapter, we will bridge the gap between mainstream personality theories and introduce the theory behind "financial personality types" or *behavioral investor types,* as I call them (also referred to as BITs). Similar to the psychological typing theories that we read about earlier, BITs are models for various types of investors. This framework has four behavioral investor types: the Preserver, the Follower, the Independent, and the Accumulator. Each of these types will be reviewed in detail; in fact, each has its own chapter in this book.

Although the framework for the creation of BITs combines elements of a number of personality theories, it is most strongly influenced by the *type theories* and *trait theories* that we read about Chapter 4. Regarding type theories, BITs are in a classification scheme similar to Hippocrates's four original types, the Kiersey types, and the Myers-Briggs types. These types of schemes tend to over-generalize about personality traits (since people are rarely only one type of person), but they are a useful tool for organizing one's thoughts about how to compare one type of person versus another. Regarding trait theories, BITs are created to emphasize a dominant orientation or dominant trait of each BIT. For example, the trait that dominates the Preserver BIT is an emphasis on limiting losses at the expense of gains. A term that could be used for this is a "loss averse" orientation. However, even the most aggressive investors sometimes find themselves being loss averse. Chapters 8 through 11 review each BIT orientation in detail.

Lastly, it is important to remember the four key points about personality we learned in Chapter 4 and how they relate to BITs. These are:

1. *Consistency:* There is generally a recognizable order and regularity to behaviors. Essentially, people act in the same ways or similar ways in a variety of situations. With BITs this is also true. The idea is that when acting out their financial personalities, people will behave in repeatable patterns, akin to the person who is trying to lose weight and goes on yo-yo diets.

2. *Psychological and physiological traits:* Personality is a psychological construct, but research suggests that it is also influenced by biological processes and needs. Although not entirely understood in the financial realm, biology can and does have an influence on financial behavior. For example, the need for items such as food, clothing, and other basic needs can influence a person's attitude toward the resources he or she needs. BITs incorporate these basic biological ideas but do not deal with them directly.

3. *Impact behaviors and actions:* Personality does not just influence how we move and respond in our environment; it also causes us to act in certain ways. This idea is the crux of why BITs were created. The only thing that really matters as it relates to financial personality is how a person behaves in relation to their money. Both practitioners and clients themselves can have ideas about how they might invest, but these ideas are essentially meaningless because no action has taken place. A concrete example here is making an investment plan but then taking no action to implement it.

4. *Multiple expressions:* Personality is displayed in more than just behavior. It can also be seen in our thoughts, feelings, close relationships, and other social interactions. BITs are not intended to be clear-cut, unequivocal descriptions of each individual's investor personality. This would be too simplistic. People's behavior is simply influenced by too many factors. They were created to make basic categorization schemes for the purpose of comparison across a large number of individual investors.

Before jumping into the nuts and bolts of how to diagnose clients into BITs, it is important for readers to understand the background of their creation. In the next section there will be a review of my original design for behavioral investor types as well as the upgrades and refinements that I have made to the process. I made these refinements to increase the usefulness of the process for both advisors and investors. The original design is still quite relevant; however, I have found the updated process easier to describe and implement.

## REVIEWING THE ORIGINAL PROCESS

When I originally created BITs, my intent was to make behavioral finance, a fairly complicated subject, easier to apply in practice for advisors working with clients and for investors interested in improving their investment decision making processes. BITs build on key concepts I outlined in some of my early papers including one published in the *Journal of Financial Planning* in March 2005 entitled "The Future of Wealth Management: Incorporating Behavioral Finance into Your Practice," as well as my book published in 2006 entitled *Behavioral Finance and Wealth Management.* BITs were designed to help advisors and investors make rapid yet insightful assessments of what type of investor they are dealing with before recommending an investment plan. The benefit of defining what type of investor an advisor is dealing with up-front is that it's easier to mitigate client behavioral surprises that can result in a client wishing to change his or her portfolio as result of market turmoil. If an advisor can limit the number of traumatic episodes that inevitably occur throughout the advisory process by delivering smoother (read here: expected) investment results because the advisor had created an investment plan that is customized to the client's behavioral make-up, a stronger client relationship can result. BITs, however, are not intended to be absolutes but rather guideposts to use when making the journey with a client; dealing with irrational investor behavior is not an exact science. For example, an advisor may find that he or she has correctly classified a client as a certain BIT, then realizes that the client has traits (biases) of another.

In my two previous works, I developed a method for applying behavioral finance in practice that I now refer to as "bottom-up." This means that for advisors to diagnose and treat behavioral biases, they must first test for all behavioral biases in the client before being able to use bias information to create a customized investment plan. For example, in my book I describe 20 of the most common behavioral biases an advisor is likely to encounter, explain how to diagnose these biases, show how to identify behavioral investor types, and finally, describe how to plot this information on a chart to create the best practical allocation for the client. But some advisors may find this bottom-up approach too time-consuming or complex, and so I developed the Behavioral Alpha method described next.

## THE BEHAVIORAL ALPHA PROCESS: A TOP-DOWN APPROACH

This method, which I call Behavioral Alpha, is a simpler, more efficient approach to bias identification that is top-down, a shortcut, if you will, that can make bias identification much easier. In this book I build further upon this methodology.

## Step 1: Identify a Client's Active or Passive Traits

Most advisors begin the planning process with a client interview, which consists mainly of a question-and-answer session intended to gain an understanding as to the objectives, constraints, and past investing practices of a client. Part of this process should include the advisor determining whether a client is an *active* or *passive* investor. Through this process you are trying to determine if the client has in the past (or currently) put his or her capital at risk to build wealth. Understanding the characteristics of active and passive investors is important because passive investors have tendencies toward certain investor biases, and active investors have tendencies toward different biases. Included below is a test that probes the active/passive nature of clients. A preponderance of "A" answers indicates an active investor and "B" answers identify passive investors.

## ACTIVE/PASSIVE TRAITS QUIZ

1. Have you earned the majority of your wealth in your lifetime?
   a. Yes
   b. No
2. Have you risked your own capital in the creation of your wealth?
   a. Yes
   b. No
3. Which is stronger: your tolerance for risk to build wealth or the desire to preserve wealth?
   a. Tolerance for risk
   b. Preserve wealth
4. Would you prefer to maintain a degree of control over your investments or prefer to delegate that responsibility to someone else?
   a. Maintain control
   b. Delegate
5. Do you have faith in your abilities as an investor?
   a. Yes
   b. No

6. If you had to pick one of two portfolios, which would it be?
   a. 80 percent stocks/20 percent bonds
   b. 40 percent stocks/60 percent bonds
7. Is your wealth goal intended to continue your current lifestyle or are you motivated to build wealth at the expense of current lifestyle?
   a. Build wealth
   b. Continue current lifestyle
8. In your work or personal life, are you generally a self-starter in that you seek out what needs to be done and then do it, or do you normally take direction?
   a. Self-starter
   b. Take direction
9. Are you "income motivated" or are you willing to put your capital at risk to build wealth?
   a. Capital at risk
   b. Income motivated
10. Do you believe in the concept of borrowing money to make money/operate a business or do you prefer to limit the amount of debt you owe?
    a. Borrow money
    b. Limit debt

## Step 2: Administer Risk Tolerance Questionnaire

Once the advisor has classified the investor as active or passive, the next step is to administer a traditional risk tolerance questionnaire to begin the process of identifying which one of the four behavioral investor type categories the client falls into. In the interest of keeping this chapter to a reasonable length, I have not included a risk tolerance questionnaire, but these are readily available. The advisor's task at this point is to determine where the client falls on the risk scale in relation to how the client falls on the active/passive scale. The expectation is that active investors will rank medium-to-high on the risk tolerance scale while passive investors will rank moderate-to-low on the risk questionnaire. Naturally, this will not always be the case. If there is an unexpected outcome, then you should defer to the risk tolerance as the guiding factor to determine which biases should be tested (see next section for more details on bias testing). At this stage, the expectation for risk tolerance and active/passive responses is contained in Figure 6.1.

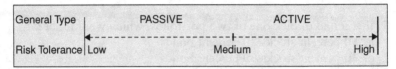

| General Type | PASSIVE | | ACTIVE | |
|---|---|---|---|---|
| Risk Tolerance | Low | | Medium | High |

**FIGURE 6.1**   Risk Tolerance and Active/Passive Scale

## Step 3: Test for Behavioral Biases

The third step in the process is to confirm the expectation that certain behavioral biases will be associated with unique behavioral investor types.
For example, if an investor is passive, and the risk tolerance questionnaire
reveals a very low risk tolerance, the investor is likely to be a Passive Preserver (now simply called a Preserver). The task at this point is to give the
client a test for biases that are associated with Passive Preservers as shown in
Figure 6.2. Likewise, if the investor is passive and the questionnaire reveals
a low-to-medium risk tolerance, the investor is likely to have biases of a
Friendly Follower (now simply called a Follower). If an investor is active
and has a medium-to-high risk tolerance, the investor is likely to be have Independent Individualist biases (now simply called an Individualist). Finally,
if an investor is active and has a high risk tolerance, the investor is likely to
have biases associated with an Active Accumulator (now simply called an
Accumulator). When the client is tested for behavioral biases of a Preserver,
for example, and the test confirms that the client has these biases, then this
will confirm the BIT diagnosis. Figure 6.2 provides an overview of the characteristics of each BIT and Figure 6.3 illustrates the entire diagnostic process
as originally created. Note that some of the biases have changed with the
updates in this book.
    One of the key things that you should get from Figure 6.2 is that at
either end of the passive/active scale, you have clients that are emotional in
their behavior. This should make intuitive sense. Passive Preserver clients,
who have a high need for security and want to provide for their heirs are

| General Type | Passive | | Active | |
|---|---|---|---|---|
| Risk Tolerance | Conservative | Moderate | Growth | Aggressive |
| Bias Type | Primarily Emotional | Primarily Cognitive | Primarily Cognitive | Primarily Emotional |
| Behavioral Investor Type | Preserver | Follower | Independent | Accumulator |
| Biases | Endowment | Hindsight | Conservatism | Overconfidence |
| | Loss Aversion | Framing | Availability | Self-Control |
| | Status Quo | Cognitive Dissonance | Confirmation | Illusion of Control |
| | Anchoring | Recency | Representativeness | Affinity |
| | Mental Accounting | Regret | Self-Attribution | Outcome |

**FIGURE 6.2**   Biases Associated with Each Behavioral Investor Type

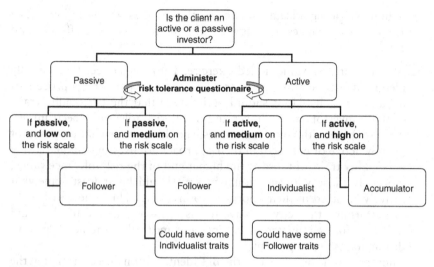

**FIGURE 6.3** The Original Behavioral Investor Type Diagnostic Process

doing so because emotion is driving this behavior. They get highly emotional about losing money and like to keep things the way they are rather than making a lot of changes. Likewise, highly aggressive investors, called Active Accumulators (now simply Accumulator), are also emotionally charged people. They typically suffer from a high level of overconfidence and believe they can control the outcomes of their investments. In between these two extremes you have the Friendly Follower (now simply called Follower) and the Independent Individualist (now simply called Independent), both of whom suffer mainly from cognitive biases, or faulty reasoning, but behave quite differently (see Figure 6.3).

## UPDATES TO THE PREVIOUS MODEL

As you can see from the process described in the last section, when I first designed behavioral investor types, I did something that built on my previous work by a natural grouping of various behavioral biases that created the foundation of each BIT. The process by which this was done was a multi-step diagnostic process of bias identification that resulted in clients being classified into one of four behavioral investor types (BITs). Bias identification, which was done near the end of the process, was narrowed down for the advisor by giving the advisor clues as to which biases a client is likely to have based on the client's BIT.

A number of significant updates to this process are as follows. The purpose of these changes is to again make the process more efficient and effective.

1. Although it is a value added exercise, I no longer feel that initially identifying active and passive traits is a crucial part of the process of identifying each BIT. It should be intuitive that the personality traits of those investors at the lower end of the risk tolerance spectrum, especially those with emotional biases, should be somewhat passive (not terribly active or engaged) in their approach to investing. Similarly, the personality traits of those at the higher end of the risk tolerance range, especially those with emotional biases, should be at least somewhat actively engaged in their approach to investing. Thus, the cost-benefit of performing the active-passive test is in my estimation too low and it is therefore eliminated. This does not mean that the active/passive distinction is not important.

2. Another significant change to the BIT identification process is that in the process outlined above, I associated emotional biases primarily with two BITS—Preservers and Accumulators. I still believe this to be quite true. However, I viewed emotional biases as essentially static and associated only with these two BITs (i.e., they were not associated with BITs dominated by cognitive biases). More recent research of mine has demonstrated that both Perservers and Accumulators can and do have the same emotional biases at certain times. For example, I mainly associated Loss Aversion bias with Perservers. In many cases this is true—Preservers' behavior is often dominated by the avoidance of losses. However, Accumulators, who may trade a lot, also get afflicted by loss aversion and a whole host of other emotional biases at various times. Furthermore, Followers and Independents may also have emotional biases at times. So investors and advisors need to be cognizant of the fact that emotional biases can appear at any time with any investor type. As we have learned in previous works, emotional biases are difficult to correct for, so often adapting to them is what is called for.

3. Perhaps the most substantial change relates to how BITS are defined. Rather than define BITs essentially by biases, I now test for general traits or orientation first for each BIT and *then* test for biases second. The first test in the Behavioral Alpha process is now for core characteristics of each BIT. Furthermore, testing for the most impactful biases is a good next step (see item 4) to maximize the value of doing this work.

4. Rather than focusing on all biases or a subset of biases for each BIT, the focus is now on one or two key biases for each BIT. Part of the reason for this change in focus is the recognition that certain biases are more meaningful than others in terms of the inability to make good decisions and stick to a financial plan to reach long-term financial goals.

## UPDATED BIT THEORY AND APPLICATION

As noted previously, the first step in BIT identification is to diagnose the orientation of an investor. Rather than testing for biases as the first step—in effect defining each BIT by the biases tested for—orientation identification is the first step. After that is determined, testing is done for one or two key biases associated with a given orientation. By doing so, advisors and investors alike can then feel confident that they have identified a key orientation and are working through the effects of a few core biases of each BIT, and they don't need to identify five or more biases. The most they will have to know for each BIT is two core biases. The reason for this simplicity is that it is not important to know *all* biases, but rather it is important to be able to identify key biases associated with each BIT, specifically those that can have a large impact on whether or not someone will be able to stick to an investment plan or not.

Remember: The main purpose in identifying BITs and the associated biases is to determine what behaviors might be present that could prevent a client or investor from reaching his or her financial goals.

Another major new insight is the recognition that cognitive biases may be relatively stable across BITS but that emotional biases are inherently unstable and, although certain biases may be associated with certain BITS, all emotional biases may be associated with any BIT at any time. Figure 6.4 illustrates this updated theory of behavioral investor types.

The updated BIT theory as outlined before is both good news and bad news. The good news is that the process of identifying BIT orientation

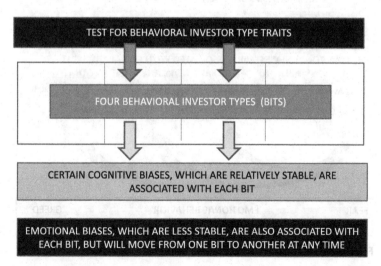

**FIGURE 6.4** Updated Behavioral Investor Type Theory

should be easier and dealing with fewer individual biases should be easier. The bad news is the realization that emotional biases are inherently unstable. This instability itself has good news/bad news elements. The good news is that we now know that we need to be on the lookout for emotional biases across all BITs. The bad news is that dealing with emotional biases is not easy; more often than not they should be adapted to—meaning they are difficult to correct. You need to be able to deal with each given emotional bias with different types of investor at any given time with varying degrees of frequency. I hope that's not too overwhelming! For example, you might be dealing with a Preserver orientation BIT with loss aversion as a core bias (i.e., this client or investor is dealing with this bias constantly, potentially in three out of four conversations). Then you might be dealing with an Accumulator BIT and be dealing with other biases more frequently, say self-control bias, and perhaps only one in ten conversations deals with loss aversion. In both cases you need to deal with loss aversion but in different frequencies and at different times. Figure 6.5 reviews the specifics of each BIT and illustrates the unstable nature of emotional biases.

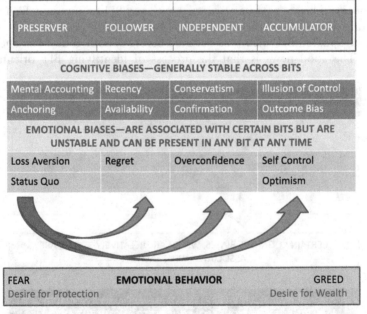

**FIGURE 6.5** Unstable Nature of Emotional Biases

## SUMMARY

In this chapter we have reviewed the behavioral investor type framework including recent modifications and improvements to the process. You should now have a usable knowledge of the BIT process that you can apply in practice. In the next chapter we will introduce specific tests that can be given to diagnose an individual investor's orientation as well as specific behavioral biases he or she might have.

# Chapter 7

# Behavioral Investor Type Diagnostic Testing

**C**ongratulations! We are now ready to apply what we have learned in the first six chapters in practice. As we observed in Chapter 5, there are two basic ways to create a personality test, objective and projective. Recall that an objective test is usually a pencil and paper questionnaire, and answers to each item are either true/false or multiple choice. These tests are considered highly structured because of the limited amount of freedom the subject has in terms of his available responses to the test's questions. In projective tests, people are presented with arbitrary, open-ended test items. Items in this kind of test are arbitrary and also the tests themselves are unstructured by design. In this chapter there are two *objective* tests that are intended to do two main things. The first is to determine the orientation of the investor—that is, what basic type of investor we are dealing with. The second is the identification of individual behavioral biases. I call the first test "Step 1" and the second test "Step 2." As noted in the last chapter, there are four basic orientations that I have identified. These again are:

1. Preserver BIT
2. Follower BIT
3. Independent BIT
4. Accumulator BIT

It is important to keep in mind that just because a person is oriented toward or identified as one BIT versus another, it does not mean that they won't have attributes of other types. For example, you might have a person that has a Preserver orientation but has Independent characteristics as well. As we will see in the next section, there are certain biases that are associated with each orientation, but just because an investor has a certain overarching orientation, such as an Accumulator, he or she may have biases of other

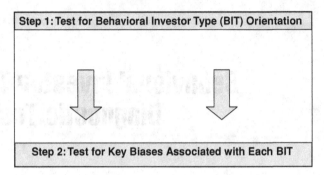

**FIGURE 7.1**   BIT Identification Process

orientations such as a Follower. For example, you might have a Follower orientation investor that demonstrates a strong tendency toward hindsight bias (a bias commonly associated with Followers). But another Accumulator oriented investor type may also have hindsight but not to the same degree. The point is that the type orientations that are the result of the test in this chapter are not meant to be taken as absolutes; they are meant to help diagnose key behavioral tendencies that can hopefully be corrected with information and advice for the purpose of attaining positive long-term financial results.

The second test in this chapter is the bias identification test. Once an orientation has been identified, it is advisable to investigate biases that are associated with a given orientation because they can be major inhibitors to successfully following an investment plan. Once again it is important to reiterate that biases associated with an investor who has a certain orientation may also be associated with another orientation. Figure 7.1 describes the two-step process using the two tests in this chapter.

## STEP 1: BIT ORIENTATION QUIZ

The first test in this chapter is an orientation for each investor type as listed in the prior section. Although the questions may seem repetitive and even perhaps being too obvious in their guiding the test taker in a certain direction, it is nonetheless important and relevant to make this initial identification. It should be said again that just because someone has one orientation it doesn't mean that they won't have traits or characteristics of another orientation. It means that this is their dominant orientation and needs to be accounted for first. Here is the test.

## BIT ORIENTATION QUIZ

1. My main role in managing my money is:
   a. To be the guardian of my wealth by not making risky investments.
   b. Actively trading my account to accumulate wealth.
   c. Doing research before investment decisions.
   d. Listening to others for advice on managing money.
2. When it comes to financial matters, I most agree with which statement?
   a. Losing money is the worst possible outcome.
   b. I should act quickly on opportunities to make money.
   c. I need to be satisfied I have taken the time to understand an investment I plan to make even if I miss opportunities by doing so.
   d. I should not be in charge of overseeing my money.
3. When deciding on an investment, I trust the advice of:
   a. My own self-discipline.
   b. My gut instincts.
   c. My own research.
   d. Someone other than myself.
4. When markets are going up, I am:
   a. Relieved.
   b. Excited.
   c. Calm and rational.
   d. Glad I am following someone's advice.
5. In the financial realm, which word best describes you?
   a. Guardian
   b. Trader
   c. Researcher
   d. Advice-taker
6. When it comes to following a plan to manage money, which best describes your thinking?
   a. If following a plan will help safeguard my assets, I will do it.
   b. Following a plan is not that important.
   c. A plan is good, but investment decisions must include my thinking.
   d. I tend to follow others' advice; so if a plan is recommended to me I will follow it or I will just listen to others' ideas.

*(Continued)*

7. I feel most confident about my money when:
   a. I can sleep at night knowing my assets are safely invested.
   b. I am invested in assets that have high appreciation potential.
   c. I make my own investment decisions or at least have input into the process.
   d. I'm invested in things that many others are invested in.
8. When a friend suggests a "sure thing" investment idea, my response normally is:
   a. I typically avoid these types of ideas.
   b. I love things like this and I can take action right away if needed.
   c. I will do my own research and then decide what to do.
   d. I will need to consult someone else before making a decision.
9. Short-term fluctuations in my portfolio make me:
   a. Panic, thinking about selling.
   b. Sense opportunity, thinking about buying.
   c. Feel in control, potentially doing nothing.
   d. Want to call someone to see how my money is doing.
10. Imagine yourself at a sporting event. Which role are you most likely to play?
   a. A defensive player.
   b. An offensive player.
   c. Strategist/Coach.
   d. Fan.

This 10-question test can identify the fundamental orientation of an investor. A preponderance of (a) responses indicates a Preserver orientation. A preponderance of (b) responses indicates an Accumulator orientation. A preponderance of (c) responses indicates an Independent orientation. A preponderance of (d) responses indicates a Follower orientation.

## STEP 2: BIAS IDENTIFICATION QUIZ

The following questions identify individual biases. When taking the quiz yourself, or giving the quiz to a client, all questions can and should be asked. Keep in mind that certain biases will be linked to certain orientations. These connections will be discussed in the next four chapters. Advice as to how to handle these biases or advise clients on these biases will also be discussed in those chapters. If you identify yourself or a client as being oriented in a certain direction, such as a Follower, and you wish to quickly dive into biases that are associated with Followers and deal with one or two right away, you might consider asking only those bias questions that are associated with that orientation. Note: I have included the type orientation with each answer provided in this section. When administering the quiz to a client, I recommend not including answers or the orientation associated with each bias.

## BIAS IDENTIFICATION QUIZ

1. When thinking about selling an investment, the price I paid is a big factor I consider before taking any action.
   a. Strongly Agree
   b. Agree
   c. Neutral
   d. Disagree
   e. Strongly Disagree
   Answer: Those who Agree or Strongly Agree with this statement are likely to be susceptible to anchoring bias (Preserver orientation bias).
2. The pain of financial loss is at least two times stronger than the pleasure of financial gain.
   a. Strongly Agree
   b. Agree
   c. Neutral
   d. Disagree
   e. Strongly Disagree
   Answer: Those who Agree or Strongly Agree with this statement are likely to be susceptible to loss aversion (Preserver orientation bias).
3. I will buy things I want even if they are not the best financial choices.
   a. Strongly Agree
   b. Agree
   c. Neutral
   d. Disagree
   e. Strongly Disagree
   Answer: Those who Agree or Strongly Agree with this statement are likely to be susceptible to self-control bias (Accumulator orientation bias).

*(Continued)*

4. Poor past financial decisions have caused me to change my current investing decisions.
   a. Strongly Agree
   b. Agree
   c. Neutral
   d. Disagree
   e. Strongly Disagree
   Answer: Those who Agree or Strongly Agree with this statement are likely to be susceptible to regret bias (Follower orientation bias).

5. I sometimes get attached to certain of my investments, which may cause me not to take action on them.
   a. Strongly Agree
   b. Agree
   c. Neutral
   d. Disagree
   e. Strongly Disagree
   Answer: Those who Agree or Strongly Agree with this statement are likely to be susceptible to endowment bias (Preserver orientation bias).

6. I often take action on a new investment right away, if it makes sense to me.
   a. Strongly Agree
   b. Agree
   c. Neutral
   d. Disagree
   e. Strongly Disagree
   Answer: Those who Agree or Strongly Agree with this statement are likely to be susceptible to availability bias (Independent orientation bias).

7. I often find that many of my successful investments can be attributed to my decisions, while those that did not work out were based on the guidance of others.
   a. Strongly Agree
   b. Agree
   c. Neutral
   d. Disagree
   e. Strongly Disagree
   Answer: Those who Agree or Strongly Agree with this statement are likely to be susceptible to self-attribution bias (Independent orientation bias).

8. When considering changing my portfolio, I spend time thinking about options but often end up changing little or sometimes nothing.
   a. Strongly Agree
   b. Agree
   c. Neutral
   d. Disagree
   e. Strongly Disagree
   Answer: Those who Agree or Strongly Agree with this statement are likely to be susceptible to status quo bias (Preserver orientation bias).

9. I am confident that my investment knowledge is above average.
   a. Strongly Agree
   b. Agree
   c. Neutral
   d. Disagree
   e. Strongly Disagree
   Answer: Those who Agree or Strongly Agree with this statement are likely to be susceptible to overconfidence (Accumulator orientation bias).

10. I trust more the advice on investment from nationally advertised firms than from smaller, local firms.
    a. Strongly Agree
    b. Agree
    c. Neutral
    d. Disagree
    e. Strongly Disagree
    Answer: Those who Agree or Strongly Agree with this statement are likely to be susceptible to framing bias (Follower orientation bias).

11. I don't easily change my views about investments once they are made.
    a. Strongly Agree
    b. Agree
    c. Neutral
    d. Disagree
    e. Strongly Disagree
    Answer: Those who Agree or Strongly Agree with this statement are likely to be susceptible to conservatism bias (Independent orientation bias).

(*Continued*)

12. I invest in companies that make products I like or companies that reflect my personal values.
    a. Strongly Agree
    b. Agree
    c. Neutral
    d. Disagree
    e. Strongly Disagree
    Answer: Those who Agree or Strongly Agree with this statement are likely to be susceptible to affinity bias (Accumulator orientation bias).

13. I tend to categorize my investments into various accounts, such as leisure, bill paying, college funding, and so on.
    a. Strongly Agree
    b. Agree
    c. Neutral
    d. Disagree
    e. Strongly Disagree
    Answer: Those who Agree or Strongly Agree with this statement are likely to be susceptible to mental accounting bias (Preserver orientation bias).

14. When reflecting on past investment mistakes, I see that many could have been easily avoided.
    a. Strongly Agree
    b. Agree
    c. Neutral
    d. Disagree
    e. Strongly Disagree
    Answer: Those who Agree or Strongly Agree with this statement are likely to be susceptible to hindsight bias (Follower orientation bias).

15. Many investment choices I make are based upon my knowledge of how similar past investments have performed.
    a. Strongly Agree
    b. Agree
    c. Neutral
    d. Disagree
    e. Strongly Disagree
    Answer: Those who Agree or Strongly Agree with this statement are likely to be susceptible to Representativeness bias (Independent orientation bias).

16. What's most important is that my investments make money; I'm not very concerned with following a structured plan.
    a. Strongly Agree
    b. Agree
    c. Neutral
    d. Disagree
    e. Strongly Disagree
    Answer: Those who Agree or Strongly Agree with this statement are likely to be susceptible to outcome bias (Accumulator orientation bias).

17. When making investment decisions, I tend to focus on the positive aspect of an investment rather than on what might go wrong with the investment.
    a. Strongly Agree
    b. Agree
    c. Neutral
    d. Disagree
    e. Strongly Disagree
    Answer: Those who Agree or Strongly Agree with this statement are likely to be susceptible to cognitive dissonance bias (Follower orientation bias).

18. I am more likely to have a better outcome if I make my own investment choices rather than relying on others.
    a. Strongly Agree
    b. Agree
    c. Neutral
    d. Disagree
    e. Strongly Disagree
    Answer: Those who Agree or Strongly Agree with this statement are likely to be susceptible to illusion of control bias (Accumulator orientation bias).

19. When an investment is not going well, I usually seek information that confirms I made the right decision about it.
    a. Strongly Agree
    b. Agree
    c. Neutral
    d. Disagree
    e. Strongly Disagree

*(Continued)*

Answer: Those who Agree or Strongly Agree with this statement are likely to be susceptible to confirmation bias (Independent orientation bias).

20. When considering the track record of an investment, I put more weight on how it has performed recently rather than on how it has performed historically.
    a. Strongly Agree
    b. Agree
    c. Neutral
    d. Disagree
    e. Strongly Disagree

    Answer: Those who Agree or Strongly Agree with this statement are likely to be susceptible to recency bias (Follower orientation bias).

## SUMMARY

So now we have the tools to diagnose ourselves or our clients as to their behavioral investor types. We have the ability to diagnose the basic orientation of an investor, and then we have the ability to identify a number of key biases that are associated with that orientation. In essence, we have the framework for broadly understanding and identifying different types of investors. But we need to keep in mind why we are doing this. The reason, as I have said over and over, is to prevent destructive behaviors from limiting our ability to reach financial goals. For readers to better understand how to use the information that these tests provide, the next four chapters will delve into the details of each BIT and how best to deal with the impediments that arise from each type. It is important to note that each BIT also has positive elements that can and should be leveraged to help attain financial goals. These positive attributes will also be reviewed.

# Three

# Explanation of the Behavioral Investor Types

**W**ith a solid background in behavioral finance, personality history and theory, and personality testing, as well as an introduction to behavioral investor type (BIT) theory and diagnostic process, we are now in a position to delve into the details of each BIT. We start with the Preserver BIT in Chapter 8, and then we move to Follower BIT in Chapter 9, Independent BIT in Chapter 10, and the Accumulator BIT in Chapter 11.

# Three

## Explanation of the Behavioral Investor Types

# Chapter 8

# The Preserver

*Name of Behavioral Investor Type:* Preserver

*Basic Orientation:* Loss averse and deliberate in decision making

*Dominant Bias Types:* Emotional, relating to fear of losses and inability to make decisions/take action

*Impactful Biases:* Loss Aversion and Status Quo

*Investing Style:* Wealth preservation first, growth second

*Level of Risk Tolerance:* Generally lower than average

**A** *Preserver* Behavioral Investor Type describes an investor who places a great deal of emphasis on financial security and preserving wealth rather than taking risks to grow wealth. Such investors are guardians of their assets and take losses very seriously. Preservers are often deliberate in their decisions and sometimes have difficulty taking action with their investments, out of concern that they may make the wrong decision. They instead may prefer to avoid risk and stick to the status quo. Preservers often obsess over short-term performance (in both up and down markets, but mostly down markets) and losses, and they also tend to worry about losing what they had previously gained. This behavior is consistent with how Preservers have approached their work and personal lives—in a deliberate and cautious way.

It is not uncommon to find older investors behaving in a way consistent with the above description. This is natural. As we age, behavior certainty of cash flow becomes paramount. As such, it is common to find Preservers focusing their wealth on taking care of their family members and future generations, especially funding life-enhancing experiences such as education and home buying. Because the focus is on financial security, Preserver biases tend to be dominated by emotion—relating to how they *feel*—rather than focusing on cognitive aspects—relating to how they *think*. Additionally, wealth level may influence Preserver behavior. Although not always the case, many Preservers that have gained wealth want to preserve it and change their attitude towards risk. This is especially true when an investor has been through a crisis that threatened his or her wealth (like in 2008 when equities dropped 37 percent for the year). The behavior biases that can affect the Preservers' ability to attain their financial goals are obsession with preserving assets and (sometimes) excessively conservative behaviors as exhibited in loss aversion, status quo, and endowment biases. Preservers can also display certain cognitive biases that relate to the same orientation, namely anchoring and mental accounting biases. What follows is a brief analysis of the positives and negatives of the Preserver BIT (Upside/Downside analysis), a description of the biases just discussed (this should be a review for most of you) and how the bias relates to the Preserver BIT as well as a quick diagnostic for each bias.

## UPSIDE/DOWNSIDE ANALYSIS

The upside is that there are certain benefits that accrue to Preserver BITs. Since Preservers are focused on preserving capital and avoiding losses, they take a somewhat conservative approach to investing. This can be a benefit in terms of lowering volatility in a portfolio, which can lead to better long-term compounded returns. Additionally, Preservers who practice savings behaviors through mental accounting (i.e., saving for retirement, for college funding, for paying bills) can accumulate long-term wealth as long as they are careful to invest in a balanced way across these various mental accounts. Preservers are also typically less likely to engage in excessive trading activity, which has been shown to be detrimental to wealth accumulation. Taking a more deliberate approach to investing has benefits in terms of having the ability to stick to a long-term plan.

The downside of the Preserver BIT has mainly to do with excessive focus on avoiding losses. Some Preservers have been known to panic during market meltdowns such as in 2000–2001 and 2008–2009 and sell out after suffering losses, only to see markets rebound in the ensuing 12 to 24 months. It is also important to note that Preservers may sell their winning investments too quickly in an effort to protect gains, which can also inhibit long-term financial success. Additionally, excessive mental accounting can lead to suboptimal portfolio construction if too much cash is held across various mental accounts such as those referenced in the previous "upside" section. Another caveat for the Preserver BIT is that they can take too much of a low risk approach to investment planning in general. For example, if Preserver BITs focus too many of their investments on cash and bonds, they may risk not reaching their financial goals if the goals call for a portfolio return between 5 and 10 percent or higher. Cash and bonds simply won't get you there. Additionally, Preserver BITs' biases are mainly emotional, which are hard to change or moderate, especially during market upheavals. During these times, investors should consider making risky investments as opposed to selling risky investments. This is counterintuitive, especially in the heat of the moment when markets are crashing, but in almost every case it is the right decision to step in to risky asset markets when there is "blood in the streets."

## BIAS ANALYSIS

As previously reviewed, the biases of Preservers are dominated by emotion. In my experience, I have found that two biases have a substantial impact on Preserver behavior: Loss Aversion and Status Quo biases. We review these now. At the end of this section we review several other Preserver biases.

### Loss-Aversion Bias

*Bias Type:* Emotional

Preservers tend to feel the pain of losses more acutely than the pleasure of gains, particularly as compared to other behavioral investor types. There are two key contexts in which loss aversion can be seen, and it is important to understand how loss aversion can apply in these situations. Some investors like to make investments in individual risky assets such as a single stock. They get a tip from a friend and buy XYZ company stock. Shortly after the investment is made, XYZ drops 20 percent due to a problem with their product line. Some rational investors will have no problem taking the loss and getting out of XYZ because the risks associated with XYZ's product line are too great to be ignored. Preservers or other investors who are subject to loss aversion will hold on to XYZ mainly because it is too painful to take the loss. These clients may hold onto losing investments too long, even when they see no prospect of a turnaround. This behavior is wealth destructing.

The other context in which loss aversion can be seen is in the *asset allocation* context. Many investors wisely choose not to invest in individual stocks but instead will invest in a diversified basket of asset classes including equities, fixed income, and perhaps some alternatives. Loss aversion bias can be seen in these investors during market meltdowns such as the one that occurred in 2008–2009. This period was tailor-made for the loss-averse client to sell out at the bottom. Equities started to fall in late 2008 and by the end of the year they were down about 20 percent. Although some loss-averse investors were scared, they could live with being down 20 percent on that portion of their portfolio. But then when 2009 began, and the first quarter marched on, equities continued their losses, accelerating down to a peak-to-trough level of down 50+ percent. In retrospect, naturally, this was the time that investors should have been considering buying equities. For some investors, this was literally a no-brainer because they kept in mind the always relevant advice of Sir John Templeton, who said "Bull markets are born on pessimism, grown on skepticism, mature on optimism, and die on euphoria. The time of maximum pessimism is the best time to buy, and the time of maximum optimism is the best time to sell."

Provide your clients with a scenario in which they buy a security and it drops 25 percent with no foreseeable rebound. Ask if they are likely to hold it until it gets back to even, or sell it and buy something with better prospects. If they hold onto the investment, they are likely to have loss aversion bias.

## Status Quo Bias

*Bias Type:* Emotional

Preservers who, as we have just learned, are loss averse, also often have difficulty when it comes to taking action on portfolio changes (status quo bias). Two examples of status quo bias are presented now.

Scenario #1: Suppose a Preserver investor, Jim, who is 50 years old, wakes up one day in September of 2008, after missing the latest bull market, and realizes he needs to embark upon a savings and investment program. He creates a financial plan (either with his financial advisor or on his own) and learns that he needs to invest in equities (the S&P 500 for purposes of this example) if he is going to reach his long-term financial goals. At present he is 40 percent in cash, 40 percent in bonds and 20 percent in equities. He needs to go to 50 percent equities according to his plan, and so he needs to sell some of his bonds and put some of his hard-earned cash to work in the equity markets. As luck would have it, he has a difficult time pulling the trigger and doesn't act. The market tumbles in late 2008 and early 2009. He can't believe how lucky he was to avoid such carnage. But he knows he needs to start investing. But when is the right time? Earlier, we learned that the right time was March of 2009, when there was blood in the streets and fear was rampant. But when fear was running rampant, Preserver investors are likely to be the most fearful of all. So there's little realistic chance that a Preserver investor like Jim, unless directed, persuaded, or otherwise told by an outside advisor to do so, will invest during a time when markets are falling precipitously. He does not invest in March 2009.

So let's say that it's now October of 2009, a full year after the crisis began. Markets have rebounded by 35 percent from the nadir in March

2009. Is this a good time to invest? Jim just missed the easy money from the rebound and now he could be entering at a time when markets might fall again. No action is taken. Now it's March 2010. Markets are up another 25 percent. Jim just missed a rally of 60 percent. Now can't be a good time. You get the point. There is always a time for Jim not to invest in equities if he is afraid of losses.

Scenario #2: Suppose a Preserver investor, Jack, had an investment/asset allocation plan going into the crisis of 2008–2009 and also had a fully invested portfolio of 40 percent equities, 40 percent bonds, and 20 percent cash. The market drops precipitously in the last quarter of 2008. Depending upon when a review might have taken place on the portfolio allocation, an investor might have been in a position to rebalance his or her portfolio. If the Preserver was in a position to rebalance in December of 2008, he may not have done so because he feared buying into a declining market. Fast forward now to the later part of the first quarter of 2009. Many investors, including Jack, are quite happy they did not rebalance in 2008. But certainly some kind of review of the portfolio has taken place between the end of the last quarter of 2008 (December 2008) and the later part of the first quarter of 2009 (March 2009). The asset allocation plan calls for the investor to rebalance his portfolio. Plain and simple: When stocks go down and fixed income goes up, it's time to rebalance back to target. March 2009 was a difficult time for any investor to rebalance, let alone Jack, who is a preserver. Many Preserver investors were "frozen in the headlights" in March 2009. Equity markets were tumbling. Fear was rampant. Status quo bias took over and no action was taken. We can replay the last example for what happened to Jack after he did not rebalance in March 2009.

In conclusion, regardless of whether we have an investor who needs to put a lot of cash to work in equities or an investor who simply needs to rebalance his portfolio, Preservers can make this a challenging process. Now that you recognize the problem, you should have a better idea of how to handle this situation if you are an investor or an advisor.

An additional tool that can help is a simple diagnostic for status quo bias: Ask your clients if they are more comfortable not taking action during times of change or whether they can embrace change with investments or life in general. If they like to keep things the same, and always take a wait and see approach, they are likely to be affected by status quo bias.

## OTHER BIASES

As we just reviewed, loss aversion and status quo biases are two highly impactful biases for Preservers. However, there are other biases that occur in Preserver BITS with some regularity. These are: endowment, mental accounting, and anchoring biases. In this section we will provide a description of each bias and a simple diagnostic.

## Endowment Bias

*Bias Type:* Emotional

Some Preservers, especially those who inherit wealth, tend to assign a greater value to an investment they already own (such as a piece of real estate or an inherited stock position) than they would if they didn't possess that investment and had the potential to acquire it. Said more simply, some investors hold onto investments that they own simply because they already own them.

A simple diagnostic for endowment bias: Ask your clients if they keep objects or investments because they already own them (through inheritance and so on) but perhaps wouldn't be interested in buying these objects or investments themselves. If so, they are likely to have endowment bias.

## Anchoring Bias

*Bias Type:* Cognitive

Investors in general, and Preservers in particular, are often influenced by purchase points or arbitrary price levels, and they tend to cling to these numbers when facing questions like "Should I buy or sell this investment?" Suppose that the stock is down 25 percent from its high that it reached five months ago ($75/share versus $100/share). Frequently, a Preserver client will resist selling until its price rebounds to the $100/share it achieved five months ago.

A simple diagnostic for anchoring bias: Ask your clients if they have ever had a problem with getting "anchored" to the pricing of an investment such as in the scenario described above. If so, they are likely to be subject to anchoring bias.

## Mental Accounting Bias

*Bias Type:* Cognitive

Many investors treat various sums of money differently based on where these sums are mentally categorized. For example, Preservers often segregate their assets into safe "buckets." If all of these assets are viewed as safe money, suboptimal overall portfolio returns are usually the result.

A simple diagnostic for mental accounting bias: Ask your clients if they tend to categorize their money by function or buckets; money for vacation, money for college funding, money for bills. If so, they are likely subject to mental accounting.

## ADVICE FOR PRESERVERS

After reviewing this section, readers might conclude that preservers are difficult to advise because they are driven mainly by the avoidance of losses, which is an emotional response to fluctuations in the value of their portfolios. Statistics have shown that long-term investments in equities, which are clearly the most volatile investment one can own, have been handsomely rewarded. Therefore, it is an investor's control of behavior around not selling at the wrong time and rebalancing at the right time that makes the difference in reaching financial goals. Preservers need good financial advice. Advisors should take the time to interpret behavioral signs provided to them by Preserver clients. Preservers need big-picture advice, and often they require behavioral coaching as opposed to strict financial or investing education. For example, advisors would probably be more effective in advising Preserver clients if they didn't dwell on details like standard deviations and Sharpe ratios, especially during times of market upheaval, or else they will lose the client's attention. Preservers need to understand how the portfolio they choose to create will deliver desired results to emotional issues such as the needs of family members or future generations. Once they feel comfortable discussing these important emotional issues with their advisors, and a bond of trust is established, they will be ready to take action. After a period of time, Preservers are likely to become an advisor's best client, because they value greatly the advisor's professionalism, expertise, and objectivity in helping them make the right investment decisions.

# Chapter 9

# The Follower

*Name of Behavioral Investor Type:* Follower

*Basic Orientation:* General lack of interest in money and investing and typically desires direction when making financial decisions.

*Dominant Bias Type:* Cognitive, relating to following behavior.

*Impactful Biases:* Recency and Framing

*Investing Style:* Passive

*Level of Risk Tolerance:* Generally lower than average but often thinks risk tolerance level is higher than it actually is.

A *Follower* Behavioral Investor Type describes an investor who is passive and often lacks interest in and/or has little aptitude for money or investing. Furthermore, Follower investors typically do not have their own ideas about investing. Rather, they may follow the lead of their friends and colleagues, or whatever general investing fad is occurring, to make their investment decisions. Often their decision making process is without regard to a long-term plan. They sometimes trick themselves into thinking they are smart or talented in the investment realm when an investment decision works out, which can lead to unwarranted risk seeking behavior. Since they don't tend to have their own ideas about investing, they also may react differently when presented more than once with the same investment proposal; that is, the way something is presented (framed) can make them think and act differently. They also may regret not being in the latest investment fad and end up investing at exactly the wrong time, when valuations are the highest.

One of the key challenges of working with Followers is teaching them how to refrain from overestimating their risk tolerance. An investment may appear so compelling that they jump in without considering the risks. Advisors need to be careful not to suggest too many hot investment ideas;

followers will likely want to do all of them. Some don't like, or even fear, the task of investing, and many put off making investment decisions without professional advice; the result is that they maintain, often by default, high cash balances. Followers generally comply with professional advice when they get it, and they try to educate themselves financially. However, advising them can be difficult at times because they don't enjoy or have an aptitude for the investment process.

It is not uncommon to find 40-year-old busy professionals who as investors behave in a way consistent with the above description. As such, it is common to find Followers doing superficial research into investing, as well as discussing investing with friends and colleagues. They might hear a stock tip from a friend and suddenly take a chance. At the same time, they may not look at their investment statements for months, simply letting them pile up in the corner, and this behavior can have disastrous results.

Followers' biases tend to be cognitive—relating well to how they *think*—rather than emotional—relating to how they *feel*. Additionally, wealth level may influence Follower behavior. Although this is not always the case, many Followers are in *wealth accumulation* mode and think that taking risks is a good thing, but they don't always think about the downside of taking these risks. This is especially true when an investor has been through a bull market such as the housing market in the past decade. Many Follower BITs saw what was happening during the housing bubble and regretted not being in the game. They decided to buy houses to "flip" in 2006 and 2007, or they bought publicly traded REITs only to see these investments crumble in 2008 and 2009 when residential housing imploded; it still has yet to return to original value. Biases of Followers tend to be cognitive: recency, hindsight, framing, cognitive dissonance, and regret.

What follows is a brief analysis of the positives and negatives of the Follower BIT (called Upside/Downside analysis), a description of the biases just discussed (this should be a review for most of you), and how the bias relates to the Follower BIT as well as a quick diagnostic for each bias.

## UPSIDE/DOWNSIDE ANALYSIS

Let's look at the upside. There are certain benefits that accrue to Follower BITs. Since Followers are not overly obsessed with money, they tend to lead their lives in a somewhat more stress-free manner than others who tend to think about money on a daily basis. Also, since investing is not necessarily at the top of their minds, Followers tend not to trade their accounts excessively, which is a big positive since trading too much has proven to be a wealth destructing activity. This low portfolio turnover can be a benefit in terms of lowering volatility in a portfolio generally, which can lead to better long-term compounded returns. Additionally, Followers may realize that they aren't good with money and make a wise decision to hire an investment advisor to help them. Advisors can help to bring discipline to the investing process, which is much needed with Follower investor types.

The downside to the Follower BIT has mainly to do with a lack of discipline during the investment process, assuming they do not hire an advisor. For example, unadvised Followers tend to place a lot of emphasis on investing in the latest investment trends—those investments that have performed well recently. This can lead to investing in asset classes at the wrong time, when prices are peaking, which can lead to wealth destruction. Followers also can think themselves intelligent when investments go up, fooling themselves into believing they are talented investors when it was a rising tide that was raising all boats. This can increase risk-taking behavior, and possibly taking on too much risk at the wrong time can create permanent losses of capital.

## BIAS ANALYSIS

The more impactful biases of Followers are Recency and Framing. These will be reviewed now.

### Recency Bias

*Bias Type:* Cognitive

Followers tend to be dissociated from the investing process, preferring instead to take an easier route to making investment decisions by either following the crowd (investing in whatever the mass audience is doing) or by following the advice of friends and colleagues. Recency bias occurs when investors look at the most recent performance of an investment and make a decision to invest based on that most recent performance. This is a very common behavior of the Follower BIT. The following is an illustration of recency bias behavior that a Follower investor can exhibit.

Technically speaking, recency bias is a cognitive bias that results from disproportionately weighting the prominence of recent events or observations versus those that occurred in the near or distant past. Suppose, for example, during a passenger liner cruise, a guest sees an equal number of green boats as blue boats from the observation deck over the duration of the trip. However, if there happens to be an excess of green boats at the end of the cruise, recency bias will likely influence the guest to conclude that there were more green boats than blue boats during the cruise.

One of the most obvious and most pernicious applications of recency bias committed by investors is the misuse of mutual fund (or other fund types) investment performance records that have had spectacular recent performance. Investors will track managers who produce temporary outsized returns during a one-, two-, or three-year period, and they may make an investment decision based only on recent experience. These investors do not pay heed to the cyclical nature of asset class returns. To counteract the effects of this bias, many practitioners wisely use what has become known as the "periodic table of investment returns," an adaptation of Mendeleev's Periodic Table of the Elements, which he conceived in his book, *The Principles of Chemistry*, completed in 1870, as shown in Figure 9.1.

As is evident by the information in Figure 9.1, asset class returns are highly variable. For example, if an investor is susceptible to recency bias, he might have decided to invest in emerging markets stocks in 1999, after seeing that style rise in that year, only to see it drop the next year by 31 percent. In 2000, 2001, and 2002 fixed income performed near the top of the chart. The next three years, it was at the bottom. Many investors fail to heed the advice offered by the chart, namely that it is nearly impossible to successfully predict which asset class will be the best performer from one year to the next, and that diversification is the most prudent investment strategy available. Practitioners would be prudent to include this chart during the initial asset allocation process with clients, emphasizing diversification over return-chasing.

A simple diagnostic for recency bias: Provide your clients with a scenario in which they examine the track record of an investment that is performing well. Ask them if they are attracted to the investment. If they are attracted, they may indeed be subject to recency bias.

## Framing Bias

*Bias Type:* Cognitive

Framing bias describes how decision makers may answer a question differently based on the way in which it is asked (framed). Technically, a decision frame is the decision maker's subjective conception of the acts, outcomes, and contingencies associated with a particular choice. The frame that a decision maker adopts is controlled partly by the formulation of the problem and by the norms, habits, and personal characteristics of the decision maker. It is often possible to frame a given decision problem in more than one way.

| | 1999 | 2000 | 2001 | 2002 | 2003 | 2004 | 2005 | 2006 | 2007 | 2008 |
|---|---|---|---|---|---|---|---|---|---|---|
| Highest Return → | Emer. Mkts 66% | Commodity 32% | Small Value 14% | Commodity 26% | Int'l Small 58% | Real Estate 33% | Emer. Mkts 35% | Real Estate 36% | Emer. Mkts 40% | Fixed Inc. -3% |
| | Int'l Large 27% | Real Estate 31% | Real Estate 12% | Fixed Inc. 10% | Emer. Mkts 56% | Int'l Small 28% | Int'l Small 24% | Emer. Mkts 32% | Commodity 15% | Small Value -29% |
| | Commodity 24% | Small Value 23% | Fixed Inc. 10% | Real Estate 4% | Small Cap 47% | Emer. Mkts 26% | Commodity 21% | Int'l Large 27% | Int'l Large 12% | Small Cap -34% |
| | Small Cap 21% | Fixed Inc. 9% | Small Cap 2% | Emer. Mkts -6% | Small Value 46% | Small Value 22% | Int'l Large 14% | Small Value 23% | Fixed Inc. 6% | Commodity -36% |
| | S&P 500 21% | Large Value 7% | Emer. Mkts -2% | Diversified Port. -6% | Int'l Large 39% | Int'l Large 21% | Diversified Port. 13% | Large Value 22% | S&P 500 5% | Divers'fied Port. -36% |
| | Diversified Port. 18% | Diversified Port. 4% | Diversified Port. -4% | Int'l Small -10% | Diversified Port. 37% | Diversified Port. 19% | Real Estate 13% | Diversified Port. 20% | Diversified Port. 5% | Large Value -37% |
| | Int'l Small 18% | Small Cap -3% | Large Value -6% | Small Value -11% | Real Estate 36% | Small Cap 18% | Large Value 7% | Small Cap 18% | Int'l Small 2% | S&P 500 -37% |
| | Large Value 7% | Int'l Small -9% | S&P 500 -12% | Int'l Large -16% | Large Value 30% | Large Value 16% | S&P 500 5% | Int'l Small 17% | Large Value 0% | Real Estate -39% |
| | Fixed Inc. 0% | S&P 500 -9% | Int'l Small -14% | Large Value -16% | S&P 500 29% | S&P 500 11% | Small Cap 5% | S&P 500 16% | Small Cap -2% | Int'l Large -43% |
| | Small Value -1% | Int'l Large -14% | Commodity -20% | Small Cap -20% | Commodity 24% | Commodity 9% | Small Value 5% | Fixed Inc. 4% | Small Value -10% | Int'l Small -47% |
| Lowest Return | Real Estate -3% | Emer. Mkts -31% | Int'l Large -21% | S&P 500 -22% | Fixed Inc. 7% | Fixed Inc. 4% | Fixed Inc. 1% | Commodity 2% | Real Estate -18% | Emer. Mkts -53% |

**FIGURE 9.1** Sample of a Periodic Table of Investment Returns

*Source:* Dimensional Fund Advisors and Thomson Financial.

A framing effect is a change of preferences between options as a function of the variation of frames, perhaps through variation of the formulation of the problem. For example, a problem may be presented as a gain (35 percent of those people with a disease will be saved by a medicine) or as a loss (65 percent of those people with a particular disease will die without the medicine). In the first case people tend to adopt a gain frame, generally leading to risk aversion, and in the latter case people tend to adopt a loss frame, generally leading to risk-seeking behavior.

A particularly relevant example of framing bias to Follower investors involves risk tolerance questionnaires.

Suppose an investor is to take a risk tolerance questionnaire for the purpose of determining which "risk category" he or she should be in. The answers to these questions are highly relevant, since the risk category will determine which types of investments will be selected. Consider the following two questions, focused on hypothetical Portfolio ABC. Over a 10-year period, ABC has historically averaged an annual return of 10 percent with an annual standard deviation of 17 percent. Recall that standard deviation is the average variation from the average return of an investment. Assuming a normal return distribution, in a given year there is a 67 percent probability that the return will fall within one standard deviation of the mean, a 95 percent probability that the return will fall within two standard deviations, and a 99.7 percent probability that the return will fall within three standard deviations. Thus, there is a 67 percent chance that the return earned by Portfolio ABC will be between –7 percent and 27 percent, a 95 percent chance that the return will be between –20 percent and 44 percent, and a 99.7 percent chance that the return will be between –41 percent and 61 percent.

Suppose that the test-taker could answer either Question 1 or Question 2 that follows. The questions both contain information about Portfolio ABC, but are framed differently.

### RISK CATEGORY QUIZ

1. Based on Table 9.1, which investment portfolio fits your risk tolerance and desire for long term return?
   a. Portfolio XYZ
   b. Portfolio DEF
   c. Portfolio ABC

**TABLE 9.1** What's Your Risk Tolerance?

| Portfolio Number | 95% Probability Gain/ Loss Range | Long-Term Return |
|---|---|---|
| XYZ | 2%–5% | 3.5% |
| DEF | −6%–18% | 6% |
| ABC | −20%–44% | 10% |

2. Assume you own Portfolio ABC, and it lost 7 percent of its value over the past year, despite previous years of good performance. This loss is consistent with the performance of similar funds during the past year. What is your reaction to this situation?
   a. Sell all of your Portfolio ABC shares.
   b. Sell some of your Portfolio ABC shares
   c. Continue to hold all of your Portfolio ABC shares.
   d. Increase your investment in Portfolio ABC shares.

Portfolio ABC may appear less attractive in the first question, where two standard deviations were used to describe the potential investments, than in the second, where only one standard deviation was used. In addition, in the second question the test-taker was reminded of previous years of good performance and that the loss was not out of line with Portfolio ABC's peers. How questions are framed can have a significant impact on how they are answered.

A simple diagnostic for framing bias: Present the previous example to your clients. Ask if they would answer the questions differently. If they do, they may be subject to framing bias.

## OTHER BIASES

As we just reviewed, recency and framing biases are two highly impactful biases for Followers. However, there are other biases that can be found to occur with Follower BITS with some regularity. These are hindsight bias, cognitive dissonance, and regret. In this section we will only provide a description of the bias and a simple diagnostic.

## Hindsight Bias

*Bias Type:* Cognitive

Followers often lack independent thoughts about their investments and are susceptible to hindsight bias, which occurs when an investor perceives investment outcomes as if they were predictable. An example of hindsight bias is the response by investors to the financial crisis of 2008. Initially, many viewed the housing market's performance from 2003 to 2007 as normal (not symptomatic of a bubble), only later to say, "Wasn't it obvious?" when the market melted down in 2008. The result of hindsight bias is that it gives investors a false sense of security when making investment decisions, emboldening them to take excessive risk without recognizing it.

A simple diagnostic for hindsight bias: Provide your clients a scenario in which they failed to make a decision, or followed the advice of others, because they did not want, in hindsight, to regret the decision.

## Cognitive Dissonance Bias

*Bias Type:* Cognitive

In psychology, cognitions represent attitudes, emotions, beliefs, or values. When multiple cognitions intersect—for example, a person believing in something only to find out it is not true—people try to alleviate their discomfort by ignoring the truth and/or rationalizing their decisions. Investors who suffer from this bias may continue to invest in a security or fund they already own after it has gone down (average down) even when they know they should be judging the new investment with objectivity. A common phrase for this concept is "throwing good money after bad."

A simple diagnostic for cognitive dissonance bias: Ask your clients to provide a scenario in which they lost money on an investment in a stock. Next ask them what the reason was for the failure. If they insist it was "not my fault" and mention other factors such as bad management, then they may be subject to cognitive dissonance bias.

## Regret Aversion Bias

*Bias Type:* Emotional

Follower investors often avoid taking decisive actions because they fear that, in hindsight, whatever course they select will prove less than optimal. Regret aversion can cause these investors to be too timid in their investment choices because of losses they have suffered in the past.

A simple diagnostic for regret aversion bias: Ask your clients if they have made investments in the past that they regret, and if that regret affects a current or future investment decision. If so, they are likely to be subject to regret aversion bias.

## ADVICE FOR FOLLOWERS

Advisors to Followers first and foremost need to recognize that Followers often overestimate their risk tolerance. Risky trend-following behavior occurs in part because Followers don't like the task of investing or the discomfort that may accompany the decision to enter an asset class when it is out of favor. They also may convince themselves that they "knew it all along" when an investment idea goes their way, which also increases future risk-taking behavior. Advisors need to handle Followers with care because they are likely to say yes to investment ideas that make sense to them regardless of whether the advice is in their best long-term interest. Advisors need to lead Followers to take a hard look at behavioral tendencies that may cause them to overestimate their risk tolerance. Because Follower biases are mainly cognitive, education on the benefits of portfolio diversification and sticking to a long-term plan is usually the best course of action. Advisors should challenge Follower clients to be introspective and provide data-backed substantiation for recommendations. Offering education in clear, unambiguous ways so they have the chance to "get it" is a good idea. If advisors take the time, this steady, educational approach will generate client loyalty and adherence to long-term investment plans.

# Chapter 10

# The Independent

*Name of Behavioral Investor Type:* Independent

*Basic Orientation:* Engaged in the investment process and opinionated on investment decisions.

*Dominant Bias Type:* Cognitive, relating to some pitfalls associated with doing one's own research.

*Impactful Biases:* Confirmation and Availability

*Investing Style:* Active

*Level of Risk Tolerance:* Generally above average but not as high as aggressive investors.

An *Independent* Behavioral Investor Type describes investors who have original ideas about investing and like to get involved in the investment process. Unlike Followers, they are not disinterested in investing and are quite engaged in the financial markets, and they may have unconventional views on investing. This "contrarian" mindset, however, may cause Independents not to believe in following a long-term investment plan. With that said, many Independents can and do stick to an investment plan to accomplish their financial goals. At their essence, Independents are analytical, critical thinkers who make many of their decisions based on logic and their own gut instinct. They are willing to take risks and act decisively when called upon to do so. Independents can accomplish tasks when they put their minds to it; they tend to be thinkers and doers as opposed to followers and dreamers.

Unfortunately, some Independents are prone to biases that can torpedo their ability to reach goals. For example, Independents may act too quickly, without learning as much as they can about their investments before making them. For example, they may mistake reading an article in a business news publication for doing original research. In their half-ready, full-on pursuit of profits, they may leave some important stones unturned that could trip them up in the end.

Independents' risk tolerance is relatively high, and so is their ability to understand risk. Independents are realistic in understanding that risky assets can, and do, go down. However, when their investments go down they don't like to admit that they were wrong or that they made a mistake (sound familiar?). Independents often do their own research and don't feel comfortable with an investment until they have confirmed their decision with research or some form of corroboration. They are comfortable collaborating with advisors, though typically using these advisors as sounding boards for their own ideas. Independents are often comfortable speaking the language of finance and understand financial terms including market and economy-related terms. They aren't afraid to delve into the details of investments, including the costs and fees of making investments.

What follows is a brief analysis of the positives and negatives of the Independent BIT (called Upside/Downside analysis), a description of the biases just discussed (this should be a review for most of you), and how the bias relates to the Independent BIT as well as a quick diagnostic for each bias.

## UPSIDE/DOWNSIDE ANALYSIS

There are certain benefits that accrue to Independent BITs. At their essence, Independents are cerebral, strong-willed, independent thinkers who aren't afraid to put their investment ideas into action by implementing them in their portfolios. Successful investing requires the fortitude to not only have original ideas but also be able to put them into action when called upon to do so; Independents can take risks and act decisively. Independents can also be contrarian investors and can be very successful, since there are many investors who are herd followers and are often not happy as a result. As they are analytical in nature, they may help themselves by finding the lowest cost service providers. They tend to be thinkers and doers as opposed to followers and dreamers.

The downside to the BIT has mainly to do with biases that can torpedo their ability to reach their financial goals. As we will see in the next section, Independents can act too quickly without taking the time to learn as much as they can about their investments before making them. They may also seek information that confirms their decisions as opposed to finding information that may contradict their hypotheses. They may also irrationally cling to their self-generated ideas as opposed to being open to new ideas that may prove they are wrong. Their analytical nature may actually work against them at times. For example, some Independents may focus too much on taxes and not enough on selecting an appropriate investing strategy. In industry parlance, this is known as letting the "tax tail wag the investment dog." The next section reviews these shortcomings in detail.

## BIAS ANALYSIS

The main objective of any investor should be to stick to a plan, and much as it is with the other types, Independents can allow their biases to impede their ability to do so. Two of the most impactful biases of Independents are Confirmation and Availability. These are reviewed now.

### Confirmation Bias

*Bias Type:* Cognitive

People tend to want to stand by the decisions they make. It's human nature. And because it makes people feel good to believe we've made the right decision, we also tend to notice those things that support our decision and opinions, and ignore those things that may contradict them. That's the essence of confirmation bias. It convinces us that what we want to believe is correct by mentally giving more weight to the factors that support our desired outcome. This behavior can be hazardous to one's wealth because we can get blindsided by information that we did not consider. The confirmation bias affects the investor by making an investment decision appear better than it actually is. An example from the last investing cycle provides a useful example.

Suppose your client, Jack, who is 43 and single, was an aggressive accumulator of real estate in the 2000s. Over these years, he had seen condominium complexes and strip malls sprout up and get bought up, and for that reason he believed that real estate would be his ticket to riches. His confirmation bias had been enforced year after year as real estate prices soared and as banks loaned money for new projects without limit. But his confirmation bias clouded his judgment. It caused him to block out potential pitfalls and focus only on the good aspects of his investment. Watching the construction industry move like it was never going to slow down, he devoted most of his portfolio to real estate and new construction, with little diversification in other areas. Like many people, he only saw the upside of the real estate boom; he didn't see it as a bubble that would eventually burst. Despite your advice to the contrary, Jack held too much in real estate investments.

Because investors with confirmation biases tend to seek out only information that confirms their beliefs about investments they have made or are about to make, they don't grasp the full picture, like Jack. He may have been peripherally aware that bad loans were being made, that the inventory of new developments was starting to outstrip the demand—both factors that should have been as valid in informing his decisions as the others. But he was able to talk himself out of their importance, rationalizing that only certain cities were being affected, and that he'd need to invest in cities that, in his mind, would never lose value like New York, Los Angeles, and Miami.

Unfortunately for Jack, and so many others who got swept away by the real estate boom of the past decade, Jack's portfolio, so heavily weighted as it was in real estate, took a nosedive when the market crashed. Had he been aware of his confirmation bias, had he chosen to see outside the realm of what he assumed to be reality, he may not have lost so much.

A simple diagnostic for confirmation bias: Provide your clients with a scenario in which they make an investment that isn't working out. Ask them if they would tend to seek information that proved they might be right in making the investment or seek information that they may be wrong. If they are attracted to information that may prove them right, they may indeed be subject to confirmation bias.

## Availability Bias

*Bias Type:* Cognitive

Another bias that weighs heavily on the investment decisions of the Independents is the availability bias. A cognitive bias, availability makes investors believe that the facts most relevant to their own lives are the ones most relevant to the success of an investment. How "available" information is to them thus somehow determines how reliable it is. When one has the availability bias, possibilities that we can easily recall and those we are most familiar with seem more likely to be true than those that are less familiar. With all the information that comes at us every day, it's so difficult to properly process it all. For that reason, we process bits of information we can easily identify and swallow, and we ignore the rest.

When it comes to investing, this behavior usually translates into making judgments based on past experiences and easily perceived outcomes, instead of taking in harder to grasp data, like statistics. Some people put a subjective slant on information instead of looking objectively at the cold, hard facts. A classic example is investing with brokers or mutual funds that do the most advertising. These firms make information available and people buy them; but are they the best? Diligent research might prove otherwise.

Availability bias can be broken down into four categories: retrievability, categorization, narrow range of experience, and resonance. These are each different twists on the same idea, but each is relevant in its own way. Try to imagine how each may apply to you or one of your Independent clients.

**Retrievability** Retrievability encompasses those ideas that come to mind most easily, and then somehow seem more credible. Following up on the earlier example, I sometimes ask new or prospective clients what they think is the "best" mutual fund company. Those who reply with one that advertises heavily, like Fidelity or Schwab, may be subject to availability bias. It usually comes as a big surprise to them to learn that many of the best-performing funds usually advertise very little, and that large asset gathering firms may underperform as assets grow larger over time.

It's also interesting to note that high-profile firms typically advertise their best-performing funds, making it seem like they're doing better than all the others. Any firm can have one or two great performing funds. But you need to look at all funds and make an overall assessment before deciding whether or not a fund family is right for you. But because this information is so retrievable, thanks to ads people have seen so often, those with availability bias may also assume it to be completely reliable.

**Categorization**  Most people like to keep the information they have stored in their brains in neat little compartments, giving them an easy framework for pulling out bits of information when they need it. The problem with this categorical thinking, however, is that it narrows the perspective of the thinker to what is already known and understood, thus limiting potential. As an example, when Americans are asked to pinpoint one country, worldwide, that offers the best investment prospects, most reply the United States because it's what they're most familiar with. Dismissing investment prospects abroad is actually a big mistake, as more than 50 percent of equity market capitalization occurs outside the United States. This is also known as home country bias.

Another aspect of categorization is that we tend to classify anything that occurred more than a couple of years ago as ancient history. For instance, if someone was in a car accident last week, they will probably be extra-cautious behind the wheel for a while, but eventually they'll slip back into the old driving habits. It's the same with investing. In the 1990s, investors ignored basic risks as they got swept up in the euphoria of the "new economy" and created the tech bubble. When the market corrected itself, these same investors lost confidence and began to over-focus on the short-term, negative results that they were experiencing, which ultimately caused the bubble to burst.

**Narrow Range of Experience**  People's experiences tend to color their decision making processes, whether it's in the realm of work, finance, or other areas. That's narrow range of experience in a nutshell. The following provides an example.

Bob works at a successful fast-growing, high-tech company. He works long, hard hours and has little contact with people in other industries. So when Bob is asked what he thinks is the industry with the most promise these days, he naturally replies that it's his own industry. After all, what else does he know? He doesn't have business relationships with people in other industries, and he doesn't seek them out. He lives in a high-tech bubble. Too bad for him because, in the long run, this translates into his not realizing that he can and should invest in other industries, and he is missing out on investment opportunities that could help diversify his portfolio.

**Resonance**    To what degree do you believe that your personal opinions are shared by others? If you like classical music, do you believe most other people do? People often favor investments, either consciously or unconsciously, that they feel resonate with their personalities—and may overlook ones that don't. Perhaps there's a big following for popular music, and money to be made in it. But not for these folks, who will miss out on those opportunities because they can only see the world through their own eyes, so to speak. In investing terms, for a bargain hunter, what would resonate most are stocks that seem to have the most value. But what they will be missing out on is the opportunity to balance these "value" stocks with ones that offer more growth potential. Because this investor is narrowly focused on what makes sense to him, value, he misses out on growth. This idea is closely related to the affinity bias discussed in other parts of the book.

## AVAILABILITY BIAS QUIZ

This is a simple quiz for availability bias.
   Answer the following four questions and review the evaluation of each question below.

1. Which do you believe is more likely, death by stroke or death by homicide?
2. What about death by falling airplane parts or death by shark bite?
3. Does the letter K appear more often as the first letter or the third letter in the English language?
4. Which claims more lives in the United States: lightning or tornadoes?

### Evaluation

1. Because death by homicide appears in the news more often than death by stroke, most believe death by homicide is more prevalent—even though death by stroke is actually 11 times more probable.
2. Because shark attacks are so sensationalized, people believe they are more common, but death by falling airplane parts is actually 30 times more likely.

3. The letter "K" occurs twice as often as a third than a first letter, but it's common to categorize words based on their initial letters.
4. More Americans are killed every year by lightning than by tornadoes, but warnings, drills, and other publicity make tornado fatalities memorable.

As we just reviewed, confirmation and availability are two highly impactful biases for Independents. However, there are other biases that can be found to occur with Independent BITs with some regularity. These are self-attribution, conservatism, and representativeness. We review these now.

## Self-Attribution Bias

*Bias Type:* Cognitive

When a decision we make works out nicely, we like to attribute the success to our own talents and foresight. And when things don't turn out as planned we like to blame bad luck and other circumstances that are out of our control. If you score a high mark on a test, do you believe this to be a direct result of your hard work and innate intelligence—and if you do poorly, do you blame the grading system of the test? If you have a tendency to believe your successes have everything to do with your talents and abilities, and that your failures are never a result of your own shortcomings, then you probably harbor the self-attribution bias.

## SELF-ATTRIBUTION BIAS QUIZ

This is a simple diagnostic for self-attribution bias.

1. After making an investment, you hear a news report that has negative implications about your purchase. How likely are you to seek information that might confirm that you've made a bad decision?
   a. Very unlikely
   b. Unlikely
   c. Likely
   d. Very likely

*(Continued)*

2. After you make a successful trade, how likely are you to put your profits to work in a quick, subsequent trade, rather than letting the money idle until you're sure you've located another good investment?
   a. When I sell a profitable investment, I usually invest the money again right away.
   b. I usually wait until I find something I really like before making a new investment.
3. Relative to other investors, how good an investor are you?
   a. Below average
   b. Average
   c. Above average
   d. Well above average

### Evaluation

1. If you replied that you were not likely to seek information that could mean you were incorrect, you probably have a self-attribution bias.
2. Investors who roll over their money without carefully plotting their next move often disproportionately attribute their successes to their own market savvy. If you answered a, you probably have self-attribution bias.
3. If you rated your investment skills "above average" or "well above average" you likely have a self-attribution bias.

When an Independent BIT's financial decisions pan out well, these investors like to congratulate themselves on their shrewdness. When things don't turn out so profitably, however, it consoles the Independent BIT to conclude that someone or something else is at fault. Neither is entirely correct. Often when things work out well and people with a self-attribution bias assess their portfolios, they end up having more confidence in their stock-picking abilities than is actually warranted—and, as a result, they may end up taking on more risks than they should. You've heard the phrase a little knowledge is a dangerous thing? In investing, it can be very painful.

Winning investment outcomes are typically due to any number of factors, a bull market being the most prominent; stocks' declining in value, meanwhile, can be equally random and complex (sometimes it is due to fraud or mismanagement, sometimes it's luck). Because they believe they have more control over these outcomes than is warranted, people with a self-attribution bias are consumed by the pride that surges when trades do well, and because they do not take a step back to figure out what they could have done wrong when trades don't do well, they tend to trade too often, resulting in a portfolio that underperforms.

## Conservatism Bias

*Bias Type:* Cognitive

Independent BIT investors with a conservatism bias tend to cling to what they already know to be true at the expense of acquiring new information. The following example illustrates this. Suppose an investor named James receives some bad news regarding a company's earnings, which contradicts another earnings estimate from the month prior, which he relied on to invest in the company. Because he has a conservatism bias, James underreacts to the new information, holding on to the original estimate instead of acting on the updated information. As a result, he ends up holding on to a stock that he's going to lose money on because he refuses to see that he could. Like James, people with conservatism bias can make bad investment decisions because they are stuck in their prior beliefs.

## CONSERVATISM BIAS QUIZ

This is a simple diagnostic for conservatism bias.

1. You live in New York City and in the fall, you forecast that the coming winter will be a snowy one. But by mid-February, no snow has fallen. What is your reaction?
   a. You say there's still time to get a lot of snow, and believe your forecast is probably still correct.
   b. You believe there still may be time for some snow, but are open to accepting that you made a wrong forecast.
   c. You realize that much of the winter is behind you and accept that your forecast was incorrect.

*(Continued)*

2. You just learned of some bad publicity surrounding a company in your portfolio, which could negatively affect the price of the stock. How do you react?
   a. You ignore the information; since you've already made the investment, you've already determined that the company will be successful.
   b. You reevaluate your reasons for buying the stock, but likely hold on to it because you've already determined that the company will be successful.
   c. You reevaluate why you originally purchased the stock, and decide your next move with the stock based on an objective consideration of all the facts.
3. You've just received news that has potentially negative implications for the price of a stock that you own. How quickly do you react?
   a. You wait for the market to communicate the significance of the information before deciding what to do.
   b. Sometimes you wait for the market to communicate the significance of the information but, other times, you act immediately.
   c. You always respond right away.

### Evaluation

If you answered either "a" or "b" to any of the questions above, you are likely susceptible to the conservatism bias.

### Representative Bias

*Bias Type:* Cognitive

The last bias that can be attributed to the Independents is the representative bias. Like the availability bias, the representative bias is strongly rooted in our desire to have the information we need to process fit into a neat framework. But the representative bias takes this tendency a step further, in that when people who harbor a representative bias encounter elements that don't fit into their categories, they try a "best fit" approach.

On the plus side, representative bias helps us quickly absorb and process new information; on the downside, it works against us as it only allows us to perceive those probabilities that fit into the framework of what we want to perceive. Think of the gambler on a winning streak. Statistically, there is no such thing as a winning streak, but try telling the gambler that when the odds are working in his favor. The gambler sees winning hand being played after winning hand, and forces this into a framework he can understand—the winning streak. But really, it's all just chance.

## REPRESENTATIVE BIAS QUIZ

This is a simple diagnostic for representative bias.

1. Jim is an ex-college baseball player who played at Notre Dame. Jim graduated from college and became a physical education teacher. Jim has two sons, both of whom are excellent athletes. Which is more likely?
   a. Jim coaches a local little league team.
   b. Jim coaches a local little league team and plays softball with the local softball team.
   If you chose b, the predictable answer, then you likely harbor a base-rate neglect representativeness bias. It is certainly possible that Jim both coaches and plays softball, but it is more likely that he only coaches little league.
   Try this one:
2. Amanda has an MBA and has started several successful businesses. She enjoys the hard work of starting a venture and then seeing the fruits of her labor. She also donates to charity whenever possible. Which is more likely:
   a. Amanda is starting a new philanthropic venture.
   b. Amanda is starting a new philanthropic venture and plans to invest in it herself.
   If you chose b, the predictable answer, then you likely harbor a base-rate neglect representativeness bias. It is certainly possible that Amanda will invest in the venture and fund it, but it is more likely that she is only starting a new philanthropic venture.

Representative bias can be broken down into two categories, base-rate neglect and sample size neglect. In base rate neglect, an investor may try to determine what the success of an investment will be by placing it within a familiar context. For example, he or she might categorize Company F as a value stock because it looks a lot like the well-performing Company A. It's the easy way out of grouping together elements that appear to be "likes"—a lot like stereotyping. You may know a lot of doctors who like to play tennis, but is it really fair to say that just because Steve is a doctor, he likes to play tennis?

In investing, when you lump like-seeming choices together, you miss out on the variables that make them distinct, which can significantly impact the success of the investment. Say George wants to add a good long-term investment to his portfolio. He gets a tip from his friend Harry about PillGene (PG), a hot, new pharmaceutical company. According to Harry, the CEO is a "mover and shaker," who's helped PG successfully market a generic drug selling so well on the Internet that several Wall Street firms have issued "buy" ratings on the stock. Satisfied, George places an order for 100 shares of PG and, equipped with little information and lots of hype, considers this hot IPO a good long-term investment.

Had George done his research, he would know that a very low percentage of IPOs actually materialize into good long run investments—that they usually make money in the first few days following the offering, and over time, tend to trail their IPO prices. Had he done his research, he would have been aware of this and may have been less quick to jump.

Sample size neglect, on the other hand, is when an investor makes a general judgment based on a set of criteria being offered to him. Remember the classical music lover? These investors incorrectly assume that small sample sizes are representative of populations (or "real" data), sometimes called the "law of small numbers."

Let's go back to George. He has a friend named Jim, who's elated about a new stockbroker who's given him three great stock picks over the last month or so, which are each up over 10 percent. George decides he needs to talk with Jim's guy. With three great picks over 10 percent in a month, he's got to be whiz. But George doesn't have the whole picture. Had George gotten all the facts, he would have learned that the broker Jim's relying on happens to be one who covers an industry that is popular at the moment, and every stock he covers has enjoyed recent success. And Jim neglected to mention that, last year, this same broker made a string of three losing recommendations.

The lesson here is that when investors don't see the whole picture, they are prone to make false assumptions based only on a few bits of available data, and ascribe universal generalities to this small cross-section of information. In investing, this could mean making investments that are headed south without realizing it, which is more common that you think. Always look at a full set of data when making decisions so this won't happen to you.

## ADVICE FOR INDEPENDENTS

Independents can be difficult clients to advise due to their independent mindset, but they are usually grounded enough to listen to sound advice when it is presented in a way that respects their independent views. As we have learned, Independents are firm in their belief in themselves and their decisions, but can be blinded to contrary thinking. As with Followers, education is essential to changing behavior of Independents; their biases are predominantly cognitive. A good approach is to have regular educational discussions during client meetings. This way, the advisor doesn't point out unique or recent failures, but rather educates regularly and can incorporate concepts that he or she feels are appropriate for the client. Because Independent biases are mainly cognitive, education on the benefits of portfolio diversification and sticking to a long-term plan is usually the best course of action. Advisors should challenge their Independent client to reflect on how they make investment decisions and provide data-backed substantiation for recommendations. Offering education in clear, unambiguous ways is an effective approach. If advisors take the time, this steady, educational approach should yield positive results.

# Chapter 11

# The Accumulator

*Name of Behavioral Investor Type:* Accumulator

*Basic Orientation:* Interested and engaged in wealth accumulation and confident in investing ability.

*Dominant Bias Types:* Emotional, relating to overconfidence and desire for influence over investment process.

*Impactful Biases:* Overconfidence and illusion of control.

*Investing Style:* Actively engaged in decision making.

*Level of Risk Tolerance:* High to very high.

The *Accumulator* behavioral investor type describes investors who are interested in accumulating wealth and are confident they can do so. These BITs have typically been successful in some business pursuit and believe in themselves enough that they will become successful investors. As such, they often like to adjust their portfolio allocations and holdings to market conditions and may not wish to follow a structured plan. Moreover, they want to influence decision making or even control the decision making process, which potentially can diminish an advisor's role. At their core, Accumulators are risk takers and are firm believers that whatever path they choose is the correct one. Unlike Preservers, they are in the race to win—and win big. Unlike Followers, they rely on themselves and want to be the ones steering the ship. And unlike Independents, they usually dig down to the details rather than forge a course with half the information that they need.

Unfortunately, some Accumulators are susceptible to biases that can limit their investment success. For example, Accumulators may be too confident in their abilities. Since they are successful in business or other pursuits, why shouldn't they be successful investors? And overconfidence sometimes leads them to think they can control the outcome of the investing process. They may discount the fact that investing outcomes are often random and full of unknown risks. Accumulators can also let their spending get out of control at times due to the "wealth effect" of having created assets that can lead to lifestyles that are more extravagant than prudent. Accumulators also may make investments based on how the opportunities they come across resonate with their personal affiliations or values.

Accumulators' risk tolerance is quite high, but when things go the wrong way (they lose money), discomfort can be very high. This discomfort may arise not only from financial loss but also from the blow to their confidence and the realization that they cannot control the outcomes of investments. Some Accumulators can be quite difficult for advisors to build close relationships with, because these clients are attempting to make their own decisions rather than relying on the advice and counsel of their advisors. These clients are entrepreneurial and often the first generation to create wealth, and they are even more strong-willed and confident than Individualists. Left unadvised, Accumulators often trade too much, which can be a drag on investment performance. Furthermore, they are quick decision makers but may chase higher risk investments than their friends. If successful, they enjoy the thrill of making a good investment. Some Accumulators can be difficult to advise because they do not believe in basic investment principles such as diversification and asset allocation. They are often hands-on and wish to be heavily involved in the investment decision making process.

What follows is a brief analysis of the positives and negatives of the Accumulator BIT (called Upside/Downside analysis), a description of the biases just discussed (this should be a review for most of you), a discussion of how the bias relates to the Accumulator BIT, as well as a quick diagnostic for each bias.

## UPSIDE/DOWNSIDE ANALYSIS

There are certain benefits that accrue to Accumulator BITs. Accumulators are confident in their abilities and as such they put their investment ideas into action. As I have said before, successful investing requires the fortitude to not only have conviction about investing ideas but also the confidence to put them into action. In short, Accumulators have the confidence to act decisively. They also understand what it takes to be successful—that is, hard work and determination to succeed. Therefore, they take the time to understand investment opportunities and examine the details of what they invest in. Lastly, they understand that accumulating wealth is about accepting risk; not all investors grasp the significance of taking risk. This is not to say that Accumulators are overjoyed when things don't work out, but they typically understand that not every decision is going to work out well.

The downside to the Accumulator BIT relates mainly to biases that concern being too confident that things will go their way and believing that no matter what happens they can exert some level of control over investment outcomes. In reality, overconfidence usually leads to poor investment results, either because these BITs feel like they can out-smart the markets on a regular basis or that they trade too much. Similarly, believing that investing outcomes can be controlled is a fallacy; there is so much uncertainty about nearly all investing vehicles that investors who believe they can control outcomes are not accepting the reality of the situation. As we will see in the next section, Accumulators also may have trouble controlling spending, may invest based on what they relate to in other parts of their lives, and be too optimistic in their investing endeavors.

## BIAS ANALYSIS

The main objective of any investor should be to stick to a plan, and much as it is with the other types, Accumulators can allow their biases to impede their ability to do so. Two of the most impactful biases of Accumulators are overconfidence and illusion of control. These are reviewed now.

### Overconfidence Bias

*Bias Type:* Emotional

Overconfidence is best described as unwarranted faith in one's own thoughts and abilities. Overconfidence manifests itself in investors' overestimation of the quality of their judgment. Many aggressive investors believe they have an above-average aptitude for selecting investments; however, similar to other investor types, they get agitated and nervous during times of market stress and make less than optimal decisions. For example, during March 2009 there were more than a few overconfident, aggressive investors who were unable to stomach the volatility of the 2008–2009 period—selling at the wrong moment, since the low point was erased in a relatively short time. Those who were advised to stick with their plans, however difficult it was and if they had the foresight and fortitude to ride out the volatility, saw their portfolios bounce back nicely. In retrospect, of course, this was an incredible buying opportunity. Advisors need to be aware of the situations in which clients may change their portfolios at the wrong time only to see the opposite of what they had intended to do occur.

People who have been successful in business and other pursuits tend to believe in themselves; this is how they became successful in the first place. But overconfidence can be a dangerous thing in the investing world. Markets can and do stay irrational for long periods of time. Just because the price of a security *should* be higher or lower doesn't mean it will change in the short run. A classic example of investor overconfidence is the case of the former executive or family legacy stockholder of a publicly traded company such as Bank of America, Enron, or Lehman Brothers. These investors often refuse to diversify their holdings because they claim insider knowledge of, or emotional attachment to, the company. They cannot contextualize these stalwart stocks as risky investments. However, dozens of once-iconic names in U.S. business, such as those named above, have declined or vanished.

## OVERCONFIDENCE BIAS QUIZ

A simple diagnostic for overconfidence bias is contained in the following questions.

1. How easy do you think it was to predict the collapse of the housing and credit bubbles of 2008–2009?
   a. Difficult
   b. Somewhat difficult
   c. Somewhat easy
   d. Easy
2. From 1926 through 2010, the compound annual return for equities was approximately 9 percent. In any given year, what returns do you expect your equity investments to produce?
   a. Below 9 percent
   b. About 9 percent
   c. Above 9 percent
   d. Well above 9 percent
3. How much control do you believe you have in picking investments that will outperform the market?
   a. Absolutely no control
   b. Little if any control
   c. Some control
   d. A fair amount of control

## Evaluation

The following are answers to these three questions. Answering C or D to any of these may indicate susceptibility to the bias.

1. If the respondent recalled that predicting the rupture of the credit and housing bubbles in 2008–2009 seemed easy, then this is likely to indicate prediction overconfidence. Respondents describing the collapse as less predictable are probably less susceptible to prediction overconfidence.
2. Respondents expecting to significantly outperform the long-term market average are likely to be susceptible to prediction overconfidence. Respondents forecasting returns at or below the market average are probably less subject to prediction overconfidence.
3. Respondents professing greater degrees of control over their investments are likely to be susceptible to certainty overconfidence. Responses claiming little or no control are less symptomatic of certainty overconfidence.

## Illusion of Control Bias

*Bias Type:* Cognitive

The illusion of control bias occurs when people believe that they can control or, at least, influence investment outcomes when, in fact, they cannot. Aggressive investors who are subject to illusion of control bias believe that the best way to manage an investment portfolio is to constantly adjust it. For example, trading-oriented investors, who accept high levels of risk, believe themselves to possess more control over the outcome of their investments than they actually do because they are pulling the trigger on each decision. Illusion of control bias can lead investors to trade more than is prudent. Researchers have found that traders, especially online traders, believe themselves to possess more control over the outcomes of their investments than they actually do. An excess of trading results, in the end, in decreased returns. Illusions of control can lead investors to maintain underdiversified portfolios because they concentrate their bets on only a few companies. Some investors hold concentrated positions in stocks because they gravitate toward companies over whose fate they feel some amount of control. That control proves illusory, however, and the lack of diversification hurts the investors' portfolios.

Illusion of control bias contributes, in general, to investor overconfidence. Investors need to recognize that successful investing is usually a probabilistic activity. A good first step is to take a step back and realize how complex U.S. and global capitalism actually are. Even the wisest investors have absolutely no control over the outcomes of most of the investments they make. Just because you have deliberately determined to purchase a stock, do you really control the fate of that stock or the outcome of that purchase? Rationally, it becomes clear that some correlations are arbitrary rather than causal. Don't permit yourself to make financial decisions on what you can logically discern is an arbitrary basis.

Another recommended step is to seek contrary viewpoints. As you contemplate a new investment, take a moment to ponder whatever considerations might weigh against the trade. Ask yourself: Why am I making this investment? What are the downside risks? When will I sell? What might go wrong? These important questions can help you to screen the logic behind a decision before implementing that decision. Lastly, it's a good idea to keep records. Once you have decided to move forward with an investment, one of the best ways to keep illusions of control at bay is to maintain records of your transactions, including reminders spelling out the rationales that underlie each trade. Write down some of the important features of each investment that you make, and emphasize those attributes that you have determined to be in favor of the investment's success.

## ILLUSION OF CONTROL BIAS QUIZ

A simple diagnostic for illusion of control bias. The following are several questions that can test for illusion of control.

1. When you participate in games of chance that involve dice—such as backgammon, Monopoly, or craps—do you feel most in control when you roll the dice yourself?
   a. I feel more in control when I roll the dice.
   b. I am indifferent as to who rolls the dice.
2. When you are playing cards, are you usually most optimistic with respect to the outcome of a hand that you've dealt yourself?
   a. A better outcome will occur when I am controlling the dealing of the cards.
   b. It makes no difference to me who deals the cards.

3. When and if you purchase a lottery ticket, do you feel more encouraged, regarding your odds of winning, if you choose the number yourself rather than using a computer-generated number?
   a. I'm more likely to win if I control the numbers picked.
   b. It makes no difference to me how the numbers are chosen.

### Evaluation

1. People who feel more confident rolling the dice themselves, rather than allowing someone else to roll, are more likely to be susceptible to illusion of control bias.
2. Question 2 parallels Question 1. People who perceive that they have more control over the outcome of a hand of cards when dealing the cards themselves are likely to be susceptible to illusion of control bias.
3. Respondents selecting a, indicating that they feel more optimistic when choosing their own lottery numbers instead of accepting randomized numbers, are likely to be susceptible to illusion of control bias.

## OTHER BIASES

Other important Accumulator biases are: affinity, self-control, and outcome. As we just reviewed, overconfidence and illusion of control biases are two highly impactful biases for Accumulators. However, there are other biases that can be found to occur with Accumulator BITs with some regularity. These are affinity, self-control, and outcome. We will review these now.

### Affinity Bias

*Bias Type:* Emotional

Affinity bias refers to an individual's tendency to make irrationally uneconomical consumer choices or investment decisions based on how they believe a certain product or service will reflect their beliefs or values. This idea focuses on the *expressive benefits* of a product rather than on what the product or service actually does for someone (the utilitarian benefits). A common example of this behavior in the consumer product realm is when one purchases wine. A consumer may purchase a fine bottle of well known wine in a restaurant or wine shop for hundreds of dollars to impress their guests, while a bottle that costs much less could be equally delicious but would not convey the same status.

## AFFINITY BIAS QUIZ

This section contains a diagnostic quiz that can help to detect susceptibility to affinity bias.

1. I invest in companies that make products I like, such as cars, watches, or clothing.
   a. Strongly disagree
   b. Disagree
   c. Agree
   d. Strongly Agree
2. I invest in companies that reflect my personal values such as environmental, social, or governance values.
   a. Strongly disagree
   b. Disagree
   c. Agree
   d. Strongly Agree

Agreeing or strongly agreeing to these questions indicates susceptibility to affinity bias.

### Self-Control Bias

*Bias Type:* Emotional

Self-control bias is the tendency to consume today at the expense of saving for tomorrow. The primary concern for advisors with this bias is a client with high risk tolerance coupled with high spending. For example, suppose you have an aggressive client who prefers aggressive investments and has high current spending needs, and suddenly the financial markets hit severe turbulence. This client may be forced to sell solid long-term investments that had been priced down due to current market conditions just to meet current expenses.

## SELF-CONTROL BIAS QUIZ

This is a diagnostic question related to self-control bias.

Suppose that you are in need of a new automobile. You have been driving your current car for seven years, and it's time for a change. Assume that you do face some constraints in your purchase, as "money doesn't grow on trees." Which of the following approaches are you most likely to take?

a. I would typically underspend on a car because I view a car as transportation, and I don't need anything fancy. Besides, I can save the extra money I might have spent on a fancy car and put it away in my savings accounts.

b. I would typically purchase a medium-priced model, with some fancy options, simply because I enjoy a nice car. I may forgo other purchases in order to afford a nice car. I don't imagine that I'd go crazy and purchase anything extravagant, but a nice car is something that I value to an extent and am willing to spend money to obtain this.

c. When it comes to cars, I like to indulge myself. I'd probably splurge on a top-of-the-line model and select most or all available luxury options. Even if I must purchase this car at the expense of saving money for the long term, I believe that it's vital to live in the moment. This car is simply my way of living in the moment.

Answering C may indicate susceptibility to self-control bias.

## Outcome Bias

*Bias Type:* Emotional

Outcome bias refers to the tendency of individuals to decide to do something—such as make an investment in a mutual fund—based on the outcome of past events (such as returns of the past five years) rather than by observing the process by which the outcome came about (the investment process used by the mutual fund manager over the past five years). An investor might think, "This manager had a fantastic five years, so I am going to invest with her," rather than understanding how such great returns were generated or why the returns generated by other managers might not have had such good results over the past five years.

## OUTCOME BIAS QUIZ

This is a simple diagnostic for assessing outcome bias:

Suppose you are contemplating making an investment in mid-cap U.S. equities. Before proceeding with an investment, you decide to research the track record of a mutual fund manager who has outperformed her index by 500 basis points per annum over the past five years.

How likely would you be to then seek information to understand what strategy was used and what kinds of risks were taken to achieve this result before investing (i.e., you might not invest if you think the manager might be taking too much risk)?

a. Very unlikely
b. Unlikely
c. Likely
d. Very likely

Answering a or b indicates susceptibility to outcome bias.

## ADVICE FOR ACCUMULATORS

Accumulator clients are often the most difficult clients to advise, particularly those who have experienced losses. Because they like to control or at least get deeply involved in the details of investment decision making, Accumulators tend to eschew advice that might keep their risk tolerance in check. They are emotionally charged and optimistic that their investments will do well, even if that optimism is irrational. Some Accumulators need to be monitored for excess spending which, when out of control, can inhibit performance of a long-term portfolio. Other Accumulator investors make investments that align with their world view but may not be the best investments for the long term.

For advisors, a reasonable approach to dealing with these clients is to take a leadership role in the situation. If the advisor lets the Accumulator client dictate the terms of the advisory engagement, they will always be at the mercy of the client's decision making (which is often emotionally driven), and the result will likely be an unhappy client and an unhappy advisor. Advisors to Accumulators need to demonstrate the impact financial decisions have on family members, lifestyle, or the family legacy. If these advisors can demonstrate to the client that they have the ability help the client make sound long-term decisions, they will likely see their Accumulator clients fall into step and be better clients that are easier to advise.

# Four

# Plan and Act

**C**ongratulations! You have completed each of the chapters describing the four behavioral investor types. It's now time to put your newfound knowledge into action! In Part IV of the book we learn practical subject that will enhance your learning and give you real world application opportunities. In Chapter 12, we discuss the fundamentals of Capital Markets and Asset Classes. Chapter 13 reviews key concepts related to asset allocation. Chapter 14 involves the financial planning process and Chapter 15 ties the entire book together with investment strategies for each behavioral investor type.

# Capital Markets and Asset Classes

*Do not worry if you have built your castles in the air. They are*
*where they should be. Now put the foundations under them.*

—Henry David Thoreau

U nderstanding the basics of the capital markets, the asset classes one can invest in, and the risks associated with each is a critical step in building a proper investment portfolio. As reviewed in Chapter 14, asset allocation is the process of determining which asset classes one will invest in and how much of each will be included in the portfolio. The right asset allocation for a given investor will depend upon how well the allocation's characteristics and behavior match the client's objectives and constraints. Regardless of the amount of risk one is willing to assume, modern portfolio theory stresses thorough diversification into different asset classes with correlations that are not perfect (i.e., they are less than 1). By doing so investors can find a way to achieve a goal return with the least amount of risk assumed or, conversely, find a way to maximize return for a given level of assumed risk.

If asset classes are so critical to portfolio design, that brings up a key question, "What exactly is an asset class?" At the core, an asset class is a group of securities that exhibit similar characteristics and behave similarly. The three main characteristics typically used to define an asset class are its *expected return, expected standard deviation,* and its *expected correlation* with other asset classes. The key to gaining the benefits of diversification is introducing lack of correlation between the asset classes used to construct the portfolio. Using a simple example for a given market environment, asset A may be increasing in value while asset B remains unchanged, and asset C is falling in value. Then, in a different market environment, A may be falling in value while B is increasing in value and asset C remains unchanged. The result is a smoothing of returns for the portfolio as a whole. However, one must remember that the accuracy of portfolio level expected return and risk (standard deviation) is only as good as the assumptions made about the expected return and standard deviation of the individual asset classes and the expected correlations among asset classes. We address the topic of generating these assumptions later in the chapter.

## OVERVIEW OF ASSET CLASSES

Asset classes can be thought of as building blocks, like the individual players that make up an American football team, as can be seen in Figure 12.1. Some of the assets play offense, trying to gain ground and increase portfolio value. Other asset classes are defensive and attempt to keep the opponent that is market volatility from eating too far into returns. Just like in football, there are many different kinds of players on each side of the ball. You might think of U.S. large-cap and even global large-cap equities as offensive linemen who do the hard but unglamorous work of just keeping the portfolio moving with market exposure. On the other hand, small-cap equities and private equity can be thought of as more glitzy running backs and receivers; they can come up with big plays, but every so often (and usually at the worst times) they can fumble and put you in a difficult position, forcing your defense to perform.

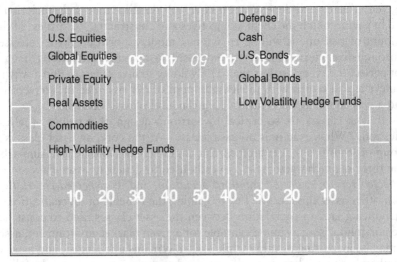

**FIGURE 12.1** Asset Classes by Position

Likewise, the defense has different types of players. Cash is like huge defensive linemen who can't be budged, but their value is susceptible to the attack of inflation. Bonds can be thought of as linebackers that do most the heavy work of protecting the portfolio from wild volatility. Finally, hedge funds are nimble players like defensive backs. At times they can come up and stop the run by being positioned defensively, but at other times they can take a risk with one-on-one coverage; they may get beat sometimes, but at others they can come up with a spectacular interception. The job of creating the portfolio goes to the head coach (the portfolio manager), and he selects the best player for each position and the right mix of teammates in order to generate a positive outcome. Figure 12.1 illustrates the football analogy used in this section.

The purpose of this chapter is to give an overview of various asset classes so that readers can gain an appreciation of not only what is possible from the capital markets, but also what tools they can use to build a portfolio to suit their specific risk and return objectives. The first step in this process is to define asset classes at a high level and then delve into details of asset classes that are used to construct portfolios.

Asset classes can be grouped into three general categories. These are: (1) capital assets, (2) economic input assets, and (3) value storage assets.

- *Capital assets:* Capital assets represent a claim on the future cash flows of a firm, and their value can be determined based on the expected net present value of those cash flows. Capital assets are normally ranked by their claim on the cash flows. For example, bonds have a higher claim relative to stocks, but because of this higher position in the capital structure they offer a lower, normally fixed, expected return, depending upon the credit quality of the issuer. By contrast, equity holders fall at the bottom of the capital structure, but these investors enjoy the unlimited upside provided by residual cash flows. Like traditional assets, the values of alternative assets, such as hedge funds and private equity funds, are largely determined as the present value of the future cash flows from the securities in which they invest and would therefore be included as part of this category.
- *Economic input assets:* Economic input assets are typically commodities that are consumed or transformed as part of the production cycle and eventually end up as useful products. Examples include metals such as copper, which is used in wiring, plumbing, telecommunications, and auto parts; grains that can be turned into food for human consumption or feed for livestock that we will later consume; energy products such as oil that is used for everything from powering cars to creating plastic in the pen that you will use to write with today.

■ *Value storage assets:* Value storage assets don't generate cash flows and are not used as economic inputs, but rather their value is only realized upon their sale. Artwork and gold are two examples of assets that store value. However, these categories are not always distinct. For example, gold could also be viewed as an economic input because it is used in both jewelry and in the manufacturing of some technology devices.

In this chapter, the focus is on *capital assets*, but we will also touch on economic inputs and stores of value. Table 12.1 summarizes the historical return and risk of a number of these asset classes. The rest of the chapter will be devoted to explaining the characteristics of each of these asset classes and then providing a simple example of portfolio construction.

These historical returns and standard deviations are also depicted graphically in Figure 12.2.

While financial services firms of every type offer a dizzying array of products across the globe to access financial markets, the basic types of capital asset investments can be broken down into three categories: equities, bonds, and real assets. Within real assets there are some economic input assets. Each of these asset classes is covered in this chapter.

**TABLE 12.1**  Historical Asset Class Returns and Risk

| Asset Class | Compound Nominal Return | Standard Deviation |
|---|---|---|
| U.S. Large Stocks | 7.6 | 15.1 |
| U.S. Mid Stocks | 10.3 | 16.7 |
| U.S. Small Stocks | 8.1 | 19.5 |
| Liquid Real Assets | 7.6 | 23.5 |
| International Large Stocks | 4.5 | 16.8 |
| International Small Stocks | 5.5 | 17.5 |
| International Emerging Market Stocks | 8.8 | 23.9 |
| U.S. Treasuries | 6.6 | 4.7 |
| U.S. Aggregate Bond | 6.7 | 3.8 |
| U.S. High-Yield Fixed | 8.4 | 9.8 |
| International Fixed Income | 7.1 | 8.6 |
| Cash | 3.3 | .06 |
| Private Equity | 14.6 | 14.0 |
| Hedge Funds | 7.0 | 6.0 |

Returns and standard deviation are for the 20 years ended 9/30/11 except for liquid real assets. Returns and standard deviation for liquid real assets are for the 15 years ended 9/30/11.
*Source:* S&P, Russell, Goldman Sachs, MSCI, Barclays, Citi, Venture Economics, Hedge Fund Research.

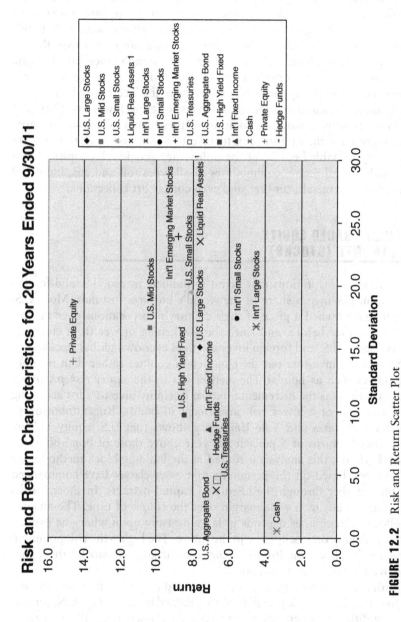

**FIGURE 12.2** Risk and Return Scatter Plot
*Source:* S&P, Russell, Goldman Sachs, MSCI, Barclays, Citi, Venture Economics, Hedge Fund Research.

Equity investments, reviewed in the next section, represent ownership (stock) in a company including its assets and the right to future earnings. Over the long term, equity investments, both public and private, have proven to be the best way to grow wealth, but they also carry significant risk. Bonds represent loans to a company or government that are repaid over the life (term) of the loan along with interest. While a bond's price can fluctuate with changes in interest rates over its life, investors will receive repayment of their loan at maturity unless the issuer defaults. Therefore, bond prices have historically fluctuated less than stocks, offering lower volatility, but also lower returns. Finally, in addition to these financial assets, investors increasingly have the opportunity to invest in real assets. Real assets are intrinsically valuable because of the utility they provide. Examples of real assets include real estate, commodities of all types (oil and gas, industrial metals, precious metals, timber), and even coin or art collections.

## PUBLICLY TRADED EQUITY INVESTMENTS (STOCKS)

Individuals and institutions that invest in publicly traded U.S. and foreign equity securities own a share of the world's business fortunes. More U.S. residents have owned a piece of their country's corporations over the last decade than ever before, and since the awakening of wealth in emerging markets, more U.S. and foreign investors than ever own global stocks.

So why do investors put their money in equities rather than in other asset classes such as bonds? The answer lies in the *equity risk premium,* which is defined as the incremental return to equity investors for accepting risk above that of a lower risk investment in bonds. Roger Ibbotson of Ibbotson Associates and Yale University shows that U.S. equity holders have enjoyed returns of 5 percent per year above those of bond holders.[1] For background, this analysis is rooted in the building-block methodology he developed based on the premiums that asset classes have commanded over one another through the history of capital markets. In short, stocks outperform bonds by a wide margin over the course of time. The amount one allocates to equities depends in large measure upon what one expects the risk premium on stocks to be in the future: The higher the risk premium, the higher the allocation. But the higher the allocation to stocks, the higher is the overall risk of the portfolio.

With regard to foreign stocks of developed countries, investors can expect to earn a similar risk premium to that earned in U.S. equities. Naturally, there are differences between these two asset classes that will cause them to behave differently over time. Equities of various countries and markets outside the United States, for example, will react differently to economic trends and capital markets activity than domestic equities. Foreign currencies also play a large role in what equity returns are actually delivered to the U.S. investor. For instance, a country such as France may deliver only a 4 percent return on its equity, but if its currency, the euro, gains strength against the dollar or other currencies of, say, 5 percent, the return to the U.S. investor will be 9 percent.

A properly diversified portfolio should hold both domestic and foreign large-capitalization equities as core portfolio holdings. A key concern, however, is the correlation between these two asset classes (and, for that matter, with nonequity asset classes), which I discuss shortly. Foreign equities have historically provided diversification benefits to investors due to a historical lack of perfect correlation with U.S. equities. Given the integration of the global economies, however, correlations have generally increased over the last two decades, and that trend may continue. Influences contributing to an increased general level of correlation among international markets are:

- An increase in the number of large multinational companies.
- Advances in communication and information technologies.
- Deregulation of the financial and banking systems of the G-7 countries, leading to major growth in international capital flows.
- Free-flowing foreign exchange between countries.

Investors should strive to keep abreast of changes in cross-country correlations. Table 12.2 shows the historical correlation between various asset classes for the five years ending June 30, 2010.

## Equity Asset Classes

The most common ways the financial services industry has to break the equity markets down into bite-size segments with similar risk and return characteristics are by: (1) stage of development of the local economy (developed, emerging, or frontier market); (2) size of the company involved (large-, mid-, or small-cap); and (3) valuation characteristic (growth or value). Some managers may be referred to as "global" and invest in equity securities across the world without significant constraints.

The global public equity universe is captured by MSCI's All-Country World Index, or MSCI ACWI. The weightings in this index are based on world market capitalization, or the aggregate market value of each company found by multiplying the number of shares outstanding by its current stock price (see Figure 12.3).

**TABLE 12.2** Historical Correlation between Asset Classes

| | S&P 500 | Russell 2000 | MSCI EAFE | MSCI EM | Barclays Agg | Citi World Bond ex US | DJ REIT | Citi 3 mo. T-Bill | DJ-UBS Commodity | HFR FoF | S&P Nat Resources | CPI |
|---|---|---|---|---|---|---|---|---|---|---|---|---|
| S&P 500 | 1.00 | 0.93 | 0.90 | 0.83 | 0.19 | 0.19 | 0.81 | 0.06 | 0.47 | 0.67 | 0.71 | 0.15 |
| Russell 2000 | 0.93 | 1.00 | 0.82 | 0.76 | 0.10 | 0.10 | 0.87 | -0.02 | 0.37 | 0.60 | 0.64 | 0.16 |
| MSCI EAFE | 0.90 | 0.82 | 1.00 | 0.93 | 0.25 | 0.34 | 0.72 | 0.11 | 0.60 | 0.79 | 0.79 | 0.18 |
| MSCI EM | 0.83 | 0.76 | 0.93 | 1.00 | 0.20 | 0.26 | 0.60 | 0.06 | 0.65 | 0.84 | 0.83 | 0.16 |
| Barclays Agg | 0.19 | 0.10 | 0.25 | 0.20 | 1.00 | 0.72 | 0.19 | -0.07 | 0.15 | 0.02 | 0.12 | -0.37 |
| Citi World Bond ex US | 0.19 | 0.10 | 0.34 | 0.26 | 0.72 | 1.00 | 0.21 | 0.09 | 0.33 | 0.04 | 0.23 | -0.10 |
| DJ REIT | 0.81 | 0.87 | 0.72 | 0.60 | 0.19 | 0.21 | 1.00 | -0.03 | 0.31 | 0.38 | 0.48 | 0.13 |
| Citi 3 mo. T Bill | 0.06 | -0.02 | 0.11 | 0.06 | -0.07 | 0.09 | -0.03 | 1.00 | 0.11 | 0.17 | 0.08 | 0.11 |
| DJ-UBS Commodity | 0.47 | 0.37 | 0.60 | 0.65 | 0.15 | 0.33 | 0.31 | 0.11 | 1.00 | 0.70 | 0.83 | 0.37 |
| HFR FoF | 0.67 | 0.60 | 0.79 | 0.84 | 0.02 | 0.04 | 0.38 | 0.17 | 0.70 | 1.00 | 0.81 | 0.31 |
| S&P Nat Resources | 0.71 | 0.64 | 0.79 | 0.83 | 0.12 | 0.23 | 0.48 | 0.08 | 0.83 | 0.81 | 1.00 | 0.25 |
| CPI | 0.15 | 0.16 | 0.18 | 0.16 | -0.37 | -0.10 | 0.13 | 0.11 | 0.37 | 0.31 | 0.25 | 1.00 |

*Source:* S&P, Russell, MSCI, Barclays, Citi, Dow Jones, Hedge Fund Research, U.S. Bureau of Labor Statistics.

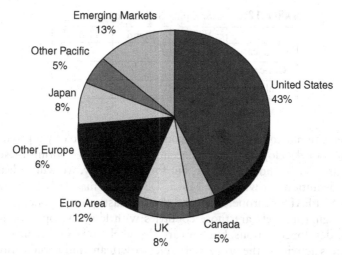

**FIGURE 12.3** MSCI ACWI Weights as of 6/30/11
*Source:* MSCI.

Some argue that other measures should be used to weight equity portfolios, such as gross domestic product (GDP). However, other approaches offer significant challenges because they don't actually represent the investable universe. In addition, over time, there has proven to be little correlation between a country's GDP growth and its equity market returns.

Within U.S. equities, the most common segmentation of the market is by both the size of the company involved and its valuation characteristic, creating the matrix style box shown in Table 12.3.

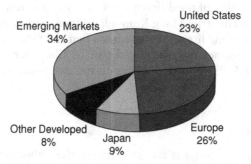

**FIGURE 12.4** World GDP in U.S. Dollars
*Source:* Ibbotson and Brinson, Investment Markets, IMF.

**TABLE 12.3** U.S. Equity Style Box Matrix

|           | Value | Blend | Growth |
|-----------|-------|-------|--------|
| Large-cap |       |       |        |
| Mid-cap   |       |       |        |
| Small-cap |       |       |        |

International equities are most commonly segmented by a given country's stage of development. The placement of countries within these categories can vary by index provider, but for consistency, we will endeavor to use the definitions provided by MSCI. Developed markets can be defined using MSCI EAFE (Europe, Asia, and the Far East) plus Canada.

Emerging markets are those countries with less developed economies than the developed nations, but who are also likely to be experiencing social or business activity in the process of rapid growth and industrialization. Often the biggest difference between developed and emerging is the liquidity of their markets and the ease at which foreign investors can access those markets. Although the term emerging market seems to imply that these countries should regularly be graduating into the realm of developed markets, only three countries (Portugal, Greece, and Israel) have graduated from emerging to developed as defined by MSCI over the past 15 years.

Frontier markets nations can be broadly defined as the least developed of the developing countries. The frontier markets offer even less liquidity, transparency, and ability for foreign investors to access their capital markets than emerging markets.

MSCI is the most widely used classification for international equities, but MSCI only covers 71 of 194 countries recognized by the U.S. State Department (24 developed markets, 21 emerging markets, and 26 frontier markets). In an oddity of the difference between the political world and capital markets, two countries Hong Kong (developed) and Taiwan (emerging) are not included in the list of 194 countries that the U.S. State Department recognizes because they are considered part of China for diplomatic relations. Figure 12.5 shows how these countries are distributed throughout the world.

## Private Equity

Equity of some companies is not available in the public markets and can only be acquired through private equity or partnership investments. Types of public equity include venture capital, buyouts, and distressed investments. Although private equity goes through periods of lackluster performance and

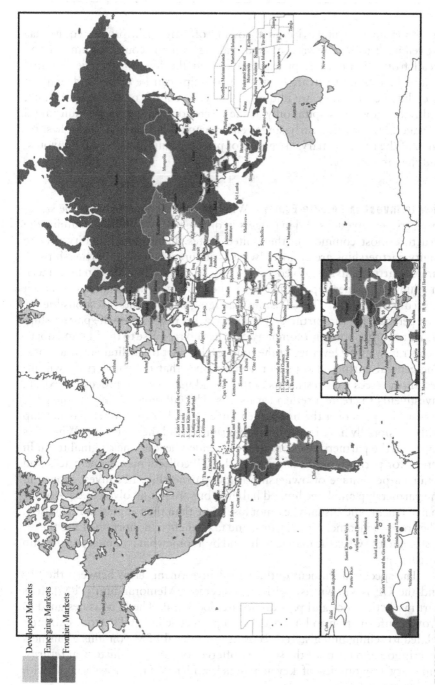

**FIGURE 12.5** World Map with Countries Identified by MSCI Classification

Developed Markets
Emerging Markets
Frontier Markets

1. Saint Vincent and the Grenadines
2. Saint Lucia
3. Saint Kitts and Nevis
4. Antigua and Barbuda
5. Dominica
6. Grenada

11. Democratic Republic of the Congo
12. Equatorial Guinea
13. São Tomé and Príncipe
14. Benin

7. Macedonia    8. Montenegro    9. Serbia    10. Bosnia and Herzegovina

funds may call capital without throwing off any cash, private equity has proven itself to be a rewarding undertaking over the course of time. If you recall from Figure 12.2, private equity had the highest average nominal return. Investing in private equity partnerships can be trying and requires discipline because they are illiquid, usually have a life of 10 years or more, and return investor capital only at the discretion of the private equity fund manager. Historically, early-stage venture capital has offered the highest returns of the three primary categories of private equity, followed by buyouts, and then mezzanine.

**How to Invest in Private Equity**   While different countries treat the structure between investors and managers in different ways, we now examine the structure most common in the United States. Institutional-quality private equity partnerships are almost always structured as limited partnerships. A limited partnership has a fixed life, usually 10 years (though it can be longer). In a limited partnership arrangement, there is a general partner (GP) and a limited partner (LP). The GP is the managing partner and is responsible for the operations of the partnership and any debts taken on by the partnership. Please note that portfolio company debt has no recourse to the LPs and documents rarely allow leverage at the fund level except to facilitate transactions. The general partner also picks the companies that the partnership will invest in, oversees its investments in them, and manages the process of exiting investments to create a return for its LPs. The GP typically invests the partnership's capital over the first three to five years, but the limited partnership will occasionally have investments that run beyond the fund's life. When this happens, the partnership term can be extended beyond the original term. In return for performing these services, the GP collects management fees and retains a percentage of ownership in the partnership. LPs invest money in the partnership and have limited liability, but are not involved in day-to-day management, and (usually) cannot lose more than their capital contribution. They receive income, capital gains, and tax benefits. In short, the LP is the investor and the GP is the manager, bound by a somewhat complex partnership agreement.

The specific document outlining the investment terms between the LPs and the GP is known as a Private Placement Memorandum (PPM). It is part marketing tool and part disclosure document. The PPM is designed to provide information to buyers (LPs) to protect sellers (GPs) from liabilities related to selling unregistered securities. A typical PPM contains a business description and terms of the security offered for sale, fees, historical returns, summary biographies of key personnel, and risk factors associated with the investment.

The PPM refers to another document called a Limited Partner Agreement (LPA), which is the actual binding agreement. The LPA establishes the rules of the operation of the fund, how the fund will be governed, and the limited partnership terms between participating parties. When there is a difference between the PPM and LPA, the LPA governs, so you should read it. A limited partnership investment is essentially a passive (flow-through) vehicle for the LP, and the LP has virtually no sway over what investments are made or the terms of the investment partnership. The higher the quality of the manager, the less power the LP has in dictating anything related to the investment process. Despite this imbalance, some LPs still try to influence the investment process, with varying degrees of success. Assuming the investor has done the requisite due diligence and decided to invest, the LP completes the subscription documents and makes a capital commitment.

All investors in a private equity fund commit a specific cash amount to be invested in the fund partnership over a specified period of time, usually 10 years. This amount is known as the limited partner's *capital commitment*. The sum of all LP capital commitments plus the GP commitment equals the total size of the fund (the general partner must also make a capital commitment to participate in the fund). In practice, the way in which LP investors make their investments is through a capital call structure, meaning that money gets *called,* usually in a three- to five-year period as the GP needs money to make investments. Such calls are due on as short as five days' notice, so sufficient funds must be available for when the capital call notices arrive. The requirement to fund a capital call is legally binding, so this kind of investing is serious business. The general partner then uses called capital to complete portfolio investments.

The good part comes when investments are realized and capital is distributed. The returns that an investor receives from a private equity fund can be both income and capital gains realized from investments (less expenses and any liabilities). Once an LP receives his initial capital investment returns, subsequent distributions are considered profits. The partnership agreement outlines both the timing of distributions to the LPs and how profits are divided among the LPs and GPs. Once a fund is substantially committed, and assuming the manager is successfully investing its funds and sees continuing opportunities in the marketplace, the GP will then go about raising its next fund and will ask its existing investors if they want to invest again, or *re-up*.

Acting as the investment manager, the GP charges a management fee to cover the costs of managing the partners' capital. The management fee (paid quarterly over the life of the fund) often tails off in the later stages of a fund's existence. The way in which fees are charged is negotiated with investors upon formation of the fund. The Blackstone Group, which has been involved in some of the biggest corporate buyouts during the latest private equity boom, has about $50 billion of assets under management and charges its investors a 1.5 percent management fee (and charges the companies it invests in other fees that it splits with investors)—not a bad business model. The firm also takes a 20 percent *carried interest* fee on profits made by its funds when it realizes profits. Carried interest is the term used to describe the profit split of proceeds to the general partner. This is the general partner's fee for carrying the management responsibility of the fund (plus the liability, if any) and for providing the necessary expertise to successfully manage the fund's portfolio of investments. There are many variations on the fees charged and the profits split between the LPs and the GP, both in the amounts and how they are calculated, but a 2 percent management fee plus a 20 percent carried interest is typical.

**Creating a Private Equity Portfolio**    Now that we have reviewed the major strategies of private equity, we are ready to create the private equity program. The first step in implementing a private equity portfolio is to decide whether an allocation to a private equity is established, and, if so, what percentage of the portfolio will be allocated there. The inclusion of private equity strategies in an individual or family office private equity portfolio is driven largely by the same factors that influence the overall asset allocation decision: return objective, risk tolerance, liquidity requirements, and time horizon, among others. The overriding consideration for most investors, however, is liquidity. Private equity capital can be tied up for many years, for which investors need to be compensated. Clients should not bother investing in private equity unless they believe they can earn a marginal return over public equity securities, which varies according to market conditions (but 500 basis points above the S&P 500 is about right).

Once an allocation to private equity is made, the next step is to determine how much money will be allocated each year. This is typically done with a cash flow private equity commitment model. In rough terms, for every percent allocation to private equity (in dollars), clients should make regular annual commitments of one-third of a percent to meet the target. Clients should not shoot for the entire allocation in one or two years. They should strive instead for *vintage year diversification*, which, as in wine collecting, helps prevent an investor from investing too much in a single bad year. Private equity returns have good years and bad years. If substantially less than a third of the commitment is invested annually, there will be a reduced likelihood of reaching a target private equity allocation within a reasonable time horizon; any more, and one risks too much allocated to a single vintage year. In addition to providing vintage year diversification, this approach allows clients to adjust commitments for the inherent unpredictability in performance and cash flows, as well as allowing the client to address changing opportunities within the broad landscape of private equity.

Once the client decides how much to allocate to private equity, the next question is how to access private equity: either by investing in direct limited partnerships having interest in underlying companies, or investing in a fund of multiple private equity partnerships (fund of funds). Which way is best depends on the amount of capital being invested, administrative capability, due diligence resources, and access to top managers. With regard to capital, there is some debate about what account size is appropriate to invest in LPs, but certainly at annual commitments of $30 million to $40 million, funds of funds are less attractive. Even at this level though, if the investor has little or no administrative help, a fund of funds might be the best option. If a direct approach is used, portfolio size may still limit the number of managers that can be used in a given year and tilt the portfolio toward managers with broader opportunity sets rather than narrowly defined specialists. If size is not an issue and direct investing is preferred, top notch due diligence is required to evaluate individual funds. Having access to top fund managers is also essential.

After deciding whether a direct or fund of funds approach will be used, the next consideration is establishing risk-and-return parameters for the private equity portfolio, similar to how one addresses the task for the entire portfolio. An investor's risk-and-return profile will play a role in selecting a manager because some private equity managers are significantly more conservative in approach than others. This is why composition of the private equity portfolio is critical to the success of the private equity investor.

Once the investor has determined the amount of the commitment, the vehicle (fund of funds or direct), and which sectors to allocate to, she must make a final decision about which private equity managers she will perform the requisite due diligence on and commit capital to.

## FIXED INCOME INVESTMENTS (BONDS)

For those unfamiliar with the basics of bonds, there are a few key characteristics that investors should be aware of. Note that for our purpose here, I sometimes use the description of a single bond for simplicity. Keep in mind that what is explained about a single bond can be extrapolated to describe groups of bonds that a bond manager could invest in. The bond characteristics you will learn about are maturity, redemption features, credit quality, interest, price (implying yield), and tax status. Together, these factors help determine the value of a bond and how well the bond (or bond manager) meets the investment objectives of a client.

## Maturity

A bond's maturity refers to the specific date on which the investor's principal will be repaid. Bonds typically mature in a period of time from one day to 30 years. The maturity ranges of bonds generally fall into three categories: short term, intermediate term, and long term. Short-term bonds have maturities of up to 5 years; intermediate-term bonds have maturities of 5 to 12 years; and long-term bonds have maturities of 12 years or more. The maturity of a bond is important because the maturity date substantially affects the price and yield of a bond, and investors take a keen interest in when their principal will be repaid.

## Bond Quality and Credit Ratings

Bond quality can range from the highest creditworthiness of U.S. Treasury securities, which are backed by the full faith and credit of the U.S. government, to below investment-grade (junk bonds), which are considered highly speculative. The way that investors and advisors can judge the quality of a bond—that is, the ability of an issuer to make its regularly scheduled interest payments and repay principal—is by relying on rating agencies that assign risk ratings to bonds when they are issued and monitor the development of these bonds during their lifetimes. These agencies rate bonds on several factors, which include the issuer's financial condition and management, quantitative and qualitative characteristics of the debt, and the general sources of repayment for interest and principal. Table 12.4 shows the ratings of the major rating agencies: Moody's Investor Service, Standard & Poor's ratings services, and Fitch IBCA agencies (the problems of these firms in view of the most recent subprime debacle notwithstanding).

As Table 12.4 indicates, the highest possible ratings are AAA from S&P and Fitch and Aaa from Moody's. Bonds rated BBB or above are

**TABLE 12.4**  Credit Ratings by Moody's, S&P, and Fitch

| Credit Risk | Moody's | S&P | Fitch |
|---|---|---|---|
| Prime | Aaa | AAA | AAA |
| Excellent | Aa | AA | AA |
| Upper Medium | A | A | A |
| Lower Medium | Baa | BBB | BBB |
| Speculative | Ba | BB | BB |
| Very Speculative | B, Caa | B, CCC, CC, C | B, CCC, CC, C |
| Default | Ca, C | D | DDD, DD, D |

*Source:* Moody's, S&P, and Fitch.

considered investment-grade; bonds with ratings BB or below are considered junk bonds, or, more politely, high-yield bonds. Although the term *junk* may imply that these bonds should be avoided, there are certainly times when these securities can and should be part of a portfolio. The best time to invest in high-yield bonds is when spreads have widened considerably; when the rate of interest paid on a junk bond is well over its long-term average spread over U.S. Treasury bonds, investors should consider them.

## Interest Rates

Bonds normally pay interest to investors twice a year (semiannually) but can also pay monthly or quarterly. Interest can be paid on a fixed basis (i.e., the rate paid doesn't change over the life of the bond); it can float (the interest rate will float with prevailing rates over the life of the bond); can be paid at maturity along with principal. Some bonds, called payment-in-kind bonds, can actually pay interest with the issuance of more bonds, but this is a creative form of high-yield financing that I won't delve into. Zero-coupon bonds, or *zeros,* pay no periodic interest, but rather pay all interest and principal at maturity, usually compounded semiannually. To compensate for the lack of current interest payments with zeros, they are sold at a deep discount from their face value. Taxable investors need to be careful if the zero they invest in is taxable, because taxes accrue annually even though interest is paid at maturity.

## Price and Yield

The price an investor pays for a bond is based on current interest rates, supply and demand, credit quality, maturity, and taxation. The yield of a bond is the return that is actually earned on the bond, based on the actual price paid and the interest payments to be received in the future. There are three main types of bond yields: current yield, yield-to-maturity, and yield-to-call. Current yield takes the price paid for the bond and divides it by the bond's interest payment. Yield-to-maturity sums the total amount of interest received on the bond from purchase until the bond's maturity, plus any gain earned if the bond is purchased below its face value (or minus any loss if it is purchased above its face value). Yield-to-call is calculated in the same way as yield-to-maturity, except that it assumes that the bond is called at the earliest point possible, and the investor receives the face value on the call date. Yield-to-maturity and yield-to-call, which are more informative than current yield, provide information on the total return received by holding the bond until it matures or it is called.

The way that bond prices move in relation to interest rate movements is often misunderstood by even professional investors and some financial journalists. When current interest rates *rise,* prices of outstanding bonds *fall* to bring the yield of existing bonds in line with higher-interest-paying new issues. The longer the maturity, the greater the risk that bond prices will fluctuate with changes in interest rates—a risk that investors will want to be compensated for. This concept can be shown by the *yield curve.* A normally shaped yield curve slopes upward and shows a fairly steep rise in yields between short- and intermediate-term issues; it shows a less pronounced rise between intermediate- and long-term issues.

If the yield curve is steep, it means the yields on short-term securities are relatively low when compared to long-term issues. If the yield curve is flat, it means the difference between short- and long-term rates is relatively small. When yields on short-term issues are higher than those on longer-term issues, the yield curve is said to be *inverted,* which suggests that bond market participants expect interest rates to decline; sometimes an inverted yield curve is a good indicator that a recession is at hand.

### Bond Redemption

Many investors focus only on the maturity of the bond and can overlook features that can have material impacts on the expected life of a bond investment, such as call provisions and put provisions. Some bonds, particularly municipal bonds, have *call provisions* that allow (or under certain circumstances, require) the issuer to repay principal on a date before the bond's maturity date. The most common reason for a bond to be called is that the issuer has an opportunity to lower its interest cost because interest rates have gone down. Rather than focusing on yield-to-maturity, good bond managers focus on yield-to-call, which hypothetically assumes that the bond is called on the earliest date the issuer could call the bond. Bonds with call provisions usually must offer a higher annual return than bonds without call provisions to compensate for the option that a bond might be called before maturity. In the opposite case, some bonds have *put provisions,* which may require the issuer to repurchase the bonds at specified times before maturity at the option of the investor. Investors will normally exercise this option when interest rates have risen since the bonds were issued (or they simply want their money returned to them).

### Tax Treatment

Different bonds naturally have different tax treatments. For example, interest on U.S. Treasury bonds is free of state and local income taxes but taxable at the federal level. Interest earned on municipal bonds is free of federal income tax, and in most cases, state and local income taxes. One might infer from this that taxable investors should always invest in tax-exempt securities. This is not always the case. The appropriateness of bond income that is taxable or tax-exempt depends on the taxable client's income tax bracket and other factors such as tax loss carryforwards and alternative minimum tax status. Another key factor is the type of account the securities are held in. Tax-deferred accounts such as company retirement accounts, 401(k)s, or IRAs should hold taxable bonds in most, if not all, cases.

## Bond Asset Classes

We now move to describing individual bond asset classes. The decision to invest in certain bond asset classes should factor in valuation as well as how the characteristics of the asset class meet the investor's objectives. Bonds can be divided up into several different segments including geographic, type, and taxability.

**U.S. Treasury and Agency Bonds**   U.S. Treasury securities are direct obligations of the U.S. government issued by the Department of the Treasury. They are backed by the full faith and credit of the U.S. government and are therefore considered to be free of credit risk. Agency securities, in contrast, are obligations of specific entities that are either part of or sponsored by the U.S. government. Agency securities do not typically have an explicit government backing, but are nevertheless viewed as having very low credit risk.[2] These bonds still carry interest rate risk, but are attractive because of their liquidity. Nearly all issues (excluding Freddie Mac and Fannie Mae) are exempt from state and local taxes.

Prior to S&P's 2011 downgrade of U.S. debt from AAA to AA+, U.S. Treasury securities were considered risk free, or to have zero credit risk. While budget and debt ceiling debates in Washington have caused concern over the trajectory of U.S. debt growth, the government's ability to raise tax revenues and print money virtually assure that that interest and principal will be paid on time even if the dollars repaid are worth less than those originally borrowed.

**Mortgage-Backed Securities (MBS)**   Mortgage-backed securities (MBS) are debt obligations that represent claims to the cash flows from pools of mortgage loans, most commonly on residential property. (SEC website; www.sec.gov/answers/mortgagesecurities.htm.) MBS can range from traditional pass through certificates to more complicated structures such as collaterized mortgage obligations (CMOs) or mortgage derivatives. A significant risk of MBS is prepayment risk; as interest rates fall, homeowners tend to refinance, causing the return of principal to investors at a time when their reinvestment options are relatively unattractive.

**Corporate Bonds**   Corporate Bonds are debt securities issued by corporations. Like Treasuries and Agency bonds, these bonds carry interest rate risk. However, due to the additional credit risk of the particular issuer, and the liquidity risk of a particular issue, they tend to have a higher yield than Treasury securities. The difference between the yield on a corporate bond compared to a similar maturity Treasury bond is referred to as the bond's "spread."

**High Yield Bonds**   High Yield Bonds, sometimes referred to as "junk bonds," are those bonds rated below investment grade (below BBB from S&P or below Baa from Moody's). These bonds typically pay higher interest rates than other bonds since they carry a higher risk of default. Entities that issue high-yield debt include many U.S. corporations, certain U.S. banks, various foreign governments, and some foreign corporations.

**Global Bonds**   Global Bonds refers to the strategy of investing in the bonds of multiple countries. In addition to being able to take advantage of the different yields offered by various countries' debts, global bond managers will attempt to use the difference in interest rates to take advantage of exchange rate movements. Exchange rates are both a key risk and an opportunity to global bond managers. There are two types of currencies: currencies pegged to the U.S. dollar and currencies that are free-floating. Pegged currency values are those that move in line with the U.S. dollar and protect it from currency risk. The value of free-floating currencies, however, fluctuates completely independently from the U.S. dollar, posing a greater risk, but also offering additional opportunities.

**Emerging Markets Local Currency Debt**   Historically, emerging market countries have issued debt denominated in U.S. dollars or euros. Recently, however, more emerging market issuers have begun issuing debt in local currencies. Like high yield bonds, many of these countries offer higher yields accompanied by lower ratings and higher default risk. Recently, local currency emerging market debt has become popular due to the expectation that their higher growth rates and trade surpluses will cause emerging currencies to appreciate versus most developed country currencies.

   The composition of emerging market debt has also improved, supporting stable growth, investment flows, exchange rates, and credit ratings. Figure 12.6 shows the growth of local currency debt as a proportion of total emerging market debt over the past 12 years.

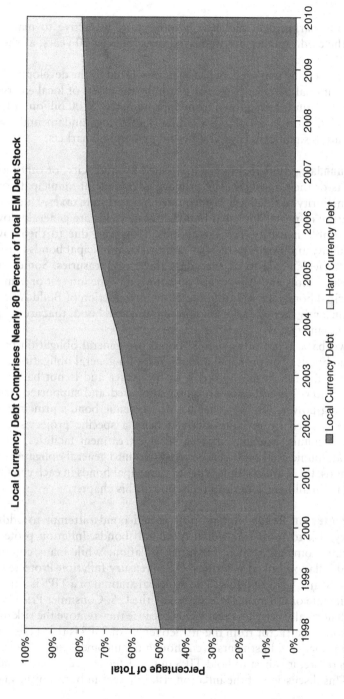

**FIGURE 12.6** Proportion of EM Debt Denominated in Local Currency
*Source:* JP Morgan, as of 10/31/10.

Emerging market debt has also become more attractive to many investors as the credit quality has improved over the past 20 years, as shown in Figure 12.7.

Finally, emerging market debt has been supported by the development of a local institutional investor base. For example, the assets of local emerging market pension funds have grown from approximately $100 billion in 1991 to over $1.4 trillion in 2010. All of these improving fundamentals have begun to lead to significant capital flows into emerging markets.

**Municipal Bonds**   Municipal bonds are issued by state, city, or other local governments or their agencies. The primary advantage of municipal bonds is that the majority of them are free from federal and state taxes. Due to the tax-free nature of most municipal bond interest, yields are generally lower than comparable maturity Treasury bonds. However, due to their lower relative liquidity and higher perceived credit risks, municipal bonds at times can trade at yields equal to or exceeding those of Treasuries. Some states (for example, Illinois and Wisconsin) do not exempt the interest of many of their municipal bonds. In addition, the 2009 introduction of Build America Bonds significantly increased the amount of municipal bonds that are subject to federal income tax.

The two basic types of municipal bonds are general obligation bonds and revenue bonds. The principal and interest of a general obligation bond is secured by the full faith and credit of the issuer and is not backed by a specific project. These bonds are voter approved and supported by the issuer's taxing power. On the other hand, a revenue bond's principal and interest are secured by revenues derived from a specific project such as toll roads, hospitals, bridges, airports, sewage treatment facilities, and so on. While all municipal bonds can be separated into general obligation and revenue bonds, there are multiple types of municipal bonds in each category; describing them all here is beyond the scope of this chapter.

**Inflation-Protected Bonds**   Inflation-protected bonds attempt to address the primary risk to most traditional (nominal) bonds. Inflation protected bonds contain some adjustment for future inflation. While many countries have issued inflation linked securities, U.S. Treasury Inflation-Protected Securities (TIPS) are the most liquid. The principal amount of a TIPS is adjusted based on the rate of inflation as measured by the U.S. Consumer Price Index (CPI). TIPS normally offer low real yields because they remove the risk of inflation. Another detractor from the attractiveness of TIPS is that taxes must be paid on principal adjustments even though the income is not actually received. Therefore, it is best to hold TIPS in tax deferred accounts whenever possible. This discussion of the inflation risk inherent in bonds brings us to

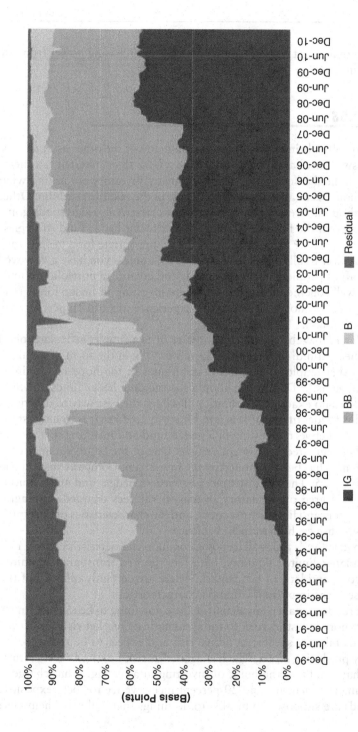

**FIGURE 12.7** Credit Quality of Emerging Market Countries
*Source:* JP Morgan, as of 12/31/10.

**171**

other assets that might help protect a portfolio's purchasing power from the scourge of inflation.

## HEDGE FUNDS

Hedge funds often bring more questions than any of the other asset classes, and the answers are rarely black and white. With their inherent tax inefficiency and limited information available, many investors are asking what the right amount is to allocate to hedge funds in the taxable portfolio. Other questions abound: Are hedge funds an asset class? Are hedge funds going to be regulated in the future? What are the different hedge fund strategies? What is a side pocket? How much leverage is appropriate for a hedge fund? The short answer to all of these questions is that unless you have a very well qualified staff of people selecting the funds and creating a portfolio of funds that work well together, you should not be investing in hedge funds (and even then success is not assured). In my experience, the top 10 percent may not be good enough.

The Merriam-Webster online dictionary does a simple, articulate job of defining a hedge fund: "an investing group usually in the form of a limited partnership that employs speculative techniques in the hope of obtaining large capital gains."[3] Despite the hoopla surrounding hedge funds, the term *hedge fund* has no exact legal definition. Perhaps the best way to describe a hedge fund is to identify what it is *not*. One way to do that is to understand the differences between investing in a hedge fund and investing in a mutual fund or other regulated investment vehicle. One of the better summaries of these differences has been compiled the Investment Company Institute, as seen in Table 12.5. The key differences between a hedge fund and a mutual fund are the degree of regulatory oversight, the fees charged, leveraging practices, pricing and liquidity practices, and the characteristics of the typical investors who use each investment vehicle.

Most hedge funds today share some common characteristics: active risk, broad mandates, limited liquidity, high fees, limited transparency, unique trading tactics, and lack of benchmark. There are certainly others, but this covers most of the important common characteristics.

Hedge funds managers, by definition, are not going to be the investment managers whom investors turn to for systematic or market risk (i.e., *beta*). Hedge funds take on specific or active risk and expect to be rewarded for doing so by producing *alpha*, which is defined as risk-adjusted excess return. Indeed, what would be the point of investing in a manager that charges a 2 percent management fee and 20 percent incentive fee for beta exposure? Hedge funds are supposed to be able to do things that will earn themselves

**TABLE 12.5** Comparison of Mutual Funds to Hedge Funds

| | Hedge Funds | Mutual Funds |
|---|---|---|
| Regulatory Oversight | Unlike mutual funds, hedge funds are not required to register with the SEC. They issue securities in private offerings not registered with the SEC under the Securities Act of 1933. Furthermore, hedge funds are not required to make periodic reports under the Securities Exchange Act of 1934. Like mutual funds and other securities market participants, hedge funds are subject to prohibitions against fraud, and their managers have the same fiduciary duties as other investment advisors. | Mutual funds are investment companies that must register with the SEC and, as such, are subject to rigorous regulatory oversight. Virtually every aspect of a mutual fund's structure and operation is subject to strict regulation under four federal laws: the Securities Act of 1933, the Securities Exchange Act of 1934, the Investment Company Act of 1940, and the Investment Advisors Act of 1940. The Investment Company Act is the cornerstone of mutual fund regulation. It regulates the structure and operation of mutual funds and requires funds to safeguard their securities, forward price their securities, and keep detailed books and records. In addition, the 1933 Act requires that all prospective fund investors receive a prospectus containing specific information about the fund's management, holdings, fees and expenses, and performance. |
| Fees | There are no limits on the fees a hedge fund can charge its investors. A hedge fund manager typically charges an asset-based fee and a performance fee. Some have front-end sales charges, as well. | Federal law imposes a fiduciary duty on a mutual fund's investment advisor regarding the compensation it receives from the fund. In addition, mutual fund sales charges and other distribution fees are subject to specific regulatory limits under NASD rules. Mutual fund fees and expenses are disclosed in detail, as required by law, in a fee table at the front of every prospectus. They are presented in a standardized format so that an investor can easily understand them and can compare expense ratios among different funds. |

*(Continued)*

**TABLE 12.5** (*Continued*)

| | Hedge Funds | Mutual Funds |
|---|---|---|
| Leverage Practices | Leveraging and other higher-risk investment strategies are a hallmark of hedge fund management. Hedge funds were originally designed to invest in equity securities and use leverage and short selling to hedge the portfolio's exposure to movements of the equity markets. Today, however, advisors to hedge funds use a wide variety of investment strategies and techniques. Many are very active traders of securities. | The Investment Company Act severely restricts a mutual fund's ability to leverage or borrow against the value of securities in its portfolio. The SEC requires that funds engaging in certain investment techniques, including the use of options, futures, forward contracts, and short selling, cover their positions. The effect of these constraints has been to strictly limit leveraging by mutual fund portfolio managers. |
| Pricing and Liquidity | There are no specific rules governing hedge fund pricing. Hedge fund investors may be unable to determine the value of their investment at any given time. | Mutual funds are required to value their portfolios and price their securities daily, based on market quotations that are readily available at market value as determined in good faith by the board of directors. In addition to providing investors with timely information regarding the value of their investments, daily pricing is designed to ensure that both new investments and redemptions are made at accurate prices. Moreover, mutual funds are required by law to allow shareholders to redeem their shares at any time. |
| Investor Qualifications | A significantly higher minimum investment is required from hedge fund investors. Under the Investment Company Act of 1940, certain hedge funds may accept investments from individuals who hold at least $5 million in investments. This measure is intended to help limit participation in hedge funds and other types of unregulated pools to highly sophisticated individuals. Hedge funds can also accept other types of investors if they rely on other exemptions under the Investment Company Act or are operated outside the United States. | The only qualification for investing in a mutual fund is having the minimum investment to open an account with a fund company, which is typically around $1,000, but can be lower. After the account has been opened, there is generally no minimum additional investment required, and many fund investors contribute relatively small amounts to their mutual funds on a regular basis as part of a long-term investment strategy. |

*Source:* www.ici.org/funds/abt/faqs.hedge.html.

unique sources of alpha, such as having better and faster access to information, superior analysis of same, the best talent money can buy, and more.

Hedge fund managers have a great deal of flexibility to pursue various investment styles, asset classes, security types, and trading techniques. For example, one of the main differences between a hedge fund manager and a traditional equity manager is that the hedge fund manager can concentrate his or her portfolio in only a few securities or have thousands of them. Those securities can be of varying sizes and styles. This flexibility affords the manager the leeway she needs to adapt to various market conditions as they change.

Perhaps the thorniest issue with investing in hedge funds is the liquidity (redemption) terms that hedge funds offer. Most hedge funds have an initial period during which the investor cannot pull money out of the fund. This is known as a *lock-up period,* the length of which varies by fund. Although lock-up terms have varied widely historically, a typical lock-up period is two years, but some are one year while others are three years; beyond three years is unusual. Even after the lock-up period has passed, investors typically can only redeem on certain dates. While these terms can appear burdensome, hedge funds often have good reasons for these types of liquidity terms. They do not want to begin engaging in a trading strategy that might take time to implement and realize value and then have investors pull money out.

Hedge fund managers charge fees that are well beyond those of traditional investment managers. Fees are divided into two areas: management fees and incentive fees. Management fees usually range from about 1 to 3 percent of assets under management. Incentive fees permit the hedge fund manager to participate in the positive performance of the fund. Incentive fees typically range from 15 to 25 percent of the annual realized or unrealized gains. There are certain hedge funds that charge well above these ranges. One of the issues with this type of fee structure, of course, is that managers have an incentive to assume excessive risk to maximize income. This is not always in the best interest of the investor. Many hedge fund managers use a tool called a *high-water mark*. A high-water mark is a measure of prior losses occurring in a fund that must be recouped by new profits before an incentive fee is paid. A few funds include a *hurdle rate,* a minimum rate of return performance level that the fund manager must achieve if he is to receive an incentive fee. Both the hurdle rate and the high-water mark are helpful to investors.

Many investors would like to know what a hedge fund is doing so they can assess the risks embedded in the manager's strategy and holdings before investing their capital. Hedge fund managers prefer not to show investors or anyone else what they are doing, mainly to protect their intellectual property: the holdings and strategies in their funds. Thus, a tension exists between investors and managers that is not easily resolved. This lack of transparency is part of what gives hedge funds their aura of mystery. Those responsible for doing due diligence on managers must penetrate this aura and uncover details. Managers are gradually getting more comfortable about revealing information. At the end of the day, trust is paramount. With such limited regulation, a hedge fund that is intent on defrauding investors will likely be able to succeed.

Hedge fund managers use three basic trading tools that go beyond traditional management so they can achieve alpha: short selling, leverage, and derivatives. Short selling allows managers to profit from declines in securities prices by borrowing someone else's shares and buying them back at a later time. Leverage, or borrowed money, is used to magnify returns on various investment strategies such as small security pricing discrepancies. Derivatives permit hedge fund managers to take meaningful positions in a certain segment of the market synthetically, or without actually owning the underlying security. These three tactics are used throughout the hedge fund world, although to varying degrees, with certain strategies using some more often than others, depending on the need.

Hedge fund managers are in the business of making money. Some in the industry refer to this as absolute returns. In the pursuit of absolute returns, hedge fund managers are unconstrained in their investment strategies. They, as such, have no formalized benchmark to beat (although some hedge fund managers do compare themselves to certain benchmarks, such as cash plus 4 percent or an individual strategy benchmark such as a convertible arbitrage benchmark).

## REAL ASSETS

Real assets represent the majority of the economic input and store of value investments we discussed earlier. Real assets are different from capital assets in that they have an intrinsic value because of the utility they provide. In the case of unexpected inflation, these assets should increase in value because of that intrinsic value. Real (or *hard*) assets, which are tangible—as opposed to financial assets, which are intangible—maintain their value over long periods of time because of their positive correlation to inflation. They usually also provide valuable diversification benefits to a portfolio. The rationale for holding real assets in an investment portfolio is to generate attractive nominal rates of return and provide a hedge against unexpected inflation. While stocks do tend to pass on the long-run effects of inflation, there have been periods (during the 1970s, for example) when inflation was high and stocks did poorly.

Real assets also tend to be inherently tax efficient because of their long holding periods, with some offering special tax advantages, such as depreciation and long-term capital gains tax rates when held for 12 months or more, and generally provide some level of cash flow during the holding period. Real estate, for example, pays out net income from operations, and timber generates a yield from harvesting trees and other fees. Oil and gas will generate income from the sale of oil and gas reserves.

## Real Estate

Real estate that is leased could still be considered a capital asset. Investments in real estate can be a way to protect against inflation based on the assumption that landowners can increase rents during periods of inflation. However, this assumption is based on the real estate market being in balance between supply and demand. Excess supply, as evidenced by vacancy rates of 10 percent plus, could make it impossible to raise rents even during periods of high inflation.

Ideally, clients with the typical low liquidity needs and long time horizon will invest in real estate the way they do in private equity: in private partnerships. As we discussed earlier, a private investment program is best achieved with vintage year diversification. As for portfolio construction of the private real estate portfolio, that is a matter of risk appetite. Generally, an investor will want a core, diversified fund as an anchor. If additional return is desired, satellite strategies such as those in the value-added and opportunistic strategies can be implemented. During the five or so years it takes to get a private strategy fully invested, liquid real estate investment trusts (although on the volatile side) can act as a proxy for private real estate while the vintage year diversification takes effect.

## Commodities

Commodities of all types (oil and gas, industrial metals, precious metals, timber) offer a hedge against inflation because commodities prices usually rise when the pace of inflation increases. As demand for goods and services increases, the price of goods and services usually rises too, as does the price of the commodities used to produce those goods and services.

There are three segments of the energy industry: the upstream, the midstream, and the downstream. Companies involved in upstream activities are exploring and extracting energy products from under the ground and beneath the ocean. Midstream companies provide the tankers and pipelines that carry crude oil to refineries. The downstream includes market participants involved in refining, marketing, and distributing energy products, including local gas stations that serve the end user. An integrated oil company is involved in two or more of these activities. Most private energy investment funds are focused on upstream and midstream activities. These funds invest in domestic oil and gas wells, with an emphasis on owning what are called *proved reserves*. As the name implies, there is evidence that oil or gas is present and is being pumped from the ground at these sites. Some funds also pursue exploration activities. Others invest in midstream assets such as pipelines and energy-related technologies. The overriding risk when investing in energy is a change in the underlying commodity price compared to the price assumed when the investment is made. Another risk factor is production costs. Most energy investments hedge price exposure for some period of time, which offers a level of protection, but can limit the upside and the inflation sensitivity.

As was mentioned earlier, the spectrum of risk and return available in the energy markets is similar to real estate strategies. In real estate, core funds derive most of their return from income. In the energy world, comparable funds are known as *royalty funds*. These funds' target returns are typically 8 to 10 percent in a stable price environment, but can increase in rising price environments. The core-plus real estate fund's energy equivalent is a *resource fund* whose primary strategy is to buy reserves and create value, mainly by cutting costs and improving operations. Returns expectations are 12 to 15 percent, net of fees. The value-added energy strategy is a resource fund or a private equity fund that invests in proved reserves and will pursue lower-risk drilling and reengineering activities to increase production. The target return on these funds is 15 percent net of fees. The last category is opportunistic. Here, the primary activity is drilling wells. This is a higher risk, higher reward scenario. Many of these investments are made by private equity funds. Expected returns in these funds are above 15 percent, but have a higher degree of risk than other types of energy funds.

Commodities are raw materials used to create consumer products and include energy, industrial and precious metals, agriculture and livestock, and soft commodities, perishables like coffee and sugar. Commodities have evolved as an asset class with the development of commodity futures exchanges and investment vehicles that track commodity indexes. Futures and options contracts can be traded on hard and soft commodities globally. This has created a tremendous demand for commodity-based investments. According to Barclays Capital, there is currently approximately $175 billion invested in allocations tracking commodity indexes. The S&P GSCI (Standard & Poor's-Goldman Sachs Commodity Index), Total Return Index, and the Dow Jones–AIG (American International Group) Commodity Index are two commonly used benchmarks that define the composition of the commodities market. Both indexes are based on a basket of collateralized commodity futures returns, rather than simply futures price returns over a period of time. Each index calculates returns from three distinct sources (hence the classification, *total return*):

- Interest earned from the cash collateral committed to trading in the futures (generally Treasury bills).
- Change in futures contract price which, when added to the above, should approximate the return on the reference index.
- Return from rolling the futures into further dated contracts as they approach expiry, which has been a positive contributor over the long term, but recently has had a negative impact.

There are four primary ways to add commodities to a portfolio:

1. Buying the physical commodity: This approach offers pure exposure to the underlying commodity, but delivery, storage, and spoilage may be problematic.
2. Investing through the futures or derivatives market: This method has predominantly been limited to large institutional investors with the resources and experience to administer complicated futures portfolios themselves, or to use a total return swap and manage the related counterparty risk.
3. Investing in pooled vehicles such as mutual funds: Until recently, mutual funds presented the most viable option for individual investors or small institutions because they provide convenient access to commodity-linked investment at reasonable costs and low investment minimums.
4. Exchange Traded Notes (ETNs): ETNs provide a new way to access difficult-to-reach markets such as commodities. ETNs are unsecured debt securities that deliver exposure to the returns of an asset class or market with the trading flexibility of an equity. ETNs linked to commodity indexes are designed to allow investors cost-effective access to the returns of popular commodity benchmarks, minus an investor fee.

## Coin or Art

Coin or art collections are stores of value that do offer some inflation protection over the long term, but they also present additional risks. The world of coin and art collecting is relatively illiquid, and prices depend on several factors that may be even less predictable than traditional markets, including supply, changes in taste, how often an item has appeared at market, condition, and collector behavior.

## SIMPLE PORTFOLIO CONSTRUCTION

Now that we have reviewed the major asset classes, it is time to learn how to put all the pieces together. Portfolio construction is the process of building a portfolio of assets that are able to perform consistently within investor's goals, through various economic and market environments, by applying a total portfolio perspective. A total portfolio perspective essentially means having a thorough understanding of how each investment within a portfolio interacts with all the other assets. In turn, it also requires understanding how this interaction impacts the overall portfolio's ability to generate more consistent risk-adjusted returns for investors. This is particularly important in this environment where investors want simplification, consistency, and portfolios that meet their objectives.

Calculating the portfolio's expected return is relatively simple; it is merely the weighted average of the individual asset class expected returns. For simplicity, we will use the historical asset class returns and standard deviations as the expected returns. However, in practice, return expectations should be adjusted to account for current valuations.

Portfolio expected return can be calculated as:

$$E[R_p] = \sum_{i=1}^{N} w_i E[R_i]$$

where  $E[R_p]$ = the expected return on the portfolio,
$N$ = the number of investments in the portfolio,
$w_i$ = the proportion of the portfolio invested in investment $i$, and
$E[R_i]$ = the expected return on investment $i$.

The portfolio's expected standard deviation is dependent not only on the expected standard deviations of the components of the portfolio, but also the correlation between those assets. Table 12.6 contains a subset of the correlations found earlier in this chapter. S&P 500 is our representative

**TABLE 12.6**  Correlation Matrix

|  | S&P 500 | Barclays Agg | Citi 3-Month T-Bill |
|---|---|---|---|
| S&P 500 | 1.00 | 0.19 | 0.06 |
| Barclays Agg | 0.19 | 1.00 | −0.07 |
| Citi 3-Month T-Bill | 0.06 | −0.07 | 1.00 |

equity class, the Barclays (formerly Lehman) Aggregate is our representative bond class, and the Citi 3-Month Treasury Bill Index is our proxy for cash.

While a little more complicated than the expected return, the variance of a portfolio of three or more assets can be written as a function of the variances of each of the assets, the portfolio weights on each, and the correlations between pairs of the assets.

The variance of a three-asset portfolio is:

$$\sigma^2(r_p) = w_a^2 \sigma^2(r_a) + w_b^2 \sigma^2(r_b) + w_c^2 \sigma^2(r_c)$$
$$+ 2w_a w_b \text{cov}(r_a, r_b) + 2w_a w_c \text{cov}(r_a, r_c) + 2w_b w_c \text{cov}((r_b, r_c)$$

and the standard deviation of the portfolio is:

$$\sigma(r_p) = \sqrt{\sigma^2(r_p)}$$

where $w_i$ = Portfolio weights on assets

$\sigma^2(r_a), \sigma^2(r_b), \sigma^2(r_c)$ = Variances of assets $a$, $b$, and $c$

$\text{cov}(r_a, r_b)$ = Covariance between pairs of assets (A&B, A&C, B&C) can be calculated from the information we already have and equals the correlation between the two assets times the standard deviation of each.

$$\text{cov}(r_a, r_b) = \rho_{ab} \sigma_a \sigma_b$$

where $\rho_{ab}$ equals the correlation between assets $a$ and $b$

Therefore, we can use combinations of assets to create an optimal portfolio for a client's given risk profile. Table 12.7 shows the expected return and standard deviation for three sample portfolios.

A basic but useful measure to compare portfolios is the Sharpe Ratio. The Sharpe ratio is a measure of return per unit of risk. Technically, the formula is return of the portfolio minus the risk-free rate divided by the standard deviation.

$$S = \frac{E[Rp - Rf]}{\sigma_p}$$

In the example above, we used the historical return on cash as the risk free rate. Since the Sharpe Ratio is a measure of excess return per unit of risk, the higher the Sharpe ratio the better.

**TABLE 12.7**  Simple Portfolio Construction

| Portfolio | A | B | C |
|---|---|---|---|
| U.S. Large Stock Weight | 80.0 | 60.0 | 40.0 |
| Lehman Aggregate Weight | 15.0 | 20.0 | 40.0 |
| Cash Weight | 5.0 | 10.0 | 20.0 |
| Portfolio Expected Return | 7.3 | 6.2 | 6.4 |
| Portfolio Expected Standard Deviation | 12.2 | 9.1 | 6.2 |
| Sharpe Ratio | 0.32 | 0.32 | 0.49 |

## SUMMARY

The intent of this chapter was to introduce the major asset classes and demonstrate how asset classes are put together to create a diversified, well-constructed portfolio. In the next chapter we delve further into the subject of asset allocation with specific emphasis on the key inputs into creating a customized allocation for an individual investor.

## NOTES

1. Roger G. Ibbotson, and William N. Goetzmann, "History and the Equity Risk Premium," April 6, 2005. Yale ICF Working Paper No. 05-04.
2. Frank J. Fabozzi, "U.S. Treasury and Agency Securities," in The Handbook of Fixed Income Securities, 7th ed., ed. Frank J. Fabozzi (New York: McGraw Hill, 2005).
3. www.merriam-webster.com/dictionary/hedge%20fund.

# Chapter 13

# What Is Asset Allocation?

*Put all your eggs in one basket—and watch that basket!*
                                                            —Mark Twain

**N**early everyone involved in advising private clients on their investments knows or has heard that asset allocation is the most important decision an investor can make vis-à-vis long-term investment performance. Importantly, a more-than-trivial number of investors and advisors either choose to ignore this sage advice or think they can pick a roster of active managers that can outperform a well diversified investment portfolio. So, if it is necessary to say it again, asset allocation is the most important decision an investor makes when designing his or her investment portfolio—period. But what many people often overlook is that asset allocation is both a quantitative (science) and qualitative (art) exercise. Because asset allocation is quantitative by nature—we talk about expected return, efficient frontier, percentages, and so on as inputs into the asset allocation selection process— there is a tendency for many to take a mostly, if not purely, quantitative approach. However, there is just as much art as there is science in selecting an appropriate asset allocation for your client. And when one factors in psychological biases, risk tolerance, multi-generational issues, and taxes, the asset allocation decision becomes even more of a subjective decision.

This chapter is intended to provide an overview of the importance of asset allocation. The chapter will be organized as follows: First, we will discuss why asset allocation is so important and review some of the academic research demonstrating how critical the asset allocation decision is for non-believers or those that may need a refresher. Next, we will discuss, without getting too technical, the importance of the assumptions that are used when modeling potential asset allocations for clients. Before moving to the importance of asset allocation, we will first define what we mean by the term. Later in the book we will discuss some asset allocations for each of the behavioral investor types.

In its simplest form, asset allocation is the process of determining how many and which asset classes will be included in a client's portfolio and the percentages that each class will represent. The right asset allocation for a client (which asset classes and in what amounts) will depend upon how well the allocation's characteristics and behavior match the client's objectives and constraints, which are typically captured in the investor's investment policy statement (IPS). Regardless of what level of risk a client is comfortable with, modern portfolio theory, which stresses diversification, tells us that our job as advisors is to obtain for our clients the best possible expected return for a given level of risk. The method used to attain this goal is to maximize the Sharpe ratio (return per unit of risk) for each portfolio allocation combination presented to the client during the asset allocation study.

Regardless of which allocation is ultimately selected, there are two types of asset allocation that are used for clients: strategic and tactical. Strategic asset allocation (SAA) means that, when integrated into the investment policy statement, the mixture of investment is intended to satisfy the client's objectives and constraints. SAA is really the seminal element of the portfolio creation and management process. The typical method of selecting the strategic allocation is through the use of an asset allocation study. This process involves presenting the client, after a thorough fact-finding and profiling session (investment policy statement inputs), with an array of possible asset allocations that may be appropriate for the client. The study presents risk and return statistics for the array of asset mixes presented so that a client can get a sense for the behavior he or she can expect from the selected allocation. Naturally, this process is not an exact science. Using historical or even forward-looking capital markets expectations cannot predict with precision how a portfolio will behave in any one year. Over the long run, however, behavior is fairly predictable using a strategic asset allocation.

Tactical asset allocation (TAA) is the process of making temporary adjustments to the asset class percentages selected in the SAA. These changes are based on projected short- to medium-term (defined as anywhere from one to five years, depending upon the time horizon of the tactical decision) relative performance of asset classes in the client's portfolio. Some may interpret this as market timing, but it is not the same thing. Market timing is defined as straying into asset classes outside the policy allocation in hopes of gaining short-term advantages. In practice, TAA can be thought of as tilting toward certain classes and away from other asset classes, while still maintaining exposure to classes that are in the client's policy allocation.

Some investment advisors don't explicitly break out asset allocation into strategic and tactical, but instead they use a combination of both as they change recommendations over time. Both strategic and tactical allocation selection are typically done using a modeling process that relies on assumptions of returns, risk, and correlations among asset classes. Many advisors don't take the time to dig into the details of these assumptions. This next section of this chapter will do this.

## THE IMPORTANCE OF ASSUMPTIONS

The most widely used implementation technique of modern portfolio theory's key tenet of diversification is *efficient frontier analysis*. Efficient frontier analysis, the process of minimizing risk per unit of return, is held in very high regard for many reasons, not the least of which is that is it based on the work of a Nobel laureate, Harry Markowitz. Mr. Markowitz's development of mean-variance optimization as a tool for investors and professionals is at the heart of asset allocation in practice. Many advisors use this tool with their clients because investors can attempt to obtain the highest Sharpe ratio in their portfolios by minimizing the volatility per unit of return by diversifying into multiple asset classes.

This process works because of a lack of perfect correlation between the asset classes in the portfolio construction; quantitatively, we call this the *covariance* among asset class pairs. Put simply, in one market environment, a given asset class may be falling while another one is rising, and another may be flat. In another market environment, the one that was flat may be rising, the one that was rising may be falling, and the one that was falling may be flat. The result is a smoothing of returns for the portfolio as a whole. We need to keep in mind, however, that the accuracy of the efficient frontier modeling process is based on assumptions of expected return, expected standard deviation (risk), and expected correlations among asset classes. The assumptions that are used for this analysis can cause the output to vary widely. Advisors need to understand the sensitivities of these assumptions so they can communicate effectively with their clients about the behavior of their clients' portfolios over time.

When advisors attempt to create efficient portfolios for their clients, they need to answer questions such as how many asset classes to include in the client's portfolio, which asset classes to use, and how much of the client's assets to allocate to each class selected. To answer these questions, advisors estimate inputs for each asset class of expected return, volatility of returns, and the correlations among all asset classes. They then optimize the mix of asset classes to create the efficient frontier, which represents the best possible combinations of risk and return for a given set of asset classes. So why all the fuss? The point is that the efficient frontier is a model in which assumptions drive the output. And assumptions of expected returns, volatility, and correlation very rarely come true to life. So advisors who want to add value to their client portfolios need to simultaneously examine history and look forward in making estimates—not an easy task. And, they need to realize that forecasts are nothing more than a best guess of the future.

The easiest way to estimate input assumptions is by using historical data. Using average return, standard deviation, and historical correlations you can back test and determine which portfolios have been optimal in the past. Obviously, using historical data only makes sense if you believe that history will repeat itself. A natural question here is, if you are going to use historical data, which historical period is best to use? Should one use a long period of time such as 100 years to capture the greatest amount of data possible, or use more mature capital market periods such as the last 30 years? And what about asset class maturity? Should one use one period for emerging markets bonds and another for Treasuries, reflecting the inception dates of these two asset classes? There is no right answer to these questions. They are a matter of judgment. There are some concepts to keep in mind, though. First, historical data should be assumed to have significant value, and changing estimates should have a clearly articulated logic. An example here is the correlation between U.S. large-capitalization equities and international large capitalization. Historically, these asset classes have been moderately correlated, but the case can be made that given the increasing integration of the global economies and capital markets, large multinational company equities will behave similarly regardless of where the companies are headquartered. Second, expected return estimates are going to have a large impact on the optimality choices of various asset mixes. Therefore, advisors need to carefully consider projected return estimates. Standard deviations and correlation assumptions have a lesser impact on optimality choices. Also, some return estimates include *alpha,* or outperformance, above an index, which typically distorts asset allocation models. Lastly, whatever methodology is used to determine assumptions should be applied consistently across asset classes.

## THE IMPORTANCE OF STRATEGIC ASSET ALLOCATION

Practitioners who rely on asset allocation to be the primary driver of returns recognize the pivotal role that strategic asset allocation plays in establishing the risk exposure a client can tolerate in his or her portfolio. One of the key benefits of the decision to diversify a portfolio into many asset classes is risk management. Although no asset allocation can prevent a portfolio from losing value in a severe market downturn, it can protect the portfolio in most market environments because when certain asset classes are falling, others are usually rising. Many advisors view asset allocation as highly important, based on a seminal article written in 1986 by Brinson, Hood, and Beebower (BHB), titled "Determinants of Portfolio Performance."[1]

BHB performed a study on the asset allocations of 91 large pension funds from 1973 to 1985. They replaced the pension funds' stock, bond, and cash selections with corresponding market indexes. The indexed quarterly returns were found to be higher than the pension plans' actual quarterly returns. The two quarterly return series' linear correlation was measured at 96.7 percent, with shared variance of 93.6 percent. On average, timing and security selection explained 6.4 percent of return variability. The contributions of timing and security selection to active returns were found on average to be negative, implying that spending time on these activities is not rewarded (on average).[2]

The authors interpreted the importance of asset allocation as the "fraction of the variation of returns over time" attributable to asset allocation on the basis of a regression analysis of the data.[3] What many financial advisors don't realize about this study is that it answered the question, "How much of the variability of returns across time for one portfolio is explained by asset allocation (or how much of a fund's volatility is explained by its policy allocation)?" rather than "What portion of a portfolio's return is explained by its asset allocation policy?"—which is really what we as advisors want to know. This may seem like an insignificant distinction, but, in fact, it is very different.

In 2000, Roger G. Ibbotson and Paul D. Kaplan answered this second and more important question in a study titled "Does Asset Allocation Policy Explain 40, 90, or 100 Percent of Performance?" Ibbotson and Kaplan used five asset classes in this study: U.S. large-capitalization stocks, U.S. small-capitalization stocks, foreign stocks, U.S. fixed-income securities, and cash, examining the 10-year returns of 94 U.S.-balanced mutual funds versus the corresponding indexed returns. After adjusting for index fund fees, the active returns failed to beat index returns. The linear correlation of monthly index returns versus the actual monthly return series was measured at 90.2 percent, with a shared variance of 81.4 percent. Asset allocation explained 40 percent of the variation of returns across funds, and explained virtually 100 percent of the level of fund returns. Ibbotson and Kaplan confirm that on average, active management (that is, market timing and manager selection) adds literally nothing to returns.[4] This does not necessarily imply that an investor cannot be successful by hiring active managers. Advisors should spend the majority of their investment policy creation time, however, on the asset allocation decision and less time on selecting active managers.

One final note is this: These studies do not include alternative investments such as hedge funds, private equity, or other private investments such as real estate or natural resources. In these asset classes, active management is almost assuredly what determines performance. In venture capital, hiring top decile (top 10 percent) managers is critical to investment success. It is not possible to invest in an index of venture capital, so manager selection is critical. In hedge funds, index returns are less than desirable. An approach that works well, therefore, is to get your active exposure in alternatives and index traditional investments, particularly highly efficient asset classes such as large-cap U.S. and large-cap international.

## CONSIDERATIONS FOR INDIVIDUAL INVESTORS

The task of determining an optimal asset allocation is a customized process for each investor and, as previously noted, is as much art as it is science. What is critical for advisors to understand is that many investors want to optimize an asset allocation for multiple objectives—and more often than not, this is simply not possible. One cannot simultaneously optimize for maximum income, maximum philanthropic donations, maximum growth, and minimal taxes. It is certainly possible to have multiple objectives and create investment strategies for each of these objectives, but optimizing a single allocation for each one is not possible. Investors need to determine what is most important to them, and, once that is established, tailor the asset allocation to their key objectives.

Perhaps the best way to illustrate the process of customizing the asset allocation is to review the categories that comprise an investment policy statement. These are return objectives, risk tolerance, and constraints such as liquidity, time horizon, taxes, legal and regulation, and unique circumstances. For clarity, there will be a segment in each of these sections called "impact on asset allocation" that will demonstrate what it is about each of these categories that affects the asset allocation process. The key is for advisors to learn how to have conversations with their clients about prioritizing investment objectives so they can recommend the most appropriate asset allocation.

### Return Objectives

It is critical that an investor's return objective be carefully defined, both quantitatively and qualitatively, with the emphasis being on the qualitative side. What advisors need to do is help their clients define exactly what it is that they want their money to do for them. Return objective is a wonderful starting point because it gets clients thinking about the broad subject of what long-term financial goals they have and how their existing wealth will help them achieve these goals. Return objectives are ironically one of the most important discussion points, but they are often backed into at the end of the process once the client has done significant thinking and planning about the question of what the family wants the money to accomplish. While quantitative measures are easy to judge ("Did I earn 9 percent or not?"), qualitative return objectives are not as easy, although they can certainly be evaluated. For example, a qualitative goal such as "to achieve returns that will provide an adequate spending income and maintain a fund's real purchasing power" can be concretely determined.

Return objective has a significant impact on the asset allocation decision. If the return objective is high, then an asset mix that emphasizes higher returns and higher-risk asset classes will be selected. If the return objective is low, then, naturally, the opposite is true. In the case of the client who is inclined toward a high return objective, advisors need to carefully assess whether the client *wants* a high return objective or *needs* a high return objective. Clients often take on more risk than is necessary simply because they think they ought to have a high return objective.

## Risk Tolerance

When creating an asset allocation policy, the natural complement to return objective is risk tolerance. As with return objectives, both qualitative and quantitative risk objectives are important considerations. Many practitioners begin the risk assessment process by administering a risk tolerance questionnaire that evaluates both quantitative and qualitative factors of an investor's risk tolerance. This usually results in the investor being categorized into one of four or five risk categories from low to high, based on the investor's willingness and ability to assume risk. But how can an advisor actually map the risk tolerance of the client to an allocation that is appropriate for the client? I believe that behavioral factors also need to be assessed because clients often overestimate their risk tolerance. In fact, I discuss this very subject later in the book. But from a purely risk assessment standpoint, there are several ways to do this. I discuss standard deviation, probability of a loss year, and shortfall risk as ways to match an allocation to risk tolerance.

Investors can quantify risk tolerance in terms of an acceptable level of volatility as measured by standard deviation of return. For example, an investor who is comfortable with the volatility associated with a standard deviation of return of 12 percent or less can eliminate allocations with greater than 12 percent volatility from consideration. The probability of a loss year is another way to quantify risk tolerance. In this method, an array of allocations can be presented to a client, some of which will have a high probability of a return that is less than zero and some of which will have a low probability of a return less than zero. A conservative investor might permit only a 10 percent chance of a negative return in any one year. A more aggressive investor might permit a 40 percent chance of a loss year in a given year. Finally, another way for an investor to quantify risk is in terms of shortfall risk, which is the risk that a portfolio's value will fall below some minimum acceptable level, such as the inflation rate or a spending rate, during a given time horizon. When shortfall risk is an important concern for an investor, an appropriate shortfall risk objective improves the description of the investor's attitude toward risk.

The willingness and ability to assume risk also have a significant impact on the asset allocation selection. Obviously, as risk tolerance increases, more risky asset classes will be included. Investors need to differentiate between the ability to assume risk and the need to take risk.

## Liquidity

Liquidity of a client's portfolio is a critical area and one that often gets overlooked. In general, significant liquidity requirements constrain the investor's ability to bear risk. The liquidity section of an investment policy statement covers two primary areas. The first area pertains to how much liquid cash is needed to meet both *anticipated* expenses and cash needs such as capital calls for private investments, and any *unanticipated* demands for cash such as medical expenses or home maintenance. The second area pertains to the overall percentage of liquid, semi-liquid, and illiquid investments that are deemed to be permissible to hold in the portfolio.

Cash requirements vary significantly for each investor, as some people depend upon portfolio returns (both income and capital gains) for their daily living expenses, while others derive income from an occupation and don't need to make portfolio withdrawals for living expenses. In the former case, a predictable living expense amount (a spend rate) constitutes a high priority for the investment portfolio. Because of their predictability, anticipated expenses are typically paid for with cash that is reserved in some portion of the investment portfolio. In the latter case, cash reserves are less of an issue because cash is not needed for a spend rate and more of the principal of the portfolio can be invested. In either case, unanticipated cash needs can be met by a cash cushion, the amount of which is client-specific. In both cases, anticipated *negative liquidity events* such as home purchases, college expenses, major philanthropic gifts, or other major expenses also need to be planned for from a liquidity perspective. *Positive liquidity events* such as inheritance or other anticipated cash inflows can also be covered in the liquidity section of the investment policy statement, assuming the family is comfortable speaking openly about such topics.

Many investors, especially those advancing in years, are sensitive to the overall level of illiquidity in their portfolios. Even though some investors have the ability, from an asset size perspective, to invest in private equity, private real estate, and natural resources investments, hedge funds, and other illiquid or semi-illiquid investments, they often want to limit the amount of overall illiquidity in the portfolio to maximize flexibility of obtaining funds when and if they are needed. Although there is no hard and fast rule, I use 50 percent of the portfolio as a natural point at which to review liquidity needs of the client. In other words, if a client's portfolio is 50 percent or more in illiquid and semi-liquid investments, it's time for a conversation about it. Some clients may put a limit like 35 or 40 percent on their portfolios.

Some investors favor liquidity, and this decision can have a significant impact on the asset allocation decision. As previously noted, those clients who limit the amount of private equity and hedge fund investing in favor of more liquid equities can expose themselves to more day-to-day volatility (depending on which asset classes are ultimately chosen). High amounts of cash and bonds can also introduce a return drag into a long-term investment portfolio.

## Time Horizon

The investment time horizon has a very large impact on the asset allocation selection. In particular, the time horizon essentially dictates the volatility that can be assumed in the portfolio. The shorter the time horizon, the less volatility the client can tolerate, and vice versa. Many advisors like to break up time horizons into short-term, medium-term, and long-term, but these phrases don't have universally accepted definitions. Whenever possible, I like to use ranges rather than absolute terms when describing a time horizon. For example, I label time horizons greater than 15 to 20 years as long-term, time horizons between 3 and 15 years as medium-term, and time horizons of less than 3 years as short-term. Medium-term can be the most open to interpretation; while I view 10 years as medium-term, some clients may perceive it as short-term and others may see it as long-term. In any event, portfolio allocations need to be constructed to account for the client's interpretation of time horizon.

A second and important aspect of time horizon is whether the investor faces a single- or multi-stage time horizon. Certain investors, particularly older clients, may be content with a single-stage time horizon such as 10 years. Some investors, however, are better suited to a multistage time horizon that may dictate different asset allocations for different time horizons.

Time horizon has a significant impact on the asset allocation decision because the time horizon selected can limit the amount of volatility that can be assumed by the client, and the type of investments the client will use. For example, a 5- to 10-year time horizon certainly has room for equities, but private equities are not going to work in this case.

## Taxes

The issue of taxes is perhaps the most universal and complex investment constraint that exists when investing for taxable clients. Taxation of income or property is a global reality and poses a significant challenge to wealth accumulation. Numerous taxes need to be dealt with: income tax, capital gains tax, wealth transfer tax, and property tax. For the purpose of this chapter, I am concerned mainly with the first two: income tax and capital gains tax. With tax burdens of such magnitude, the individual investor must approach the investment process from an after-tax perspective. Just to give readers an idea of the global reality of taxes, Table 13.1 illustrates the top marginal tax rates that existed around the world as of 2005.

Taxes negatively affect portfolio performance in two ways: periodically and cumulatively. The preferable method (if any taxation can be called preferable) is cumulative, which occurs when taxes are paid at the end of a given measurement period. Less preferred are periodic payments, which occur when a tax is assessed periodically throughout a measurement period; here, the beginning balance of the next period is reduced by the amount of the tax paid, and therefore funds that would otherwise compound at the portfolio growth rate do not do so. Table 13.2 highlights the effects of these two tax strategies on portfolio performance. At the top of the chart, a periodic tax of 20 percent, similar to an annual marginal income tax rate, is applied against investment returns (10 percent, in this case) over five years. In the lower part of the chart, a tax of 20 percent is subtracted from the beginning and ending balances (i.e., cumulative investment return) at the end of the five-year holding period, similar in concept to a capital gains rate tax. The difference in the ending balance of the portfolio values shows the benefit of deferring tax payments.

Given these two types of tax effects, the job of the advisor is to minimize or eliminate, to the extent legally possible, the tax burden that occurs during the investment process. Tax strategies are naturally unique to each client, depending upon the content of current IRS regulations and the client's place of residence. Although tax minimization strategies often involve complex considerations, two basic strategies are fundamental and can be applied

**TABLE 13.1** Tax Rates Around the World

| Country | Income Tax | Gains Tax | Wealth Transfer Tax |
|---|---|---|---|
| Brazil | 27.5% | 15.0% | 8.0% |
| Canada (Ontario) | 46.4% | 23.2% | 0.0% |
| Chile | 40.0% | 17.0% | 25.0% |
| China (PRC) | 45.0% | 20.0% | 0.0% |
| Egypt | 32.0% | 0.0% | 0.0% |
| France | 48.1% | 27.0% | 60.0% |
| Germany | 42.0% | 50.0% | 50.0% |
| India | 30.0% | 20.0% | 0.0% |
| Israel | 49.0% | 25.0% | 0.0% |
| Italy | 43.0% | 12.5% | 0.0% |
| Japan | 37.0% | 26.0% | 70.0% |
| Jordan | 25.0% | 0.0% | 0.0% |
| Korea | 35.0% | 70.0% | 50.0% |
| Mexico | 30.0% | 30.0% | 0.0% |
| New Zealand | 39.0% | 0.0% | 25.0% |
| Pakistan | 35.0% | 35.0% | 0.0% |
| Philippines | 32.0% | 32.0% | 20.0% |
| Russian Federation | 35.0% | 30.0% | 30.0% |
| South Africa | 40.0% | 10.0% | 20.0% |
| Taiwan | 40.0% | 0.0% | 50.0% |
| United Kingdom | 40.0% | 40.0% | 40.0% |
| United States | 35.0% | 35.0% | 47.0% |

*Data source:* Ernst & Young.

to almost every client. These are tax-deferral strategies and tax-reduction strategies.

**Tax-Deferral Strategies**    As we learned in the last section, periodic tax payments significantly inhibit the growth of a taxable portfolio. Taxable investors should always seek to defer taxes so that the time during which investment returns can be reinvested and compound can be maximized. Two strategies that facilitate this concept are *low turnover* and *tax loss harvesting*. Investment managers who focus on low turnover, which in effect means more buying and holding versus trading the portfolio, extend the average holding period of investments, which postpones the triggering of taxable gains. Tax loss harvesting focuses on realizing capital losses to offset taxable gains while maintaining the investment performance of the portfolio. Both low turnover and tax loss harvesting strategies are intended to keep capital gains realization to a minimum, resulting in deferred tax payments.

**TABLE 13.2** Comparison of Periodic and Cumulative Tax Effects

| | Year | Beginning Balance | 10% Annual Return | Less 20% Tax | Ending Balance | Gain | Cumulative Gain |
|---|---|---|---|---|---|---|---|
| Periodic Tax  20% | 1 | $1,000,000.00 | $100,000.00 | $20,000.00 | $1,080,000.00 | $ 80,000.00 | |
| | 2 | $1,080,000.00 | $108,000.00 | $21,600.00 | $1,166,400.00 | $ 86,400.00 | $ 166,400.00 |
| | 3 | $1,166,400.00 | $116,640.00 | $23,328.00 | $1,259,712.00 | $ 93,312.00 | $ 259,712.00 |
| | 4 | $1,259,712.00 | $125,971.20 | $25,194.24 | $1,360,488.96 | $100,776.96 | $ 360,488.96 |
| | 5 | $1,360,488.96 | $136,048.90 | $27,209.78 | $1,469,328.08 | $108,839.12 | $ 469,328.08 |
| Cumulative Tax  20% | 1 | $1,000,000.00 | $100,000.00 | — | $1,100,000.00 | $100,000.00 | |
| | 2 | $1,100,000.00 | $110,000.00 | — | $1,210,000.00 | $110,000.00 | $ 210,000.00 |
| | 3 | $1,210,000.00 | $121,000.00 | — | $1,331,000.00 | $121,000.00 | $ 331,000.00 |
| | 4 | $1,331,000.00 | $133,100.00 | — | $1,464,100.00 | $133,100.00 | $ 464,100.00 |
| | 5 | $1,464,100.00 | $146,410.00 | — | $1,610,510.00 | $146,410.00 | $ 610,510.00 |
| | | | | Tax | $ (122,102.00) | | $(122,102.00) |
| | | | | | $1,488,408.00 | | $ 488,408.00 |

*Data source:* Ernst & Young.

**Tax-Reduction Strategies** If taxes cannot be deferred, opportunities may remain to reduce their impact. When income tax rates exceed the capital gains tax rate, as they do in the current U.S. tax code (and in a number of countries, as seen earlier in Table 13.1), advisors can recommend investment managers who employ a strategy of investments that are focused on capital gains versus ordinary income. Because the capital gains tax is assessed only at the time of sale, such strategies may also benefit from tax deferral as well as the lower tax rate. Investments that eliminate taxes altogether can also be employed in the portfolio. Tax-exempt bonds, for example, are the quintessential tax avoidance investment vehicle. Tax-exempt securities typically offer lower returns or involve higher expenses (including higher transaction costs) relative to taxable alternatives, and they are attractive only when the following relationship holds: Tax-free return > [Taxable return × (1 − Tax rate)].

Taxes have a huge impact on asset class and manager selection. The following are key considerations. For equity asset classes, indexing (versus active management) is an excellent choice because of its inherent tax efficiency. Long-term capital gains asset classes (at the time this chapter was written) are preferred over short-term capital gains (income tax) oriented asset classes. Here, hedge funds may take a lesser role in the taxable portfolio as do Treasury Inflation-Protected Securities, neither of which are particularly tax-sensitive investments. Real estate and energy, which are longer-term asset classes, are also excellent choices for the taxable portfolio. Optimizing a portfolio for *after-tax* returns is the best way to approach the asset allocation decision. I discuss asset location later in the book; this discussion will focus on the best location for certain investments on the basis of obtaining the best tax treatment.

## Legal and Regulatory Environment

In the context of the asset allocation process, legal and regulatory constraints, with the exception of taxes, most frequently involve working with pools of investment capital that have some sort of legal restriction(s) on them, such as trusts or family foundations. I focus on trusts for the purpose of this chapter.

The use of trusts to implement investment and estate planning strategies is very common among affluent clients, and advisors need to familiarize themselves with these strategies. In short, a trust is a legally established entity that holds and manages assets in accordance with specific guidelines. A trust is the legally recognized owner of whatever assets are held and is subject to taxes in the same ways that individuals are taxed. These assets vary and can include equities, bonds, real estate, real assets, and even art or coins. Trusts are not an investment strategy but are a way to implement an investment or estate planning strategy. The appeal of a trust is the flexibility and control afforded to the grantor, who can delineate how trust assets will be managed and distributed, both before and after his or her death.

The framework for investment decision making within a trust often revolves around the conflicting needs and interests of current income beneficiaries versus those who will ultimately receive the corpus or principal of the trust, called the *remaindermen*. This conflict presents the trustee and portfolio manager of a trust with a challenge. Current income beneficiaries will typically desire that the trustee maximize current income through the selection of income-producing assets. The remaindermen beneficiaries will favor investments with long-term growth potential, even if this reduces current income. The trustee is responsible for considering the needs of both groups, under guidelines and criteria provided by the trust document. Most trustees have adopted the principles of modern portfolio theory and use a total return approach, which permits distributions from realized capital gains as well as income-oriented investments.

As is seen in this last section, legal and regulatory constraints can and do affect the asset allocation decision. In the case of trusts, there are often conflicting interests that must be managed, and the ultimate asset allocation selection can be greatly affected. Advisors need to work with these restrictions and simultaneously satisfy the needs of their clients, which is challenging but certainly possible.

## Unique Circumstances

All investors have unique circumstances that present challenges to their investment advisors. These circumstances constrain portfolio choices and add wrinkles to the asset allocation selection process. Such situations might include a concentrated equity position, certain business interests that need to be considered in the context of the overall portfolio, real estate holdings outside the liquid portfolio, socially responsible guidelines, or a host of others. Investors need to consider carefully their unique circumstances because they can have a lasting impact on the asset allocation, which may lead to certain asset classes being either under- or overrepresented in the portfolio.

Some wealthy investors may have assets that they want accounted for when they create an asset allocation. These can be real estate holdings, concentrated equity positions, large bond portfolios, private business investments, and so on. If an ultimate asset allocation that excludes certain asset classes is selected, then the client needs to understand that the behavior of that allocation will be choppier or less even than that of a well-diversified portfolio. When taken as a whole, however, the portfolio may be just fine—or it may not, in the case of a concentrated equity position that is declining in value. When reporting on the portfolio, UAC advisors may be wise to include these assets in the reports to demonstrate the effect that unique circumstances had on the overall investment performance.

## WHY ASSET ALLOCATION IS SO IMPORTANT

By including asset categories with investment returns that move up and down under different market conditions within a portfolio, an investor can protect against significant losses. Historically, the returns of the three major asset categories have not moved up and down at the same time. Market conditions that cause one asset category to do well often cause another asset category to have average or poor returns. By investing in more than one asset category, you'll reduce the risk that you'll lose money and your portfolio's overall investment returns will have a smoother ride. If one asset category's investment return falls, you'll be in a position to counteract your losses in that asset category with better investment returns in another asset category.

### The Magic of Diversification

The practice of spreading money among different investments to reduce risk is known as diversification. By picking the right group of investments, you may be able to limit your losses and reduce the fluctuations of investment returns without sacrificing too much potential gain.

In addition, asset allocation is important because it has a major impact on whether you will meet your financial goal. If you don't include enough risk in your portfolio, your investments may not earn a large enough return to meet your goal. For example, if you are saving for a long-term goal, such as retirement or college, most financial experts agree that you will likely need to include at least some stock or stock mutual funds in your portfolio. On the other hand, if you include too much risk in your portfolio, the money for your goal may not be there when you need it. A portfolio heavily weighted in stock or stock mutual funds, for instance, would be inappropriate for a short-term goal, such as saving for a family's summer vacation.

### Getting Started

Determining the appropriate asset allocation model for a financial goal is a complicated task. Basically, you're trying to pick a mix of assets that has the highest probability of meeting your goal at a level of risk you can live with.

As you get closer to meeting your goal, you'll need to be able to adjust the mix of assets.

If you understand your time horizon and risk tolerance—and have some investing experience—you may feel comfortable creating your own asset allocation model. "How to" books on investing often discuss general rules of thumb, and various online resources can help you with your decision. For example, although the SEC cannot endorse any particular formula or methodology, the Iowa Public Employees Retirement System offers an online asset allocation calculator. In the end, you'll be making a very personal choice. There is no single asset allocation model that is right for every financial goal. You'll need to use the one that is right for you.

Some financial experts believe that determining your asset allocation is the most important decision that you'll make with respect to your investments—that it's even more important than the individual investments you buy. With that in mind, you may want to consider asking a financial professional to help you determine your initial asset allocation and suggest adjustments for the future. But before you hire anyone to help you with these enormously important decisions, be sure to do a thorough check of his or her credentials and disciplinary history.

## Changing Your Asset Allocation

The most common reason for changing your asset allocation is a change in your time horizon. In other words, as you get closer to your investment goal, you'll likely need to change your asset allocation. For example, most people investing for retirement hold less stock and more bonds and cash equivalents as they get closer to retirement age. You may also need to change your asset allocation if there is a change in your risk tolerance, financial situation, or the financial goal itself.

But savvy investors typically do not change their asset allocation based on the relative performance of asset categories—for example, increasing the proportion of stocks in one's portfolio when the stock market is hot. Instead, that's when they "rebalance" their portfolios.

## Rebalancing 101

Rebalancing is bringing your portfolio back to your original asset allocation mix. This is necessary because over time some of your investments may become out of alignment with your investment goals. You'll find that some of your investments will grow faster than others. By rebalancing, you'll ensure that your portfolio does not overemphasize one or more asset categories, and you'll return your portfolio to a comfortable level of risk.

For example, let's say you determined that stock investments should represent 60 percent of your portfolio. But after a recent stock market increase, stock investments represent 80 percent of your portfolio. You'll need to either sell some of your stock investments or purchase investments from an underweighted asset category in order to reestablish your original asset allocation mix.

When you rebalance, you'll also need to review the investments within each asset allocation category. If any of these investments are out of alignment with your investment goals, you'll need to make changes to bring them back to their original allocation within the asset category.

There are basically three different ways you can rebalance your portfolio:

1. You can sell off investments from overweighted asset categories and use the proceeds to purchase investments for underweighted asset categories.
2. You can purchase new investments for underweighted asset categories.
3. If you are making continuous contributions to the portfolio, you can alter your contributions so that more investments go to underweighted asset categories until your portfolio is back into balance.

Before you rebalance your portfolio, you should consider whether the method of rebalancing you decide to use will trigger transaction fees or tax consequences. Your financial professional or tax advisor can help you identify ways that you can minimize these potential costs.

## WHERE TO FIND MORE INFORMATION

For more information on investing wisely and avoiding costly mistakes, please visit the Investor Information section of the SEC's website. You also can learn more about several investment topics, including asset allocation, diversification, and rebalancing in the context of saving for retirement by visiting FINRA's Smart 401(k) Investing website as well as the Department of Labor's Employee Benefits Security Administration website.

You can find out more about your risk tolerance by completing free online questionnaires available on numerous websites maintained by

*(Continued)*

investment publications, mutual fund companies, and other financial professionals. Some of the websites will even estimate asset allocations based on responses to the questionnaires. While the suggested asset allocations may be a useful starting point for determining an appropriate allocation for a particular goal, investors should keep in mind that the results may be biased towards financial products or services sold by companies or individuals maintaining the websites.

Once you've started investing, you'll typically have access to online resources that can help you manage your portfolio. The websites of many mutual fund companies, for example, give customers the ability to run a "portfolio analysis" of their investments. The results of a portfolio analysis can help you analyze your asset allocation, determine whether your investments are diversified, and decide whether you need to rebalance your portfolio.

## SUMMARY

The purpose of this chapter is to demonstrate the importance of asset allocation and to provide some tools to help you through the process. In concert with a good investment plan is a solid financial plan. In the next chapter we will review the key components of a financial plan as well as offer some resources that are available to help create a financial plan.

## NOTES

1. Gary P. Brinson, L. Randolph Hood, and Gilbert L. Beebower, "Determinants of Portfolio Performance," *Financial Analysts Journal* (July/August 1986): 39–44.
2. Ibid.
3. Ibid.
4. Roger G. Ibbotson and Paul E. Kaplan, "Does Asset Allocation Policy Explain 40, 90, or 100 Percent of Performance," *Financial Analysts Journal* (January/February 2000): 26–33.

# Chapter 14

# Financial Planning: A Crucial Step

**F**inancial planning is not the same thing as asset allocation, which we reviewed in the last chapter. Advising clients in financial planning is distinctly different from investment advisory. Financial planning is just as it sounds—a plan or a roadmap to reach numerous financial goals. Asset allocation is the implementation of one part of the plan. Financial planning may mean different things to different people. For one person, it can mean providing for a comfortable retirement, while for another it may mean saving money for a college education for a child or grandchild. Financial planning can even extend to insurance analysis and planning choices, career (job) decisions, or may simply be used to plan a budget. Everyone should have some kind of financial plan. As the old saying goes, "He who fails to plan, plans to fail."

Fortunately, there are resources available to help one make and execute a plan. Some of these resources are free while others require a monetary investment. I will discuss some resources for those who wish to do it themselves, but the focus of this chapter, including the steps in the financial planning process to be detailed later, will be from the viewpoint of those working with financial advisors. Hiring a financial planner to aid in the development of a financial plan is not necessary, but it is certainly recommended. There are free online resources such as fpanet.org, books like this one, software programs, and other resources available to help a person make a plan. The decision to hire a financial planner may depend on many things, including the net worth of the individual in need of planning; generally it makes more sense to hire a planner the higher one's wealth level. And, naturally, if you are a "do-it-yourself" type you may prefer to—do it yourself! But financial planning techniques can be useful even for these people in the form of monthly budgeting. A budget can be very helpful in terms of identifying what is actually spent each month and ways to trim or eliminate unnecessary or out-of-control expenses. Financial potholes will inevitably come your way—stock market downturns, recessions, job layoffs, car wrecks, or the cost of an unexpected illness. You may not be able to avoid these potholes, but you can certainly minimize their financial impact.

## WHAT IS FINANCIAL PLANNING?

Financial planning is the process of meeting life's financial goals through the proper management of one's finances. Life goals vary from person to person and from wealth level to wealth level. For most people, top financial goals include buying a home, saving for children's education, and planning for retirement. For others, wealth transfer goals and charitable goals come into play. Your goals can be short-term—for example, paying a credit card off in six months; medium-term—such as saving for a down payment on a house in two years; or long-term—such as sending your kids to college in 15 years. In most cases, the financial planning process consists of six key steps as outlined by the Certified Financial Planning Board (CFPB), which will be reviewed later. This framework helps people do three key things:

1. Identifies one's current financial status, where one is today: for example, by listing everything one owes (liabilities) and the value of everything one owns (assets).
2. Articulates one's future financial objectives (life goals).
3. Documents what steps are needed to reach those goals (the plan).

The entire process involves collecting important financial information—which should be on a computer instead of on paper—and analyzing it to see where spending and saving (or lack of saving) are taking place. By providing structure and direction to one's financial life, a financial plan can be instrumental in reaching goals. A plan allows one to understand how each financial decision affects every other financial decision. For example, if someone decides to pay down extra money each month to pay off the mortgage early, he or she may be lessening the ability to invest in a college savings plan. Or a decision about funding a child's education may affect when and how the parent meets retirement goals. Or an investment decision may have tax consequences that are harmful to the estate plans. Remember that all financial decisions are interrelated. By viewing each financial decision holistically, an individual can more easily consider short- and long-term effects on financial goals. A plan also helps the person adapt to life's constantly changing circumstances, and it gives a sense of confidence in knowing when goals are on track and when they are not on track.

Many people wisely employ the services of financial planners to aid them in their quest to reach their goals. For those of you unfamiliar with this type of service, a professional financial planner is a practitioner who provides advice and guidance to a client on a wide spectrum of financial planning issues. The reasons you might want to use a planner are as follows:

- You lack certain expertise in the area of personal finances. For example, a planner can help evaluate the level of risk in an investment portfolio or adjust a retirement plan due to changing family circumstances.
- You need a second opinion about a financial plan created on your own or by a planner who may not be doing a great job.
- You don't have time to do your own financial planning.
- An immediate need or major life event such as a birth, inheritance, or major illness comes up and you need professional advice.
- You have not been looking at finances holistically, but only addressing certain parts of a typical plan.

In making the decision to work with a planner, there are six key steps that can help clients through the financial planning process. We will review these now.

## WORKING WITH A FINANCIAL PLANNER

When working with a financial planner, the financial planning process consists of the following six steps. If possible, each of these steps should be followed.

### Step 1: Establish and Define the Client-Advisor Relationship

Financial planners need to detail the process by which they will deliver the financial planning service and should clearly explain and document both their responsibilities as well as those of the client. Planners shall also fully explain the fees and expenses involved and how they are paid and by whom. The client and planner should agree on a minimum length of time they will commit to work with each other and on how decisions will be made.

### Step 2: Gather Client Data and Set Financial Goals

The financial planner will get from the client all information about his or her financial situation. The planner and client shall together define the client's personal and financial goals, understand the client's time frame to accomplish the goals, and discuss risk tolerance as well as other aspects of risk management.

## Step 3: Analyze and Evaluate Current Financial Status

The financial planner shall analyze the information provided by the client to assess the client's current situation and determine steps necessary to meet goals. Depending upon what services the client desires, this could include analyzing assets, liabilities, and cash flow, current insurance coverage, investments, or tax strategies.

## Step 4: Develop and Present Financial Planning Recommendations and Scenarios

The financial planner offers planning recommendations that address financial objectives based on the information provided. The planner then reviews the recommendations with the client so that the client makes informed decisions. The planner listens to concerns and revises the financial plans accordingly.

## Step 5: Implement Financial Planning Recommendations

The client and the planner should agree on how the recommendations will be implemented. The planner and client then decide how plans will be carried out and how the planner will coordinate the process with other advisors such as attorneys and accountants.

## Step 6: Monitor and Update the Financial Planning Recommendations

The client and planner then agree on who will monitor progress toward reaching goals. Should the decision be made that the planner will lead the process, the client must establish periodic reviews, typically quarterly. During reviews, updates and/or adjustments to the recommendations are made if necessary.

When deciding which financial planner to work with, it is important to know what differentiates one planner from another. Financial planners may or may not be certified and offer varying levels of experience. The main reason that people decide not to go it alone, even if they have the skills to do so, is that they may not be good at executing a plan. Furthermore, some people are good at executing plans in general but when it comes to plans involving themselves they have difficulties. People often delay planning for the future because they feel pressure to live on a day-to-day basis; they would eventually like to plan, but for now it needs to be on the back burner. But before hiring a planner, it is important to understand with whom you are dealing and what the choices are. For example, it is important to differentiate a certified financial planner (CFP) from a planner who is not a CFP, since the CFP is the most widely held and most rigorous financial planning designation in the industry. Equally important is understanding how an advisor gets paid and to what standards he or she is held while dispensing financial advice.

## WHAT IS A CERTIFIED FINANCIAL PLANNER?

To earn the Certified Financial Planner (CFP) designation, candidates must meet the following requirements: education, examination, work experience, and continuing education (including ethics).[1] Each of these areas will now be reviewed.

### Education

To fulfill the educational requirement of the CFP, candidates must complete course training in the following topic areas in order to be able to sit for the 10-hour CFP Board Certification Examination. The following broad topics are further broken down into nearly 100 subtopics centered on integrated financial planning.

- General Principles of Finance and Financial Planning
- Insurance Planning
- Employee Benefits Planning
- Investment and Securities Planning
- State and Federal Income Tax Planning
- Estate Tax, Gift Tax, and Transfer Tax Planning
- Asset Protection Planning
- Retirement Planning
- Estate Planning

In addition, a bachelor's degree (or higher), or its equivalent in any discipline, from an accredited college or university is required to attain CFP certification. The bachelor's degree requirement is a condition of initial certification; it is not a requirement to be eligible to take the CFP Certification

Examination. For questions about whether or not an individual has the right to use such a designation, call 1-800-CFP-MARK (1-800-237-6275). To be authorized to use the designation, the candidate must pay an ongoing certification fee; however, there are different rules for international candidates and one may inquire about these issues at the number given above as well.

## Examination

The CFP Certification Exam is a 10-hour multiple-choice exam, divided into one four-hour session and two three-hour sessions the following day. The exam includes three major case problems and is designed to assess the candidates' abilities to apply their knowledge of the aforementioned areas to financial planning situations. The exam was set as a requirement in 1993, and at that time CFPs were grandfathered without having to pass this exam.

Individuals holding certain approved professional designations by the CFP Board, for example, Certified Public Accountants (CPA), Chartered Financial Analysts (CFA), Chartered Certified Accountants (ACCA), Chartered Accountants (CA), Chartered Wealth Managers (AAFM), and Chartered Life Underwriters (CLU) are entitled to register for and take the exam without completing the education requirements.[2] This is done by "challenging" the exam by using the CFP-board's challenge status. International degrees may be substituted for a U.S. degree if they receive equivalency from a third-party organization.

## Work Experience

After passing the CFP exam, the candidate must demonstrate extensive experience in the financial planning field. The CFP Board defines work experience as "the supervision, direct support, teaching, or personal delivery of all or part of the personal financial planning process to a client"[3] and such experience must fall within one or more of the following six primary elements of financial planning:

- Establishing and defining the client relationship.
- Gathering client data and goals.
- Analyzing and evaluating the client's financial status.
- Developing and presenting financial planning recommendations and alternatives.
- Implementing the financial planning recommendations.
- Monitoring the financial planning recommendations.

Even after students pass the exam and meet one or more of the six primary elements of financial planning, they must also have completed the following:

- Three years' full-time or equivalent (2,000 hours per year) part-time experience in the financial planning field.
- Be approved by the CFP Board during initial certification, which also involves an extensive background check, including an ethics, character, and criminal check.

## Ethics and Continuing Education

The final components of the CFP requirements are the ethics and continuing education requirements. CFP holders and candidates are required to adhere to the CFP Board Code of Ethics and Professional Responsibility and to the Financial Planning Practice Standards. The CFP Board has the right to enforce these guidelines through its Disciplinary Rules and Procedures. To maintain certification, license holders are also required to complete continuing education requirements on an ongoing basis in addition to paying a licensing fee every two years.

So, you can see that a CFP is a well-qualified provider of financial planning advice. But there is another key issue that one needs to be aware of when selecting an advisor. This is whether or not your advisor is a fiduciary or not. It is important to know that the government does not regulate financial planners as financial planners; instead, it regulates planners as stockbrokers, insurance agents, or investment advisors, depending on the services they provide.

## Fiduciary versus Suitability

Although it is unlikely, a CFP is not necessarily 100 percent committed to putting his or her clients' financial interests first. The word "fiduciary" means someone who is committed to putting the client's financial interests ahead of his or her own. Certain advisors, by definition, are required to be fiduciaries. Others are held to a "suitability" standard, which means that they are supposed to reasonably believe that the investment and insurance products they want clients to buy are appropriate for their situation.

"Many investors do not realize that their trusted financial 'advisor' may be nothing more than a salesman, with only an obligation to make suitable recommendations but without any legal responsibility to act in the customer's best interest,"[4] said consumer advocate Barbara Roper, director of investor protection for the Consumer Federation of America. The federation's surveys show that the majority of people who work with a financial advisor trust that they are receiving sound advice. In the financial services world, there are three job titles that automatically connote a fiduciary standard:

- Attorney
- Certified Public Accountant (CPA)
- Registered Investment Advisor (RIA)

There are several other job titles that indicate the opposite. Stockbrokers (also known as "registered representatives") or insurance agents are allowed to put their own interests, or those of their firm, ahead of the client's interests. With that said, there are excellent advisors who are not fiduciaries.

## How Advisor and Firm Are Compensated

Regardless of what type of company or person with which a client has decided to work, it is critical to understand how the advisor and advisory firm are compensated. Although many top quality financial service companies have determined that their clients want objective advice, these companies still have in place commission-based sales business models. Some firms call their commission-based employees "advisors," "financial advisors," or "fee-based consultants," but these people may not adhere to a fiduciary standard. There has been government involvement in this issue without much clarity, unfortunately. In 2005, the Securities and Exchange Commission, which regulates brokerages and financial planners, made permanent a rule that allowed brokers to avoid registering as investment advisors—which would require them to uphold fiduciary standards—as long as the advice they gave was "incidental" to their primary business of selling investments.[5] Later, in a staff letter, the SEC said that an advisor could play more than one role with a client; an advisor could agree to a fiduciary duty in order to create a financial plan, then switch back to the non-fiduciary role of broker when actually buying investments to execute the plan. Clear as mud, right? Therefore there is currently no uniform method by which "financial planners" are paid. A planner can be paid a salary by the company for which he works; can charge fees based on an hourly rate, a flat rate, or a percentage of assets; can receive commissions paid by a third party from the products sold to the client to carry out the financial planning recommendations; or can receive a combination of fees and commissions, whereby fees are charged for the amount of work done to develop financial planning recommendations, and commissions are received from any products used in executing the financial plan.

There are some questions a potential client can ask to clear up exactly how an advisor is paid:

Question 1: Are you a fiduciary—meaning that you are legally obligated to act in my best interests at all times? Will you put that in writing?

Question 2: Is the way in which you conduct business subject to any conflicts of interest, and if so, will you disclose them? Will you disclose all relationships, compensation, incentives, or other factors that could potentially interfere with your ability to act in my best interests?

Question 3: In what ways are you compensated? Do you receive commissions, referral fees, or other financial incentives?

You may find that your advisor is not a fiduciary but you may decide to work with him or her anyway. If your broker has done well for you, for example, you may be comfortable continuing to follow his or her tips. But you still need to keep in mind that this advisor is not a fiduciary and may put his or her interest ahead of yours.

## WHO CAN PROVIDE FINANCIAL PLANNING SERVICES?

The government does not regulate financial planners as financial planners; instead, it regulates them by the services they provide. For example, a planner who also provides securities transactions or advice is regulated as a stockbroker or investment advisor. As a result, the term "financial planner" may be used inaccurately by some financial advisors. To be sure that you are getting financial planning advice, ask if the advisor follows the six steps discussed previously.

### Different Advisors Who May Offer Financial Planning

In addition to providing clients with general financial planning services, many financial planners are also registered as investment advisors, or they hold insurance or securities licenses that allow them to buy or sell products. Some planners may have you use more specialized advisors to help you implement their recommendations. With the right education and experience, each of the following advisors could take you through the financial planning process. Ethical financial planners will refer you to one of these professionals for services that they cannot provide, and they will disclose any referral fees they may receive in the process. Similarly, these advisors should refer you to a planner if they cannot meet your financial planning needs.

As we now know, anyone can call himself or herself a financial planner. A financial planner should focus on your needs first before recommending a course of action. Most planners have been trained to take a broad look at your financial situation, while accountants, investment advisors, brokers, or insurance agents may focus on a particular area of your financial life. Always ask a financial advisor what qualifies him or her to offer financial planning services. A "good" financial planner is someone who uses the financial planning process to help a client identify and reach financial goals. The good planner typically adopts a "big-picture" view of their clients' financial situation and makes planning recommendations about how to reach financial goals. The competent planner looks at all of the client's financial aspects: budgeting, taxes, cash flow, savings for various objectives, recommending or selecting investment managers, insurance, and risk management as well as retirement planning. There are different types of advisors that a client can work with who offer advice but may come at the advice from different angles. For example, some advise in the context of working with a client on a single issue such as investments, insurance, or taxes, and they provide or attempt to provide holistic advice at the same time. In general, financial planners who provide holistic or "big-picture" planning differentiate themselves from other advisors who are specialists in one unique aspect of a person's financial life. Regardless of the preferred approach, it is important to get a qualified advisor. We will review now some other advisors that might work for you. You could hire an accountant (CPA), estate planning attorney, insurance agent, broker, or private banker. Registered investment advisors may offer planning services, but these will not be covered here.

## Accountant (CPA)

An accountant is a fiduciary that provides advice on tax matters and helps you prepare and submit tax returns to the Internal Revenue Service. All accountants who practice as Certified Public Accountants (CPAs) must be licensed by the state(s) in which they practice. In addition to preparing income taxes, they can be a good resource for business and financial matters. Business owners especially can benefit from the advice of a good CPA, and that advice can extend to personal matters such as insurance advice or planning for the costs of college. Business owners are especially aware of the importance of proper record keeping, budgeting, and so on, and they know how critical it is to make the correct financial decisions. A qualified CPA can be a good fit for this situation. In terms of locating a qualified CPA, there are resources that can help. Personal referrals are very helpful. Other than personal referrals, there are many CPA associations and networking groups that can provide good referrals, such as the local state society of CPAs or the American Institute of CPAs.

## Estate Planning Attorney

Estate planners advise you on estate taxes or other estate planning issues and put together a strategy to manage your assets at the time of your death. While attorneys, accountants, financial planners, insurance agents, or trust bankers may all provide estate planning services, you should seek an attorney to prepare legal documents such as wills, trusts, and power-of-attorney forms. Many estate planners hold the Accredited Estate Planner (AEP) designation. Every adult should have the following four basic documents: will, general durable power of attorney, medical power of attorney, and a living will (also called a medical directive). A financial planner can guide you and refer you to an estate planning attorney to draft these documents.

## Insurance Agent

Insurance agents are licensed by the state(s) in which they practice to sell life, health, property, casualty, or other insurance products. Many insurance agents hold the Chartered Life Underwriter (CLU) designation. Financial planners may identify and advise you on your insurance needs, but can only sell you insurance products if they are also licensed as insurance agents. Insurance prevents financial catastrophes, so do not put off getting it. Insure what you cannot comfortably afford to replace. For most people, that means having the following insurance: auto, renters or homeowners, liability, health, disability, and life insurance (if someone depends on you financially). Take advantage of the insurance offered to you at your job and supplement it with insurance you buy on your own. Shop for the best price, but make sure you buy from a reputable, financially sound insurance company.

## Investment Advisor

Anybody who is paid to provide securities advice must register as an investment advisor with the Securities and Exchange Commission or relevant state securities agencies, depending on the amount of money he or she manages. Because financial planners often advise people on securities-based investments, many are registered as investment advisors who are fiduciaries.

Investment advisors cannot sell securities products without a securities license. For that, you must use a licensed securities representative such as a stockbroker (see next section). A good RIA firm can and does work with other advisors such as a CPA and an attorney to provide holistic planning advice.

## Stockbroker

Also called registered representatives, stockbrokers are licensed by the state(s) in which they practice to buy and sell securities products such as stocks, bonds, and mutual funds, and are typically not fiduciaries. They generally earn commissions on all of their transactions. Stockbrokers must be registered with a company that is a member of the National Association of Securities Dealers (NASD) and pass NASD-administered securities exams such as the Series 7. Brokers come in all different types; some provide financial planning advice using software programs while others sell only securities. Individual decisions as to which broker to work with are critical to success in working with brokers.

## SUMMARY

Financial planning can be a very good way to meet one's financial goals. It is possible to do it yourself, but working with a planner is highly recommended. Following are some final thoughts on best practices toward meeting financial goals:

1. Set measurable financial goals.
2. Understand the effects your financial decisions have on other financial issues.
3. Reevaluate your financial plan periodically.
4. Start now and with what you've got—don't assume financial planning is for when you get older or just for wealthy people.
5. Take charge and look at the big picture; you are in control of the financial planning engagement, and financial planning is more than just retirement planning!
6. Don't confuse financial planning with investing.
7. Do not expect unrealistic returns on investments.
8. Set specific targets of what you want to achieve and when you want to achieve results. For example, instead of saying you want to be "comfortable" when you retire or that you want your children to attend "good"

schools, you need to quantify what "comfortable" and "good" mean to you so that you'll know when you've reached your goals.

9. Financial planning is a dynamic process. Your financial goals may change over the years due to changes in your lifestyle or circumstances such as inheritance, marriage, birth, house purchase, or change of job status.

10. If you are working with a financial planner, be sure you understand the financial planning process and what the planner should be doing. Provide the planner with all of the relevant information on your financial situation. Ask questions about the recommendations offered to you and play an active role in decision making.

## FOR MORE INFORMATION ON FINANCIAL PLANNING

For further questions on financial planning, contact:

Certified Financial Planner Board of Standards, Inc.
1670 Broadway, Suite 600, Denver, Colorado 80202-4809
Consumer Toll-Free Number: 888-CFP-MARK
www.CFP.net/learn

## NOTES

1. www.cfp.net/learn/knowledgebase.asp?id=15.
2. www.pearltrees.com/#/N-f=1_2647419&N-fa=2623537&N-p=192069 92&N-play=0&N-s=1_2647419&N-u=1_260396.
3. http://financetrain.com/required-work-experience-for-cfp-certification.
4. Liz Pulliam Weston, "Can You Trust Your Financial Adviser?" *MSN Money Online* (2009), http://articles.moneycentral.com (accessed December 28, 2010).
5. Ibid, 3.

# Chapter 15

# Investment Advice for Each Behavioral Investor Type

*We should take care not to make the intellect our god; it has, of course, powerful muscles, but no personality.*

—Albert Einstein

**W**e are at the last chapter and now ready to apply everything we have learned in the book, especially what we have learned in the last three chapters. In this chapter we go about the task of creating an asset allocation program that is modified for each behavioral investor type. In Chapter 12, we learned about how the capital markets operate and how to invest via asset classes. In Chapter 13, we learned about asset allocation and how to create an investment plan. In the previous chapter, we learned about the importance of financial planning and how it can be critical to investing success. In this chapter, we put it all together and demonstrate how to modify an investment plan for each behavioral investor type. We start with an introduction to the concept of behaviorally modified asset allocations (BMAA), which is also referred to as best practical allocation.

For today's financial advisor, private banker, or generalist wealth management practitioner (hereafter "financial advisor"), creating viable and unique investment solutions in response to the array of financial situations and personalities clients present is the heart and soul of the job. Sometimes the job is easy: The client being advised appears rational in his or her approach—that is, he or she seems to understand the importance of asset allocation and has reasonable return expectations. For these clients, the typical method for arriving at an asset allocation is to administer a risk tolerance questionnaire and use financial planning software to create a mean-variance-optimized asset allocation program. At other times, financial advisors encounter irrational behaviors in their clients. Irrational clients do such things as overestimate their risk tolerance, be unrealistic in their return expectations, or generally behave in a way that makes advising them difficult because they are not grounded in rational investment principles and are resistant to learning them. Most advisors have no trouble in the former case, the easy clients. In the latter case, however, some advisors get frustrated and impatient when confronted with an irrational client. In these situations, risk tolerance questionnaires and mean-variance software are often ineffective.

Understanding and applying behavioral finance solutions can help clients to meet their financial goals. But many advisors are often vexed by their clients' decision making process when it comes to allocating their investment portfolio. Why? In a common scenario, a client, in response to short-term market movements, such as what we witnessed in late 2008 and early 2009 and more recently in the fall of 2011, and to the detriment of the long-term investment plan, demands that his or her asset allocation be changed. This kind of behavior is a lose-lose situation for both the advisor and the client. The client loses because their portfolio is likely to underperform when they stray from their asset allocation policy targets (witness those who "sold out" in March 2009 only to see the market rebound dramatically). The advisor loses because he or she becomes ineffective and can even be blamed for the decision to change allocation even if it was the client's idea.

## FOUNDATIONS OF BEST PRACTICAL ALLOCATION

Nobel prize-winner Daniel Kahneman and co-author Mark Riepe, who have made significant contributions to behavioral finance, describe financial advising as "a prescriptive activity whose main objective should be to guide investors to make decisions that serves their best interest."[1] Serving the best interest of the client may be the recommendation of an asset allocation that suits the client's natural psychological preferences, and it may not be one that maximizes expected return for a given level of risk. More simply, a client's *best practical allocation* may be a slightly underperforming long-term allocation recommendation that the advisor believes that client can comfortably adhere to. Conversely, another client's best practical allocation may be one that goes against his or her natural psychological tendencies, but the client may be well served to accept more risk than he or she might otherwise be comfortable with, in order to attain a higher return for that level of risk. Note here that allocation recommendations are still on the efficient frontier; they may move up or down it based on the client's behavioral make-up. Our goal as advisors should be to find the best practical allocation for each individual client.

Developing proper guidelines for incorporating biases in asset allocation decisions involves answering central questions:

- When should advisors attempt to moderate the way clients naturally behave to counteract the effects of behavioral biases so that they can fit a predetermined asset allocation? (For purposes of this book, we will call this moderating a client.)
- When should advisors create asset allocations that adapt to clients' biases, so that clients can comfortably abide by their asset allocation decisions? (For purposes of this book, we will call this adapting to a client.)

The decision to *moderate* or *adapt* an asset allocation to fit a client's biases is covered in the next section.

## GUIDELINES FOR DETERMINING WHEN TO MODERATE AND WHEN TO ADAPT

What follows are two guidelines that financial advisors can use when deciding when to attempt to moderate (that is, to change) the behavior of their client to meet the "rational" asset allocation that was created by the financial advisor, or when to change a "rational" asset allocation the advisor would otherwise recommend in order to adapt to a client's behavioral biases.

The first guideline is this: The financial advisor's decision whether to moderate or adapt to a client's behavioral biases during the asset allocation process depends in large part on the client's wealth level. Specifically, the wealthier the client, the more the advisor is safely able to adapt the asset allocation to the client's behavioral biases. The less wealthy, the more the advisor should attempt to moderate a client's biased behavior to match a rational asset allocation.

The rationale for this guideline has to do with a concept called "standard of living" risk. If a client is at risk for outliving his or her assets, or seriously jeopardizing his or her standard of living based on their current asset allocation, this is a major problem that needs to be carefully considered by the advisor. No advisor wants to be responsible for causing a client to become destitute. If biased behavior, then, is likely to endanger a client's standard of living, regulating the client's behavior is likely to be the best course of action. This can be the case for both too conservative and too risky allocations. On the other hand, if a client bears no standard of living risk (that is, the client's standard of living is highly unlikely to be jeopardized and will remain in the 99.9th percentile unless there is a market crash of unprecedented proportions), irrational biases become a lesser consideration, and adapting the rational allocation to the client's irrational behaviors may be the more appropriate action. In other words, destitution constitutes a far graver investment failure than a client's inability to amass the greatest possible fortune.

The second guideline is this: The financial advisor's decision whether to moderate or adapt to a client's behavioral biases during the asset allocation process also depends fundamentally on the type of behavioral biases being exhibited by the client. Specifically, clients exhibiting cognitive biases, which stem from illogical reasoning, should be moderated, while those clients exhibiting emotional biases, which stem from impulsive feelings, should be adapted to.

The rationale for guideline 2 is straightforward. As we have learned, behavioral biases fall into two broad categories, cognitive and emotional, though both types yield irrational decisions. Because cognitive biases stem from illogical reasoning, better information and advice can often correct them. Conversely, because emotional biases originate from impulsive feelings or intuition—rather than from conscious reasoning—they are difficult to correct. Financial advisors need to understand this difference, because if they attempt to correct biases that they have little chance of correcting, they will become frustrated and ineffective. Cognitive biases include heuristics, such as anchoring and adjustment, availability, and representativeness biases. Other cognitive biases include selective memory and overconfidence. Emotional biases include regret, self-control, loss aversion, hindsight, and denial. We have discussed these biases in earlier chapters.

Figure 15.1 is a visual depiction of guidelines 1 and 2. For advisors who encounter less wealthy clients exhibiting cognitive biases, the best course of

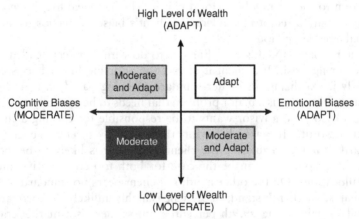

**FIGURE 15.1** Description of Guidelines 1 and 2

**TABLE 15.1** Adapt and Moderate Recommendations

|                   | Bias Type—Cognitive | Bias Type—Emotional |
| ----------------- | ------------------- | ------------------- |
| High Wealth Level | Modest Asset Allocation Change | Stronger Asset Allocation Change |
| Low Wealth Level  | Typically Recommend the Rational Asset Allocation | Modest Asset Allocation Change |

action is typically to attempt to change the behavior of the client to meet the rational asset allocation that the advisor might normally recommend. At higher levels of wealth, for those clients exhibiting emotional biases, advisors should modify the rational asset allocation recommendation and adapt to the client's behavioral biases. For clients at low levels of wealth who exhibit emotional biases, and for clients at high levels of wealth who exhibit cognitive biases, advisors should offer a blended recommendation. How might this blended recommendation be accomplished? The short answer is that a client's asset allocation may not change as much, for example, for a higher wealth client exhibiting emotional biases as when adapting to a higher wealth client who exhibits cognitive biases. In the case of a less wealthy client with strong emotional biases, the advisor might modify a client's asset allocation decision modestly, rather than recommending the rational asset allocation as an advisor would for a less wealthy person exhibiting cognitive biases. Table 15.1 summarizes the *adapt and moderate* actions advisors can take with their clients.

## BEST PRACTICAL ALLOCATION FOR PRESERVERS

We will now put these ideas into concrete action by examining each behavioral investor type and how one might think about creating a behaviorally modified asset allocation (BMAA) for each one. We will begin with the Preserver BIT. For purposes of simplicity, we will not be considering standard of living risk in this chapter. For more complete case studies including the analysis of standard of living risk, see my other book, *Behavioral Finance and Wealth Management.* Our process will be to review the basics of each BIT, discuss the primary biases at work and how we incorporate these biases into our allocation recommendation, and then discuss how to modify an asset allocation based on these biases. This analysis is being presented from the point of view of the advisor. If you are an individual investor, you can read the analysis from the point of view of the investor, and I hope it will make sense in terms of trying to help you understand how to create an allocation based on your particular circumstances.

Preservers place a great deal of emphasis on financial security and preserving wealth rather than taking risks to grow wealth. Some Preservers obsess over short-term performance and are slow to make investment decisions because they aren't entirely comfortable with change (which is consistent with the way they have approached their professional lives), being careful not to take excessive risks. Many Preservers are focused on taking care of their family members and future generations, especially funding life-enhancing experiences such as education and home buying. Because the focus is on family and security, Preserver biases tend to be emotional rather than cognitive. As age and wealth level increase, this BIT becomes more common. Behavioral biases of a Preserver tend to be emotional, financial security–oriented biases such as endowment bias, loss aversion, and status quo. Preservers also often exhibit cognitive biases such as anchoring and mental accounting.

Suppose you are beginning an engagement with a new client, Stan. You give him a standard of risk tolerance quiz and determine that he is a conservative investor. After that, you give him a test for behavioral biases of conservative clients. Based on the answers to the bias questions you determine that Stan is a Preserver. Some of your other clients are conservative but they are not biased as Stan is. The object of this exercise is to see how to create a BMAA for a Preserver versus a non-biased or mildly biased conservative investor. Generally, this can mean that a Preserver should accept less risk in his portfolio than those clients without bias. Since Stan is a Preserver, he is not predisposed to taking on additional risk to his portfolio anyway. This makes working with a Preserver an easier task than with some other BITs.

The following analysis presents two investment programs, one for Steve (a non-biased conservative investor) and one for Stan (a Preserver). You are using Steve's portfolio allocation as a baseline for creating Stan's. Your basic task is to assess a retirement goal for Stan and the risk associated with the return needed to reach that goal. When working with actual clients, you will need to adjust this analysis to suit your purposes.

As we know, Preserver clients:

- Are driven by emotion.
- Generally want a conservative portfolio anyway.

For Stan, a Preserver, we are going to make an assumption that he may have difficulty sticking to a portfolio with a probability of a loss year at greater than 15 percent. For Steve, a conservative client, 15 percent may

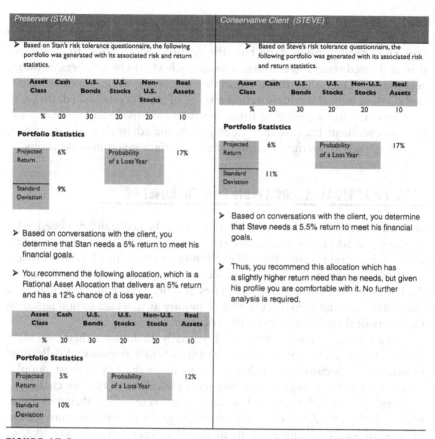

**FIGURE 15.2** Comparison of Preserver BMAA to Non-Biased Client's Asset Allocation

be too conservative and the number can be a bit higher. So let's examine Figure 15.2 and analyze how Stan's portfolio might compare to Steve's.

Without getting too caught up in the details of the numbers, you can see that Stan has a more conservative allocation than Steve, which will likely permit him to reach his financial goals. This is an example of how one adjusts an allocation for the Preserver BIT. In the next section we review advice for working with the Preserver BIT.

After reviewing this section, readers might correctly conclude that Preservers don't like volatility. This is true; they may feel more comfortable with a lower risk allocation. Also, advisors should take the time to interpret behavioral signs provided to them by Preserver clients. Preservers need big-picture advice and advisors shouldn't dwell on details like standard deviations and Sharpe ratios or else they will lose the client's attention. Preservers need to understand how the portfolio they choose to create will deliver desired results to emotional issues such as family members or future generations. Once they feel comfortable discussing these important emotional issues with their advisor, and a bond of trust is established, they will take action. After a period of time, Preservers are likely to become an advisor's best clients because they value greatly the advisor's professionalism, expertise, and objectivity in helping make the right investment decisions.

## BEST PRACTICAL ALLOCATION FOR FOLLOWERS

In the last section, we learned how to create a behaviorally modified asset allocation or BMAA (also referred to as Best Practical Allocation) for a Preserver behavioral investor type. We will now continue this learning process by examining the Follower. Our process will be the same. We will review the basics of the Follower and the biases at work with Followers, present a client scenario, and then discuss how to modify an asset allocation based on the behavioral characteristics of the Follower.

Followers are passive investors who usually do not have their own ideas about investing. They often follow the lead of their friends and colleagues in investment decisions, and they want to be in the latest, most popular investments without regard to a long-term plan. One of the key challenges of working with Followers is that they often overestimate their risk tolerance. Advisors need to be careful not to suggest too many hot investment ideas—Followers will likely want to do all of them. Some don't like, or even fear, the task of investing, and many put off making investment decisions without professional advice; the result is that they maintain, often by default, high cash balances. Followers generally comply with professional advice when they get it, and they educate themselves financially, but can at times be difficult because they don't enjoy or have an aptitude for the investment process. Biases of Followers are cognitive: recency, hindsight, framing, cognitive dissonance, and regret.

Suppose you are beginning an engagement with a new client, Amy. You give her a standard risk tolerance quiz and determine that she is a *moderate* risk tolerant investor. After that, you give her a test for behavioral biases of moderate clients. Based on the answers to the bias questions, you determine that Amy is a Follower. Some of your other clients are *moderate* in their risk tolerance but they are not biased like Amy. The object of this exercise is to see how to create a BMAA for a Follower versus a non-biased or mildly biased *moderate* investor. Generally, this can mean that a Follower should accept less risk in her portfolio than those clients without bias. Since Amy is a Follower, she may overstate her risk tolerance. This makes working with a Follower somewhat more challenging than with some other BITs.

The following analysis presents two investment programs, one for Bill (a non-biased moderate investor) and one for Amy (a Follower). You are using Bill's portfolio allocation as a baseline for creating Amy's. Your basic task is to assess a retirement goal for Amy and the risk associated with the return needed to reach that goal. When working with actual clients, you will need to adjust this analysis to suit your purposes.

As we know, Follower clients:

- Are driven by cognitive biases.
- Tend to overestimate their risk tolerance.

For Amy, a Follower, we are going to make an assumption that she may have difficulty sticking to a portfolio with a probability of a loss year at greater than 25 percent. For Bill, a moderate client, 25 percent may be too conservative and can be a bit higher. So let's examine Figure 15.3 and analyze how Amy's portfolio might compare to Bill's.

Without getting too caught up in the details of the numbers, you can see that Amy has a more conservative allocation that Bill, which will likely permit her to reach her financial goals. This is an example of how one adjusts an allocation for the Follower BIT.

Advisors to Followers first and foremost need to recognize that Followers often overestimate their risk tolerance. Risky trend-following behavior occurs in part because Followers don't like situations of ambiguity that may accompany the decision to enter an asset class when it is out of favor. They also may convince themselves that they "knew it all along" when an investment idea goes their way, which also increases future risk-taking behavior. Advisors need to handle Followers with care because they are likely to say yes to investment ideas that make sense to them regardless of whether the advice is in their best long-term interest. Advisors need to lead Followers to take a hard look at behavioral tendencies that may cause them to overestimate their risk tolerance. Because Follower biases are mainly cognitive, education on the benefits of portfolio diversification and sticking to a long-term plan is usually the best course of action. Advisors should challenge Follower clients to be introspective and provide data-backed substantiation for recommendations. Offering education in clear, unambiguous ways so they have the chance to "get it" is a good idea. If advisors take the time, this steady, educational approach will generate client loyalty and adherence to long-term investment plans.

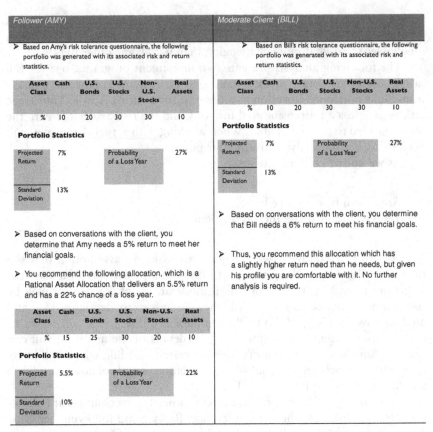

**FIGURE 15.3** Comparison of Follower BMAA to Non-Biased Client's Asset Allocation

## BEST PRACTICAL ALLOCATION FOR INDEPENDENTS

In the last section, we learned how to create a behaviorally modified asset allocation or BMAA (also referred to as Best Practical Allocation) for a Follower behavioral investor type. We will now continue this learning process by examining the Independent. Our process will be the same. We will review the basics of the Independent and the biases at work with Independents, present a client scenario, and then discuss how to modify an asset allocation based on the behavioral characteristics of the Independent.

An Independent is an active investor with medium-to-high risk tolerance who is strong-willed and an independently minded thinker. Independents are self-assured and trust their instincts when making investment decisions;

however, when they do research on their own, they may be susceptible to acting on information that is available to them rather than getting corroboration from other sources. Sometimes advisors find that an Independent client made an investment without consulting anyone. This approach can be problematic because, due to their Independent mindset, these clients often irrationally cling to the views they had when they made an investment, even when market conditions change, and thus making advising Independents challenging. They often enjoy investing, however, and are comfortable taking risks, but often resist following a rigid financial plan.

Some Independents are obsessed with trying to beat the market and may hold concentrated portfolios. Of all behavioral investor types, Independents are the most likely to be contrarian, which can benefit them—and lead them to continue their contrarian practices. Independent biases are cognitive: conservatism, availability, confirmation, representativeness, and self-attribution.

Suppose you are beginning an engagement with a new client, Leo. You give him a standard risk tolerance quiz and determine that he is a *growth-oriented* risk tolerant investor. After that, you give him a test for behavioral biases of moderate clients. Based on the answers to the bias questions you determine that Leo is an Independent. Some of your other clients are *growth-oriented* in their risk tolerance but they are not biased like Leo. The object of this exercise is to see how to create a BMAA for an Independent versus a non-biased or mildly biased *growth* investor. Generally, this can mean that an Independent should accept less risk in his portfolio than those clients without bias. Since Leo is an Independent, he may want to make investments in his portfolio outside of a recommended plan, which may change the risk level in his overall portfolio without his realizing it. This makes working with an Independent somewhat more challenging than with some other BITs.

The following analysis presents two investment programs, one for Jack (a non-biased growth investor) and one for Leo (an Independent). You are using Jack's portfolio allocation as a baseline for creating Leo's. Your basic task is to assess a retirement goal for Leo and the risk associated with the return needed to reach that goal. When working with actual clients, you will need to adjust this analysis to suit your purposes.

As we know, Independent clients:

- Are driven by cognitive biases.
- May make investments outside of a recommended plan.

For Leo, an Independent, we are going to make an assumption that he may have difficulty sticking to a portfolio with a probability of a loss year at greater than 35 percent. For Jack, a non-biased *growth* client, 35 percent may

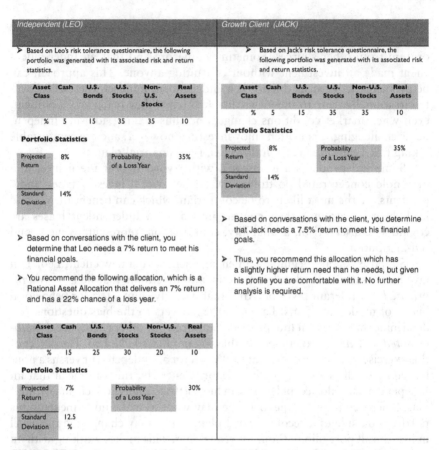

**FIGURE 15.4** Comparison of Independent BMAA to Non-Biased Client's Asset Allocation

be just fine. So let's examine Figure 15.4 and analyze how Leo's portfolio might compare to Jack's.

Without getting too caught up in the details of the numbers, you can see that Leo has a more conservative allocation than Jack, which will likely permit him to reach his financial goals. This is an example of how one adjusts an allocation for the Independent BIT.

Independents can be difficult clients to advise due to their contrarian mindset, but they are usually grounded enough to listen to sound advice when it is presented in a way that respects their Independent views. As we have learned, Independents are firm in their belief in themselves and their decisions, but can be blinded to contrary thinking. As with Followers, education is essential to changing behavior of Independents; their biases are predominantly cognitive. A good approach is to have regular educational discussions during client meetings. This way, the advisor doesn't point out unique or recent failures, but rather educates regularly and can incorporate concepts that he or she feels are appropriate for the client. Because Independent biases are mainly cognitive, education on the benefits of portfolio diversification and sticking to a long-term plan is usually the best course of action. Advisors should challenge Independents to reflect on how they make investment decisions and provide data-backed substantiation for recommendations. Offering education in clear, unambiguous ways is an effective approach. If advisors take the time, this steady, educational approach should yield positive results.

## BEST PRACTICAL ALLOCATION FOR ACCUMULATORS

In the last section, we learned how to create a behaviorally modified asset allocation or BMAA (also referred to as Best Practical Allocation) for an Independent behavioral investor type. We will now continue this learning process by examining the Accumulator. Our process will be the same. We will review the basics of the Accumulator and the biases at work with Accumulators, present a client scenario, and then discuss how to modify an asset allocation based on the behavioral characteristics of the Accumulator.

The Accumulator is the most aggressive behavioral investor type. These clients are entrepreneurial and often the first generation to create wealth, and they are even more strong-willed and confident than Independents. At high wealth levels, Accumulators often have controlled the outcomes of non-investment activities and believe they can do the same with investing. This behavior can lead to overconfidence in investing activities. Left unadvised, Accumulators often trade too much, which can be a drag on investment performance. Accumulators are quick decision makers but may chase higher risk investments than their friends. If successful, they enjoy the thrill of making a good investment. Some Accumulators can be difficult to advise because they don't believe in basic investment principles such as diversification and asset allocation. They are often hands-on, wanting to be heavily involved in the investment decision making process. Biases of Accumulators are overconfidence, self-control, outcome, affinity, and illusion of control.

Suppose you are beginning an engagement with a new client, Bob. You give him a standard risk tolerance quiz and determine that he is an *aggressive growth-oriented* investor. After that, you give him a test for behavioral biases of aggressive clients. Based on the answers to the bias questions you determine that Bob is an Accumulator. Some of your other clients are *aggressive growth-oriented* in their risk tolerance but they are not biased like Bob. The object of this exercise is to see how to create a BMAA for an Accumulator versus a non-biased or mildly biased *aggressive growth* investor. Generally, this can mean that an Accumulator should accept less risk in his portfolio than those clients without bias. Since Bob is an Accumulator, he may believe that he can control the outcome of his investments or be overly optimistic about the prospects, which may change the risk level in his overall portfolio without his realizing it. This makes working with an Accumulator somewhat more challenging than with some other BITs.

The following analysis presents two investment programs, one for Brandon (a non-biased aggressive growth investor) and one for Bob (an Accumulator). You are using Brandon's portfolio allocation as a baseline for creating Bob's. Your basic task is to assess a retirement goal for Bob and the risk associated with the return needed to reach that goal. When working with actual clients, you will need to adjust this analysis to suit your purposes.

As we know, Accumulator clients:

- Are driven by emotional biases.
- May believe they can control the outcomes of their investments.
- May be overly optimistic about the prospects for their investments.

For Bob, an Accumulator, we are going to make an assumption that he may have difficulty sticking to a portfolio with a probability of a loss year at greater than 45 percent. For Brandon, a non-biased *aggressive growth* client, 45 percent may be just fine. See Figure 15.5.

Aggressive clients are the most difficult clients to advise, particularly those who have experienced losses. Because they like to control or at least get deeply involved in the details of investment decision making, they tend to eschew advice that might keep their risk tolerance in check. And they are emotionally charged and optimistic that their investments will do well, even if that optimism is irrational. Some Accumulators need to be monitored for excess spending which, when out of control, can inhibit performance of a long-term portfolio. The best approach to dealing with these clients is to take control of the situation. If the advisor lets the Accumulator client dictate the terms of the advisory engagement, they will always be at the mercy of the client's emotionally driven decision making, and the result will likely be an unhappy client and an unhappy advisor. Advisors to Accumulators need to demonstrate the impact financial decisions have on family members,

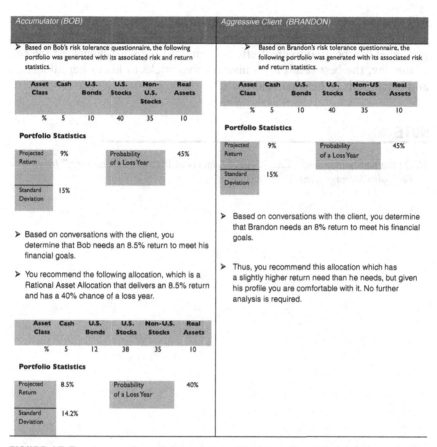

**FIGURE 15.5**  Comparison of Accumulator BMAA to Non-Biased Client's Asset Allocation

lifestyle, or the family legacy. If these advisors can prove to the client that they have the ability help the client to make sound long-term decisions, they will likely see their Accumulator clients fall into step and be better clients that are easier to advise.

## SUMMARY

The intent of this chapter is to demonstrate how to create a behaviorally modified asset allocation for each behavioral investor type. Naturally, you will need to adapt this process to real-world clients who will likely be different from the ones presented in this chapter. Nevertheless, the concepts presented can be used to great effect when working with clients. At the end of the day, the best result is an investor that sticks to his or her allocation and reaches his or her financial goals.

## NOTE

1. Daniel Kahneman and Mark Riepe, "Aspects of Investor Psychology," *Journal of Portfolio Management* 24 (1998): 52–65.

# Index

Printed in the United States
By Bookmasters